Powerful Practices
for Supporting
English Learners

Fern: Dedicated with great love to my family who has always stood by my side, no matter the distance or the direction.

Stephaney: To Võ Văn Vinh, my light and rock, and to Robert D. Ray, an Iowa governor who changed lives through his compassion and unprecedented leadership when others failed to act.

Paula: To the many talented and dedicated teachers in Toronto and across Canada who threw open their classroom doors wide and welcomed me so I could learn from them, and to my late father, himself a refugee, who started me on my journey of wanting to work with newcomers.

And with deep gratitude for our colleagues, educators, and professionals everywhere who strive to effect more equitable outcomes for culturally and linguistically diverse students and families.

Powerful Practices for Supporting English Learners

Elevating Diverse Assets and Identities

Fern Westernoff

Stephaney Jones-Vo

Paula Markus

Foreword by Jim Cummins

CORWIN

FOR INFORMATION:

Corwin
A SAGE Company
2455 Teller Road
Thousand Oaks, California 91320
(800) 233-9936
www.corwin.com

SAGE Publications Ltd.
1 Oliver's Yard
55 City Road
London EC1Y 1SP
United Kingdom

SAGE Publications India Pvt. Ltd.
B 1/I 1 Mohan Cooperative Industrial Area
Mathura Road, New Delhi 110 044
India

SAGE Publications Asia-Pacific Pte. Ltd.
18 Cross Street #10-10/11/12
China Square Central
Singapore 048423

Program Director and Publisher: Dan Alpert
Senior Content Development
    Editor: Lucas Schleicher
Associate Content Development
    Editor: Mia Rodriguez
Production Editor: Gagan Mahindra
Copy Editor: Karin Rathert
Typesetter: C&M Digitals (P) Ltd.
Proofreader: Susan Schon
Indexer: Integra
Cover Designer: Candice Harman
Graphic Designer: Candice Harman
Marketing Manager: Sharon Pendergast

Printed in the United States of America

Library of Congress Cataloging-in-Publication Data

Names: Westernoff, Fern, 1960- author. | Jones-Vo, Stephaney, author. | Markus, Paula, author.

Title: Powerful practices for supporting English learners : elevating diverse assets and identities / Fern Westernoff, Stephaney Jones-Vo, Paula Markus.

Description: Thousand Oaks, California : Corwin, [2021] | Includes bibliographical references and index. |

Identifiers: LCCN 2020046712 | ISBN 9781544380094 (paperback) | ISBN 9781544380100 (epub) | ISBN 9781544380124 (epub) | ISBN 9781544380117 (pdf)

Subjects: LCSH: English language—Study and teaching—Foreign speakers. | Multilingual education—United States. | Multilingual education—Canada. | Culturally relevant pedagogy—United States. | Culturally relevant pedagogy—Canada. | Immigrant students—United States. | Immigrant students—Canada. | Community and school—United States. | Community and school—Canada.

Classification: LCC PE1128.A2 W47 2021 | DDC 428.0071—dc23
LC record available at https://lccn.loc.gov/2020046712

This book is printed on acid-free paper.

SUSTAINABLE FORESTRY INITIATIVE
Certified Chain of Custody
Promoting Sustainable Forestry
www.sfiprogram.org
SFI-01268

21 22 23 24 25 10 9 8 7 6 5 4 3 2 1

Contents

Foreword

Jim Cummins
University of Toronto

During the past 30 years, I have given a large number of workshops and conference presentations in both North America and Europe to educators of multilingual students who are learning the language of instruction. Although each context is unique in multiple respects, similar questions were raised by participants over and over again:

- How can you tell if a student who doesn't appear to be making adequate progress has a learning handicap or is just going through the normal process of learning the school language (L2)?

- How can students utilize their home language (L1) to transfer knowledge to the school language when they have missed out on schooling and have minimal literacy skills developed in L1?

- How can we involve parents in their children's education when the parents don't speak any English and are not highly literate in their L1?

- How can I teach for crosslinguistic transfer when there are multiple languages in my classroom, and I don't speak any of these languages?

- How can I get my principal and 'mainstream' or subject matter teachers to understand that it typically takes at least five years for students to catch up academically and the ESL teacher can't simply 'fix' the students in just one year?

I would do my best to answer these and many other questions, but I was acutely aware that my answers were always partial and not fully satisfactory, even to me. I frequently tried to let myself off the hook by saying (legitimately!) that many of these issues have emerged relatively recently, and research doesn't provide definitive answers that will apply in every context. There are no formulaic answers to many of these questions, no book that we can just pull off the shelf that will point us in the right direction.

That is, until now. As I was reading *Powerful Practices for Supporting English Learners*, I found myself engaging in retrospective fantasies, reliving those question and answer sessions and being able to tell committed teachers and school administrators that much of what they need to know to support English Learners will jump out at them from the pages of this lucid, unpretentious, and inspirational book.

The book is lucid, but in no way formulaic. It doesn't tell us what to do—instead, it shares with us successful initiatives and creative projects that other teachers have carried out, working individually in their classrooms and collectively as a school community. The book stimulates us to think about how we might adapt some of these strategies in our own unique contexts. It also invites us to extend our own identities as *educators*. We are not simply passive conduits for the transmission of pre-packaged curriculum into the minds of generic students. We are also far more than just recipients of research findings generated by our university colleagues with the expectation that we will 'mobilize' this knowledge in our schools and classrooms.

Rather than providing us with definitive formulas, the authors have shared with us narratives of educators, working together creatively with students and families, who transform 'problems' into possibilities, who define learners not by what they lack (e.g., knowledge of the school language) but by what they are capable of achieving, and who, in the process, define themselves as advocates of all that is best in humanity and as generators of knowledge and insight. The inspirational educational initiatives that you will read about in these pages were not dreamt up by researchers on the basis of rigorous scientific studies—they emerged from the imagination of brilliant educators who were familiar in general terms with much of the relevant research, but who went far beyond the research in pushing the boundaries of what was conventionally considered possible. For example, several of the instructional examples illustrate how teachers can engage students' multilingual resources and teach for crosslinguistic transfer even when they themselves don't speak the home languages of their students. Researchers didn't generate this knowledge—teachers did.

The book is unpretentious because it has been written by teachers for teachers—it uses a language that we all understand and doesn't try to complexify basic educational principles that are ultimately fairly evident to all committed educators. For example, the vast majority of educators, many of whom work in challenging conditions, will agree with the foundational principles that run through every page of this book:

- *You connect instruction to students' lives;*

- *You get to know and respect the students who are in your classrooms;*

- *You identify and build on the personal, cognitive, and linguistic assets that students bring to the school's learning community;*

- *You respect students' families and the diverse communities they represent, and you reach out to involve them as partners in their children's education;*

- *You continue to expand your professional knowledge and you learn from the students you are teaching, the families who have entrusted their children to your care, and the colleagues with whom you share the journey.*

I truly believe that this book will make a significant difference in the lives of students, families, and educators. The *powerful practices* that it so clearly describes have the potential to create not only powerful learning, but also powerful learners and powerful educators.

Over many years, I have explored the idea of schools as sites where teachers and students *negotiate identities* (e.g. Cummins, 1986, 2001). Schools in many countries, including Canada and the United States, share a shameful history of racist practices designed to exclude Indigenous and minoritized students from educational and social advancement. These schools were permeated by what I called *coercive relations of power* where power is exercised by a dominant individual, group, or country to the detriment of a subordinated individual, group, or country. I contrasted this notion of 'power over' with *collaborative relations of power* that reflect the sense of the term *power* that refers to *being enabled* or *empowered* to achieve more. Within collaborative relations of power, power is not a fixed quantity but is generated through interaction with others. The more empowered one individual or group becomes, the more is generated for others to share. The process is additive rather than subtractive. Within this context, 'empowerment' can be defined as *the collaborative creation of power*.

The powerful instructional practices documented in this book clearly constitute 'effective instruction' but we can understand *why* they are so effective only when we view them through the lens of identity negotiation and the collaborative creation of power. When emergent bilingual students create multimodal and multilingual identity texts that find their place in the school library side by side with the books of experienced and accomplished authors, they are telling the world, and more importantly themselves, that they are more than simply learners of English. When educators at Crescent Town Elementary School in Toronto organize a potluck community *iftar* event (a meal that breaks the fast each night during Ramadan), they are creating an interpersonal space within which power is being collaboratively generated for students, families, and educators themselves.

It is my expectation that this book will act as a catalyst for schools to more clearly articulate what they stand for—what concept of *education* is embodied in the interactions that take place within the walls of the school. For educators within these schools, collegial discussion of the powerful practices vividly described in these pages will open up new instructional possibilities that not only *express* our identities as educators but also *expand* and *re-create* these identities.

REFERENCES

Cummins, J. (1986) Empowering minority students: A framework for intervention. *Harvard Educational Review* 56, 18–36.

Cummins, J. (2001) *Negotiating Identities: Education for Empowerment in a Diverse Society*. 2nd edn. Los Angeles: California Association for Bilingual Education.

Acknowledgments

We gratefully acknowledge the support, guidance, and encouragement from our team at Corwin: Dan Alpert, Program Director and Publisher, Equity and Professional Learning; Lucas Schleicher, Senior Content Development Editor; and Mia Rodriguez, Associate Content Development Editor.

We would also like to thank the following people and agencies whose dedication to students from diverse backgrounds provided us with much inspiration.

Qudsia Ahmad

Judith Arrowood

Vanessa Barnett

Donna Beaton

Ryan Bird

Sally Bliss

Kay Cairns

Katie Campana

Jenny Cheng

Roma Chumak-Horbatsch

Grace Chung

CultureLink, Toronto, Ontario

Andrea DeCapua

Sukayna Dewji

Peter Dorfman

Carol Doyle-Jones

Rose Egolet

Jennifer Fannin

Frances Ferguson

Laurel Fynes

Mandi Gerland

Yasmin Hasan

Heartland Area Education Agency, Iowa

Susan Hind

Shirley Hu

Shannon Hutchison

Janet Jundler

Ellen-Rose Kambel

Artemis Kapakos

Farida Kassum

Sandra Katz

Ann Kong

Thursica Kovinthan Levi

Ashley Lam

Stephanie Ledger

Emmanuelle Le Pichon-Vorstman

Lisa McDonald

Martha McGloin

Sandra Mills-Fisher

Shamira Mohamed

Mike Montanera

Alyssia Montesino

Genine Natale

Jo Nieuwkerk

Marlene Neri

Sharon Newmaster

Kaila O'Callaghan

Sheila Pinto

Hetty Roessingh

Tammy Ross

Jennifer Shields

Angela Sioumpas

Cecilia Song

Elena Soni

Jan Stewart

Fei Tang

Betty Ann Taylor

Denise Taylor-Edwards

Toronto District School Board

Jeanette Voaden

Tu Vuong

Dan Warden

Nadine Williams

Grace Wong

Ann Woomert

PUBLISHER'S ACKNOWLEDGMENTS

Corwin gratefully acknowledges the contributions of the following reviewers:

Ina Berard
Kindergarten Teacher
Greater Essex County District School Board
Windsor, ON

Hope Edlin
Teacher
Bethel Elementary School
Simpsonville, SC

Lynn Farrugia
ESL Program Coordinator
Edmonton Public Schools
Edmonton, AB

Karen Kozy-Landress
Speech/Language Pathologist
Brevard Public Schools
Merritt Island, FL

Maija Leipala
ESL Teacher
Thames Valley District School Board
London, ON

Jeffrey Robinson
Learning Coordinator, ESL/ELD K–8
Thames Valley District School Board
London, ON

Joanne Shimotakahara
Retired Chief Speech-Language Pathologist, East Office
Toronto District School Board
Toronto, ON

Laura Von Staden
Teacher
School District of Hillsborough County
Tampa, FL

Susan Woo
Literacy Consultant
Edmonton Regional Learning Consortium
Edmonton, AB

Theresa Young
Speech-Language Pathologist, M.Cl.Sc., Reg. CASLPO, SLP(C), CCC-SLP
Sound Communication
Parry Sound, ON

About the Authors

Fern Westernoff is a speech-language pathologist with over thirty-five years of experience at the Toronto District School Board. She served on the Immigrant Assessment Team, which prompted her to pursue doctoral studies regarding bilingualism and second language learning at The Ontario Institute for Studies in Education/University of Toronto. She co-instructed in the Kindergarten Early Language Intervention (KELI) Program, where she was also a co-program leader supporting the development of the program. Fern continues to publish and present widely in Canada, the United States, and Israel regarding cultural and linguistic diversity and communication disorders in education.

Stephaney Jones-Vo is president of Starfish Education, LLC, focusing on equity for English Learners. With over a decade of Title III grant directing, refugee sponsorship, and K–12 ESL classroom teaching experience, she served as an English Learner and Diversity consultant at a regional state education agency supporting multiple school districts to increase English Learner achievement. She has designed and facilitated ESL endorsement and cultural competence courses at several universities. A frequent presenter in the United States and in Canada, she has co-authored multiple books, chapters, and articles; designed and delivered a variety of adult ESL classes for specific purposes and in the workplace, and advocated widely for English Learners.

Paula Markus served as the ESL/ELD Program Co-ordinator with the Toronto District School Board from 2001 through 2017. She is currently a sessional lecturer in the Master of Teaching Program at the Ontario Institute for Studies in Education/University of Toronto, preparing pre-service teachers to support English Learners. Paula is the founder of the annual "Celebrating Linguistic Diversity" Conference, Ontario's largest professional gathering of K–12 teachers of English Language Learners for the past two decades. She continues to be an invited presenter at school districts and conferences across Canada and the United States.

Introduction

Have you ever been invited to a friend's party that included a bit too much of their unique office talk? Sure, it was wonderful to join the celebrations, even if you did not really participate much in the discussions. No doubt after a while, you might become a bit disillusioned with making small talk. You might start losing interest. You might even begin daydreaming or mentally going through your to-do list while unconsciously murmuring words of agreement. This distractedness can mirror the feelings of students from culturally and linguistically diverse backgrounds who often do not recognize their experiences, background knowledge, cultures, or home languages represented in the curriculum or visible in the school community. Students who have very little opportunity to connect to what is happening in the classroom may begin to feel detached, uninvolved, unimportant, or devalued. Perceiving that they are excluded from the school community, these learners may disconnect from school entirely.

Over the past decades, classroom demographics have continued to evolve, becoming increasingly culturally and linguistically diverse. As a result, all teachers share the responsibility of supporting diverse learners in their classrooms, including English Learners. Educators appreciate how critical it is for students and families to see their backgrounds, experiences, and lives authentically present in the classroom, school, and community. Organically incorporating culturally and linguistically responsive educational practices is an essential element of today's schools. The purpose of this guide is to articulate a foundation of culturally and linguistically responsive core practices that break through boundaries, bridging the gap between research and application. Building on educators' current competencies in supporting linguistically and culturally diverse learners, this guide aims to illuminate meaningful ways to engage learners and to promote their achievements inside and outside of school.

As authors who have partnered on a range of educational projects over the years, we are a trio who embrace the unique perspectives that each brings to our shared work on behalf of English Learners and their families. We have chosen to focus our collaboration on this book through a collective interprofessional, transnational, and asset-based lens.

Interprofessional: An interprofessional perspective allows professionals from different disciplines and backgrounds to integrate their knowledge and skills. Through collaboration with colleagues, interprofessional initiatives can enrich professional practices, build capacity (Fairbairn & Jones-Vo, 2016), promote creative problem solving, and lead to increased opportunities and options for clients and students (Geva, Barsky, & Westernoff, 2000). Dove and Honigsfeld (2020) maintain that systemic collaboration among professionals effectively advances the educational outcomes of students from culturally and linguistically diverse backgrounds. When a variety of differently prepared professionals combine their expertise and insights, they can create a uniquely effective team for serving English Learners. Classroom teachers, teachers of English as an additional language, special education teachers, teaching assistants, paraprofessionals, speech-language pathologists, psychologists, social workers, school counselors, coaches, and administrators all contribute to the betterment of services for students. The process of working in tandem with others is not always easy, but the outcomes can be extraordinary.

The effort to co-create this guide is an example of interprofessional collaborative work, highlighting the four core principles of teamwork proposed by Dove and Honigsfeld (2020): common purpose, shared mindset, supportive environment, and diverse team membership. It incorporates our work as practitioners from the teaching and speech-language pathology professions who have worked with young children, teenagers, and both seasoned and pre-service educators situated in a variety of American and Canadian school districts. Together, we bring a combined century of knowledge, training, and experience in public and private education, teaching English as an additional language, communication sciences and disorders, professional consultation, teacher and clinical training, and educational administration; work that encompasses meeting the needs of language learners and educators at the systems/organizational level as well as in day-to-day classroom learning.

Transnational: With differences in national policies, procedures, and history, the transnational approach infused by Canadian and American authors allows the weaving together of diverse practices, experiences, research, and national leadership. Both American and Canadian perspectives can include an emphasis on multicultural, multilingual pedagogy, a focus on curriculum, and the use of large-scale assessment data to drive improved student achievement. It is the authors' intent to spotlight powerful instructional and support practices from contexts both north and south of the 49th parallel rather than to provide a comparative perspective. This transnational perspective will also be reflected through the spelling used in this guide. While most of the writing reflects American spelling conventions (e.g., color, favor, center), Canadian conventions are used when discussing Canadian contributions, names, and quotes (e.g., colour, favour, centre). The use of spelling from different nations in one publication is rather unique and is an example of how we have tried to blend transnational perspectives as well as language use.

Asset-Based: An ongoing worldwide movement focuses on the notion of positivism in a number of different disciplines. Positive psychology is gaining in popularity beyond the field of psychology and is reflected in both the fields of speech-language pathology (e.g., Holland & Nelson, 2014) and education (e.g., Zacarian & Staehr Fenner, 2020). Asset-based approaches value and elevate student resources and talents rather than focus on deficits or what the student has not achieved. In the case of English Learners, an asset-based approach means viewing all the internal riches and personal linguistic and cultural contributions that students bring into the classroom as transcending any perceived lack of knowledge or skills. An asset-based approach means acknowledging and integrating students competencies and skills, or in the words of Moll, Amanti, Neff, and Gonzalez (1992), their "funds of knowledge." The educational use of funds of knowledge significantly impacts how students define themselves, as described in a related concept of "funds of identity" (Esteban-Guitart & Moll, 2014). An asset-based perspective serves students best and begins with the language we use when talking about students (Sánchez-López & Young, 2018). For example, when we say "He is fluent in Tamil and is developing English" rather than "He doesn't speak English," we are focusing on the student's skills and potential. This is one example of maintaining an asset-based perspective in our views of students, which then carries into our interactions with others. By purposefully and consistently recognizing students' experiences and backgrounds as strengths, educators establish a collective asset-based approach to pedagogy that promotes more authentic integration of cultural and linguistic resources into daily classroom activities. Highlighting these assets in the classroom, while positioning the English Learner as expert when possible, empowers students to find their voices and a new sense of belonging.

THE ORGANIZATION OF THIS BOOK

Researchers and educators agree that strong relationships between students and caring people are crucial for the emotional, academic, linguistic, and social growth of students (e.g., Asgedom & Even, 2017; Cummins, 1996; Kottler, Kottler, & Street, 2008; Zacarian & Staehr Fenner, 2020). Students interact directly and indirectly with a network of people who support their education to various degrees of connection and influence. For example, students interact with relatives in their immediate and extended family, with teachers and classmates in the classroom and around the school, as well as with others who make up their wider school and neighborhood communities. These multifaceted relationships are closely intertwined; each exerts significant influence on the others. For example, administrative decisions affect what teachers do in the classroom, which in turn impacts student learning; a family crisis influences a student's readiness to learn, which may then alter teacher expectations. Teachers become increasingly culturally competent by learning from their students, the benefits of which can then can be shared with other teachers, cascading greater understanding into the wider school community. The resulting unique inter-relationships can be depicted in the English Learner Interconnected Ecosystem Model presented below.

FIGURE INTRO 1 English Learner Interconnected Ecosystem Model

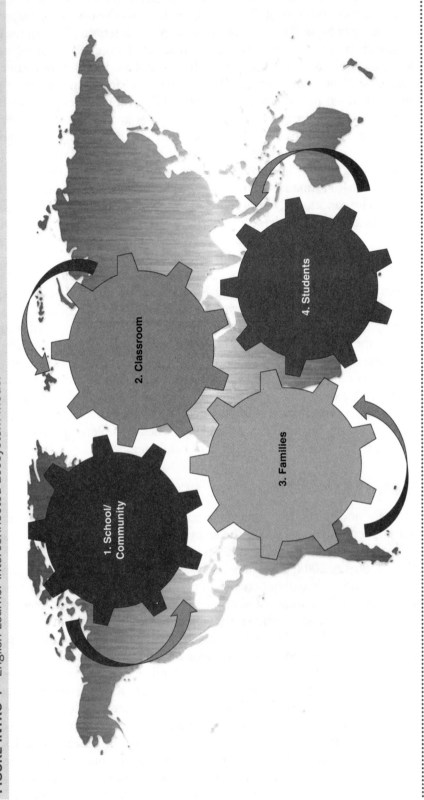

The spheres of school/community, classroom, families and students can be envisioned as four separate, large gears, all connecting and interacting to advance student well-being and achievement. When any part of the mechanism is not working to capacity, the entire ecosystem bears the burden of slower forward movement and progress. To best support English Learners, educators can facilitate smooth meshing and interaction among the gears by using culturally and linguistically responsive understanding and practices. This guide explores each large gear of the English Learner Interconnected Ecosystem Model as a separate chapter. We recognize that depending on one's role, experiences, and responsibilities, some readers may have a greater interest in one chapter over another. You may not currently serve all the different types of learners that are included in this guide. But one day you might. Perhaps an idea, comment, or perspective might inspire you to innovate new professional partnerships and projects.

Each chapter is organized based on a repeated pattern of three parts: (1) What We Know, (2) What It Might Look Like, and (3) Making It Your Own. Each chapter begins with What We Know: an overview of research highlighting the linguistic, cognitive, academic, social, and emotional rationale for inclusion of home languages and cultures as a keystone in culturally responsive education. As with all learning, what we already know provides the basis for additional learning. For this reason, each chapter goes on to ask salient questions, building on current knowledge and exploring additional ideas and applications. These questions can be represented by smaller gears internal to the chapter, showing us what we want to know next about that particular area of investigation. Each chapter will include a visual overview of the questions, for reference purposes.

What It Might Look Like provides a variety of responses to each question using effective and pragmatic Powerful Practices, which are also pictured in visual overviews. Powerful Practices are the cogs of the gears: actions, activities, programs, and interventions that we have curated from educational interactions, observations, classroom practices, professional reading, as well as work and life experiences. To highlight the Powerful Practices, we include examples of implementation using descriptions, photos, explanations, vignettes, sample lesson plans, links to related websites, videos, interviews, and so forth. Sometimes the Powerful Practices are written with specific details about actual practices, sometimes they are portrayed as an amalgamation of activities or contextualized as a narrative. Because many of the Powerful Practices come from our experiences, they often reflect our geography and work lives in Ontario, Canada, and the states of Iowa and Georgia. While we are proud of these models of innovation and records of success, it is important to keep in mind that the Powerful Practices described in this guide are not meant to be a definitive or exhaustive list. No doubt you have Powerful Practices of your own that would be significant contributions to each chapter. Our hope is that the Powerful Practices will provide a catalyst for growing and expanding the support in your educational context for English Learners and their families. Rather than replicating the Powerful

Practices, we hope that you can use them as springboards and liberally adapt them to your particular setting. To facilitate this process, each Powerful Practice concludes with an application component—Making It Your Own—designed to promote educator reflection with activities such as exercises, brainstorming, thought-provoking questions, and further reading.

To better personalize and operationalize the English Learner Interconnected Ecosystem Model, you are invited to complete the provided template on page 255 of this guide, where you will find a working copy of the English Learner Interconnected Ecosystem Model. First, using your own professional knowledge, try brainstorming facts, ideas, thoughts, and musings about your students, families, classroom, school, and community context and jot them inside the appropriate large gear. As you work through the chapters, you can add to each gear with appropriate culturally and linguistically responsive ideas from the Powerful Practices, as well as with your additional thoughts. This brainstorming and labelling will support you to fully consolidate your own version of the model and how it can work in your own context. We will prompt you to add to this model after each chapter. You can do this by yourself, or perhaps you would prefer some professional dialogue with like-minded colleagues sharing this professional learning journey. Read a chapter and then get together to discuss and add to each gear in a professional book club format. By the end of reading and completing this guide, you will have had the opportunity to create your own personalized ecosystem model to support your students in reaching their fullest potential.

In Chapter 1, we examine practices pertaining to the school and community. Specifically, we answer the following questions:

A. What are some ways that schools can provide a welcoming environment for all students, families, and the local community?

B. How might initial assessment and reception services be offered to newcomer students and their families?

C. What are some ways to facilitate integration of students and families into school and the larger community?

D. What have we learned so far about supporting English Learners attending school from a distance?

In Chapter 2, we focus on the classroom and instruction by answering the following questions:

A. What components of meaningful instruction are needed to support English Learners in every classroom?

B. What are some ways to expand students' connections to new learning in an additional language?

C. What are some ways to embrace languages that we do not speak in the classroom?

D. How might we show that it is important for students to continue to develop the home language?

In Chapter 3, we look at connecting with families, as we answer the following questions:

A. What are some ways to support families who are adjusting to life in a new country?

B. What are some ways to collaborate with parents?

C. What are some ways to partner with parents to support both the home language and English language development?

D. What are some ways to communicate with parents when we do not speak their languages?

In Chapter 4, we answer the following questions revolving around some specific needs of the student:

A. What are some ways to ensure that English Learners maintain high levels of engagement in language learning?

B. What are some ways to support English Learners with exceptional needs?

C. What additional considerations are needed to help newcomers with a range of circumstances thrive and be successful?

D. What are some ways to support students with limited or interrupted formal schooling?

E. What are some ways to support newcomers who may be experiencing trauma?

We present many essential questions distributed across four chapters. But there are two more key questions—one in the introduction for grounding our efforts and one in the conclusion for reflecting on the work that we have achieved. Let's begin with the first question, which only you can answer:

Question #1: What are my goals in using this guide?

1. _____

2. _____

3. _____

FIGURE 1.1 School/Community: Overview

CHAPTER 1

School and Community

WHAT WE KNOW

Schools in Canada and the United States often serve as the portal for receiving and serving young English Learners. Some of these students are newcomers, while others are native to the country but perhaps have not yet acquired full command of the language of classroom instruction. In the United States where the population is estimated over 330 million people (United States Census Bureau, 2020), a majority of schools throughout all fifty states have enrolled English Learners (Lynn, 2018). Comprising nearly 10% of students in U.S. public schools and nearly 25% of students in California alone (Ruiz Soto, Hooker, & Batalova, 2015), English Learners "are the fastest-growing student population in the United States, growing 60% in the last decade, as compared with 7% growth of the general student population" (Grantmakers for Education, 2013).

"It is crucial . . . that these students, and all students, have equal access to a high-quality education and the opportunity to achieve their full academic potential. We applaud those working to ensure equal educational opportunities for EL [English Learner] students, as well as the many schools and communities creating programs that recognize the heritage languages of EL students as valuable assets to preserve" (U.S. Department of Justice and U.S. Department of Education, 2015, p. 1).

Canada, a country of just over 37.5 million people, is also experiencing significant growth of English Learners, welcoming approximately 321,000 newcomers in 2018, its largest annual influx in more than a century (Argitis & Hertzberg, 2019). The city of Toronto in Ontario, Canada, considered the most culturally diverse city in the world, is home to the Toronto District School Board (TDSB), which serves students from over 190 different countries, speaking over 115 different languages. Thirty-four percent of the students speak one or more non-English languages as a home language, while 22% speak both English and a non-English home language at home. The remaining 44% of students speak English as their sole home language (Toronto District School Board, 2013). All ten Canadian provinces and three territories have enrolled English Learners to varying degrees. Also reflecting exponential English Learner impact, Vancouver reports that over sixty schools in their school board have a majority English Learner enrolment.

The Calgary Board of Education in the province of Alberta identifies approximately 25% of their students as English Learners (Skelton, 2014).

The spectrum of English Learners in Canada is comprised of a variety of smaller groups that reflect a wide representation of cultural and linguistic backgrounds, including newcomers and refugees from around the world, indigenous peoples in communities where primarily indigenous languages are spoken (First Nations, Métis, and Inuit), children from French-speaking communities outside of Quebec, and children from Canadian communities where another language is spoken, such as the Mennonite and Hutterite (Markus, n.d.) communities.

In the United States, where the majority of English Learners are speakers of Spanish, English Learners also lay claim to a vast variety of cultural and linguistic backgrounds. While English Learners in the United States are partly composed of newcomers or refugees, their languages also might reflect state history, from multigenerational Spanish speakers, to German-speaking migrants in Montana, former refugees of Vietnam and their second or third generations whose first language is Vietnamese, or people speaking Ilokano in Hawaii or Yupik languages in Alaska (Bialik, Scheller, & Walker, 2018; Lynn, 2018), to name only a few.

Due to the dramatically increasing presence of diverse cultures and languages in classrooms and communities, schools experience urgency to explicitly connect English Learners with achieving academic accomplishments so they may continue their success in post-secondary studies or in the workplace. Today's classrooms demand different and fully inclusive ways of conducting the business of education. Classroom teachers often recognize that strategies for instruction and assessment intended for non-English Learners are insufficient to meet the linguistic and cultural needs of English Learners. Since the scales have already tipped under the weight of increased English Learner enrollment in many classrooms, instructional research, data interpretation, guidelines for learning to read in English, engagement with parents and families, indeed every aspect of school, must be informed by facts that are English Learner-specific and focused. It is not appropriate or effective to simply apply the same instructional strategies or approaches used for non-English Learners and expect success for all students. For example, when a district, agency, or school employs instructional coaches, those coaches should be expected to possess training about language acquisition and experience relevant to English Learners. When school principals or superintendents are hired, they should be prepared with deep knowledge about English Learners and their families to create an equitable and caring environment where all are welcome and supported to achieve high standards.

The enrollment of even one English Learner in a school constitutes a mandate for their equitable opportunity and treatment. This directive requires conscious attention to the way school is conducted so that English Learners and their families see themselves reflected and capable of achieving success to the same extent as all other students. Whether English Learners are gifted, have limited or interrupted educations, are second or third generation immigrants, have special education needs, are undocumented or documented refugees, are children of parents with work visas, are adopted, or fit any other description of English Learner, each deserves the same opportunity in reaching full developmental potential along with all of their peers. Accordingly, this means that all aspects of school, including classroom activities, texts and materials, school activities, special programming, extracurricular activities, parental communication and involvement, and community efforts must visibly take into account and explicitly engage English Learners and their families in an equitable fashion. To highlight this developing sensibility of equitable inclusion, the U.S. Department of Education and the U.S. Department of Justice jointly issued a letter of guidance in 2015 to all superintendents at the helm of public school districts laying out expectations in line with current policy and laws. The letter stated that, "In addition to ensuring EL students have access to the core curriculum, SEAs [state education agencies] and school districts must provide EL students equal opportunities to meaningfully participate in all programs and activities of the SEA or school district—whether curricular, co-curricular, or extracurricular. Such programs and activities include pre-kindergarten programs, magnet programs, career and technical education programs, counseling services, Advanced Placement and International Baccalaureate courses, gifted and talented programs, online and distance learning opportunities, performing and visual arts, athletics, and extracurricular activities such as clubs and honor societies" (U.S. Department of Justice and U.S. Department of Education, 2015, p. 18).

While many teachers of English Learners have received training in research-based pedagogy designed to promote the development of both language and content knowledge, significant variability in teacher preparation, as well as local requirements that govern educational practices for English Learners, diverge throughout Canada and the United States. This unevenness in educational programming for English Learners, as well as in teacher preparation programs for those serving English Learners, highlights the lack of coherence between teachers' preparation for working with English Learners and knowledge about how to serve the diverse students who actually populate contemporary classrooms. In addition, teachers of English Learners are not only expected to possess pedagogical skills but are often called upon to expand their reach by addressing various concomitant issues related to living conditions, food security, cultural adjustment, mental health issues, family communication, and so much more.

Areas with the most rapid current growth generally tend to have less experience educating the English Learner population, which can cause seasoned teachers to struggle with their level of confidence in being prepared to support and teach English Learners who currently make up their classrooms.

Such teachers can benefit greatly, as can their students, from exploring the notion of affirming student identities.

To enable English Learners' engagement with literacy, Cummins, Mirza, and Stille (2012) highlight, among other things, the importance of teachers connecting with students' lives and affirming student identities in a myriad of ways. This "English Learner-specific" approach, which explicitly considers and responds to the unique background characteristics and distinctive data related to English Learners as it contrasts with that of non-English Learners, plays a critical and essential role in the classroom engagement and academic achievement of English Learners.

Despite the aforementioned challenges in some locales, countless educators succeed in making a profound daily difference in English Learners' and their families' lives by enacting and building foundational dispositions of empathy and professionalism within their classroom and community contexts (Jones, Weissbourd, Bouffard, Kahn, & Ross Anderson, 2020). Such is the intent of the Powerful Practices described in this book: to share ways for educators to expand profound daily difference-making interactions in students' and families' lives.

The authors of this book concur that empathy serves as essential grounding for the implementation of the Powerful Practices, fueling advocacy and inspiring informed responses. Empathetic, knowledgeable, and prepared educators embrace their essential roles with English Learners, advocating for and learning together with their students and their families while promoting student success and academic achievement. Such responsive practitioners also often serve as the most critical factor in students' success at school and beyond through their daily choices and actions (Brayko, 2018; Staehr Fenner & Snyder, 2017; Wright-Maley & Green, 2015). Maintaining this responsiveness became even more critical during the spring of 2020.

In the interest of public health due to the COVID-19 pandemic, schools required that teachers educate all students by maintaining their classrooms via distance learning. Such a monumental instructional shift challenged teachers not only to quickly become adept with distance education technology and pedagogy but also to adapt their classroom approaches and strategies for communicating a welcoming and friendly stance that conveys emotional comfort and safety during unprecedented and particularly stressful times. Teachers of English Learners in the United States and Canada, from populous provinces and states to rural areas, reached out in pioneering efforts to ensure that English Learners continued to sense recognition and inclusion as a valued part of their classroom and school community. Likewise, clinicians in educational settings, such as speech-language pathologists, psychologists, and social workers, quickly learned how to adapt their services to telepractice technology, in order to provide continued support for students and families. Their professional regulatory boards, whose mandate is to protect the public, also rallied to guide clinicians by drafting standards for virtual care (e.g., American Speech-Language and Hearing Association, 2020). Educational professionals recognized the urgent need to balance student and family emotional wellness during a particularly stressful and vulnerable time in history, with the need to help some gain access to technology and to provide effective quality education and interventions in new and exciting ways.

To accomplish such social and emotional continuity between the distance learning platform and students and families at home, educators must first respond to the essential question, *In what myriad of ways can we communicate our foundational environment of caring and responsiveness, reduce anxiety, engage families in meaningful activities, provide resources, and make personal connections, as well as cover content and language development, when our students are learning from their homes?* The answers to this question include strategies that are only as limited as teachers' imaginations and actions. In this chapter, we share some useful resources and describe adaptable ideas innovated by educators in the early stages of reaching out to effectively maintain the personal threads of connection that foster equity, inclusion, and learning in a virtual context.

After establishing and maintaining an appropriate learning environment for English Learners, teachers must attend to many additional challenges. Against the rapidly increasing and diversifying demographic backdrop, other competing instructional needs have been heaped onto teachers' plates in the United States and Canada. Common Core standards, individual state and provincial content standards, English language development standards, such as those developed by WIDA (2020c) and English Language Proficiency Assessment for the 21st Century (ELPA21) (2018) in the United States, the Alberta K–12 ESL Proficiency Benchmarks (Alberta Government, 1995–2020a), and Steps to English Proficiency (Ontario Ministry of Education, 2015), as well as federal guidelines, high stakes assessments, special education mandates, reading instruction expected of teachers not previously trained as reading teachers—the dizzying range of teachers' responsibilities can seem overwhelming. Teachers of English Learners who are able to weave targeted English language development standards together with content standards can simultaneously promote students' progress through the stages of language acquisition, as well as advance content learning. When both of these sets of instructional standards are blended together by artful teachers in grade-level and content area classrooms, appropriate instruction and assessment of English Learners thrives. In a smart combination of both sets of standards and an economy of effort, students simultaneously learn language when it is rooted in content learning (Alberta Government, 1995–2020b; Larson & Lau, 2016; Ontario Ministry of Education, 2015; Van Viegen Stille, Jang, & Wagner, 2015; WIDA, 2020a).

While each of the ten Canadian provinces and three territories manage educational policies, including those related to English Learners, independently of the federal Canadian government based on the Constitution, the United

States Department of Education (USDE) is the ultimate source of oversight of education in all states, providing federal education guidance and compliance monitoring, complemented by each state's department of education. In practical matters, populous states might function more independently while other states tend to share costs and expertise by joining together in consortia, such as WIDA (2020c) or ELPA21 (2018), to develop materials such as English Learner assessments and standards or learning targets.

To set the stage for overall successful interactions with English Learners and their families across a spectrum of cultures and languages, the most essential action that schools can undertake is to provide a welcoming environment. A warm and friendly atmosphere where families can seek resources or assistance, volunteer, ask questions, and more, will attract families to the school and can be part of an overall strategy of inclusion. Further, such an appealing environment reduces students' anxiety, allowing them to focus on new learning. Finally, since parent involvement in children's education correlates highly with increased achievement, consistently communicating emotional comfort, safety, welcome, and respect as foundational in the school environment is essential to support family involvement (Staehr Fenner & Snyder, 2017).

Inextricably linked to welcoming and interacting with English Learners and their families in culturally and linguistically responsive ways is the identification of students' individual starting points in their English learning journey. Wide variability in the English language experience of individual English Learners across grade levels underscores the necessity for accurate initial assessments. Consistent identification of instructional entry points allows students to clearly demonstrate their progress and growth in a standards-based format. Further, assessment data enables educators to match instruction with demonstrated student needs. Similarly, when rich individual background data is accurately interpreted and shared, teacher collaborators throughout the school can consistently facilitate appropriate scaffolding and supports. Teachers are then empowered to provide adjusted linguistic expectations promoting student engagement in grade-level content at their current levels of English language development, even while "pushing" and supporting students to higher levels of language performance and content learning.

When serving newcomer and refugee students who may have experienced a range of challenges, including the psychological impact of trauma, sensitivity and information are key. Teachers' awareness and focused attention to lesson design, as well as ways to best support such students and families, may also be needed. Together, educators can form a network of responsive supporters that mirror a schoolwide stance and attitude of inclusion and compassion.

Turning attention next to practical instructional considerations, we suggest ways for teachers to productively engage English Learners in the simultaneous development of language and content learning within their own classrooms. Many of the Powerful Practices described in this chapter rely on one or more of the following three important features: student motivation, relevance, and interaction with peers. When teachers embed these key features in their lessons, students tend to experience high impact on their language development and content learning, increased engagement and interest through context and personal connections, and increased voluntary socialization with others to advance language learning and relationship building (Bernard, 2010; Mousa, 2018; Saeed & Zyngier, 2012).

In this chapter, we explore focused approaches to inclusion of English Learners and their families in schools and communities, as we answer the following key questions:

A. What are some ways that schools can provide a welcoming environment for all students, families, and the local community?

B. How might initial assessment and reception services be offered to newcomer students and their families?

C. What are some ways to facilitate integration of students and families into school and the larger community?

D. What have we learned so far about supporting English Learners attending school from a distance?

FIGURE 1.2 Question A Overview

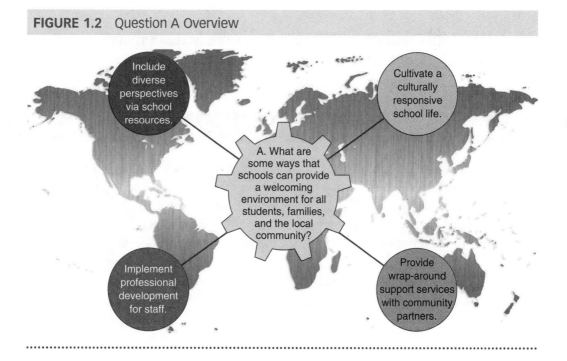

A. WHAT ARE SOME WAYS THAT SCHOOLS CAN PROVIDE A WELCOMING ENVIRONMENT FOR ALL STUDENTS, FAMILIES, AND THE LOCAL COMMUNITY?

- Powerful Practice 1: Cultivate a culturally responsive ethos that permeates every facet of school life.

- Powerful Practice 2: Provide wrap-around support services for newcomer students and their families in tandem with education and community partners.

- Powerful Practice 3: Implement professional development for staff to increase knowledge, build empathy, and support inclusion of newcomer students and families in all aspects of school.

- Powerful Practice 4: Prioritize the inclusion of books and resources representing diverse perspectives throughout the school and community.

Powerful Practice 1: Cultivate a culturally responsive ethos that permeates every facet of school life.

What It Might Look Like

Experienced teachers of English Learners know that learning is kick-started only when students feel relaxed enough in a new school and classroom environment to attend to the demands required by active learning, especially in another language. By putting both students and families at ease through seizing every opportunity to demonstrate welcome and inclusion, the school starts an intentional relationship-building process to best foster learning and student achievement, as well as parent and community engagement.

Many schools in Canada and the United States exhibit an equitable and inclusive mindset throughout their buildings and environments. A thoughtful school administrator's vision that is shared by all staff, accomplished through collective daily actions, can set an all-embracing tone for a culturally responsive school. Meet Tammy Ross, award-winning retired principal of Toronto's highly diverse Crescent Town Elementary School, where the majority of the students are English Learners. Tammy shared a few of her school's success stories in the following interview.

FIGURE 1.3 Tammy Ross

Authors: Tammy, what do you consider some of the most important factors for a school to be able to create an inclusive environment where students from diverse linguistic and cultural backgrounds can meet with success?

Tammy: We had high expectations for the teachers and in turn they were having high expectations for the kids. The kids were able to match or surpass Canadian-born kids in other schools in provincial testing. If these kids (English Learners) were able to do it, there's a reason; it's the quality of the teaching; it's the high expectations. The kids can do it; that's the message that we try to share with our staff and our parents.

Teachers used to think our kids can't do this because they don't have the language skills, and we moved our thinking to the point of recognizing the language skills the children have right now. What are we going to do to move them forward? So it's a shift in thinking.

When we were hiring people, we were looking for staff with experience supporting English Learners and also who were open to learn and had the idea that every child can learn. And also open to working with families. Ninety-four percent of our kids came from homes where another language was spoken. We tried to look for staff who spoke the languages of the community. Most of the staff did speak another language, whether it was one of the ones spoken in the community or another language. We tried to find people who reflected

(Continued)

(Continued)

the community but also people who had the compassion to understand what newcomer families were experiencing.

Coming there, I really had to be open to learning about the community. I had a lot of support in that way from staff, teachers, the community, our settlement worker. For example, if a parent in the community died, they would explain to me what the protocol was, and we would go into the community to visit them. When a child was sick for an extended period or we unfortunately had some tragedies with the parents and children in the community, we would go and do visits and bring food and show our respect for the families. We gained respect from the community by doing those visits.

We had these two little boys who would run away every day, and every day we would go to their home where they would be having tea and sit with the parents and try to help and get the kids to come back to school. These two little boys hadn't been to school before, and it was snowing and cold. They were just afraid.

I tried to be visible. In the morning, I would stand on the bridge to the school and say hello and welcome, and I think parents appreciated that. If I could, I would do that at the end of the day too, and say "see you tomorrow." Research shows it's so important that kids feel that someone is welcoming them to school and they feel like part of the community. If I knew personal things about the parents or family, I could say something. When I retired, a parent said to me: "Who's going to remind my son to wear his boots in the wintertime when you're gone?"

I think it's really important to consider the whole family and that there are varying needs depending on where they come from. Understanding the children's needs through their families. How teachers had to adjust what they're doing. If the mother came and said my son saw his father being shot, you understand more about why that child is behaving in a certain way. Not necessarily giving advice but trying to understand where the kids are coming from.

It's that trust too. Trust the people around you who know the community but who also understand your values and what you want to do for the school moving forward. Being honest with the community is so important too. For me to say to them, I really don't know, can you help me, can you teach me?

Building relationships from the get-go is so important. A smile does a lot. The people who were my front line people in the office—you want them to be welcoming and have smiling faces for everybody who comes into the school. I would sometimes talk with the office staff and tell them that they were the first faces that many of these families dealt with when they came to Canada, they had to be welcoming and kind. Then a parent who's having a really hard time will feel comfortable enough to have a conversation, which might lead to helping them. The school secretary was very open to sharing with parents about her own experiences as a new immigrant to Canada. Sometimes parents would come into the school just to sit and talk with her.

We used to do *Snuggle Up and Read* on Tuesdays from 6:00 to 7:00 p.m., once a week. The teacher–librarian would open the school library and parents could come with their kids to read and take books home. We also had the parents reading the multilingual parts of the books to the kids. We could get fifty or sixty people coming on an evening. Different teachers would sign up to read to the kids; grandparents too. The school became a community hub where people enjoyed coming during off-school time. It was also a way of demonstrating what we were doing with books in school so that parents could feel they could do that at home as well.

We've also done things like a neighbourhood walk with the staff so they could see where the community was living. We arranged to do a walk through the neighbourhood to look at all the resources that are available and to see where the kids were coming from. We also walked out of the community to where the subway is and farther away to see where the community services were. This way the staff were aware of what was offered for families. And to see where the kids are hanging out after school is interesting! It started a different conversation for teachers; for instance, there was a roof garden in one of the community service organizations. After seeing it, one of the teachers got her students to go there and plant.

As expressed in her brief interview highlighting essential principles of her successful leadership, Tammy's tenure consistently modeled specific goals. Her leadership embodied maintaining high expectations for her teachers and staff; serving as a reliable presence and trusted advocate visible throughout the school day; setting high expectations for students; recognizing students' current language skills as a starting point to build upon; developing a hiring policy that rewards multilingual skills and welcoming dispositions; modeling personal engagement with families and community during difficult or stressful events; and developing familiarity with the whole family's story as a means of accurately understanding and supporting students.

In both similar and divergent ways, other culturally responsive school leaders in the United States and Canada have enacted a multiplicity of impactful ideas achieving powerful outcomes in their contexts. For example, as a manifestation of welcoming and including new students and families, educators and students at one Iowa school focused on identifying kind actions that anyone could perform to convey a sense of belonging and caring to newcomers. A lead teacher combined all of her students' co-created ideas in a project called *Acts of Kindness Through a Cultural Lens*. Their suggestions were

FIGURE 1.4   Acts of Kindness Through a Cultural Lens Bookmark

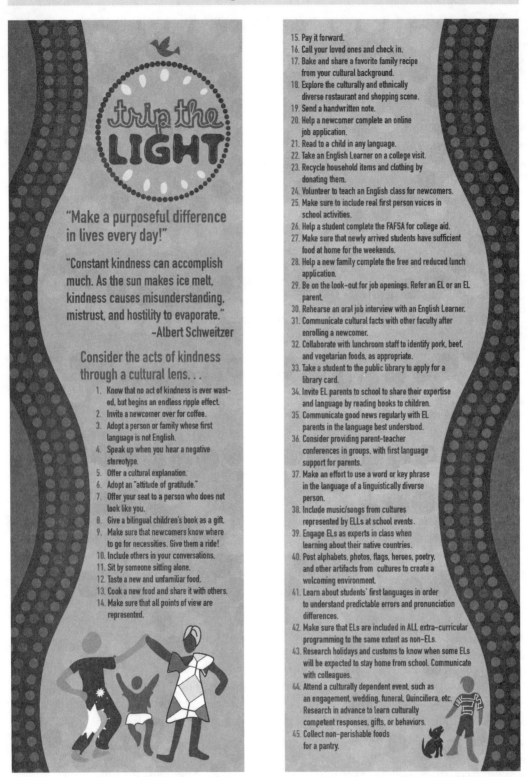

trip the LIGHT

"Make a purposeful difference in lives every day!"

"Constant kindness can accomplish much. As the sun makes ice melt, kindness causes misunderstanding, mistrust, and hostility to evaporate."
–Albert Schweitzer

Consider the acts of kindness through a cultural lens...

1. Know that no act of kindness is ever wasted, but begins an endless ripple effect.
2. Invite a newcomer over for coffee.
3. Adopt a person or family whose first language is not English.
4. Speak up when you hear a negative stereotype.
5. Offer a cultural explanation.
6. Adopt an "attitude of gratitude."
7. Offer your seat to a person who does not look like you.
8. Give a bilingual children's book as a gift.
9. Make sure that newcomers know where to go for necessities. Give them a ride!
10. Include others in your conversations.
11. Sit by someone sitting alone.
12. Taste a new and unfamiliar food.
13. Cook a new food and share it with others.
14. Make sure that all points of view are represented.
15. Pay it forward.
16. Call your loved ones and check in.
17. Bake and share a favorite family recipe from your cultural background.
18. Explore the culturally and ethnically diverse restaurant and shopping scene.
19. Send a handwritten note.
20. Help a newcomer complete an online job application.
21. Read to a child in any language.
22. Take an English Learner on a college visit.
23. Recycle household items and clothing by donating them.
24. Volunteer to teach an English class for newcomers.
25. Make sure to include real first person voices in school activities.
26. Help a student complete the FAFSA for college aid.
27. Make sure that newly arrived students have sufficient food at home for the weekends.
28. Help a new family complete the free and reduced lunch application.
29. Be on the look-out for job openings. Refer an EL or an EL parent.
30. Rehearse an oral job interview with an English Learner.
31. Communicate cultural facts with other faculty after enrolling a newcomer.
32. Collaborate with lunchroom staff to identify pork, beef, and vegetarian foods, as appropriate.
33. Take a student to the public library to apply for a library card.
34. Invite EL parents to school to share their expertise and language by reading books to children.
35. Communicate good news regularly with EL parents in the language best understood.
36. Consider providing parent-teacher conferences in groups, with first language support for parents.
37. Make an effort to use a word or key phrase in the language of a linguistically diverse person.
38. Include music/songs from cultures represented by ELLs at school events.
39. Engage ELs as experts in class when learning about their native countries.
40. Post alphabets, photos, flags, heroes, poetry, and other artifacts from cultures to create a welcoming environment.
41. Learn about students' first languages in order to understand predictable errors and pronunciation differences.
42. Make sure that ELs are included in ALL extra-curricular programming to the same extent as non-ELs.
43. Research holidays and customs to know when some ELs will be expected to stay home from school. Communicate with colleagues.
44. Attend a culturally dependent event, such as an engagement, wedding, funeral, Quinciñera, etc. Research in advance to learn culturally competent responses, gifts, or behaviors.
45. Collect non-perishable foods for a pantry.

SOURCE: Heartland Area Education Agency, https://www.heartlandaea.org/

printed on bookmarks and distributed to teachers and students throughout the school. Large posters of the Acts of Kindness were displayed in the front lobby of the school, along with multilingual Welcome to Our School posters. The Acts of Kindness initiative was a regular subject of discussion during homeroom periods. Administrators dedicated time in weekly staff meetings for teachers to report on kind gestures observed in action. As such, the thoughtful and welcoming practices became part of the school's fabric and served as norms of behavior for everyone in the school.

Physical spaces of any school can offer additional avenues for communicating a culturally responsive ethos. For example, an administrative team in a TDSB high school, whose population was evolving to include many newly arrived Muslim students, designed a foot-washing station in two washrooms to streamline the process for students preparing for midday prayers. Many schools and colleges now routinely dedicate spaces for students so that they can seamlessly perform their religious duties on campus during the school day. Other schools have conducted projects for making use of their physical spaces to visibly support an increased sense of inclusion and welcoming from the moment of entry. Simply transforming a corner of the foyer or main office into a parent welcome area, stocked with beverages, newspapers, magazines, and informational materials in the community languages of the school presents a natural gathering place where parents and other visitors begin to feel a sense of belonging. Along with having ready interpretation services, visible efforts such as these signal to students, families, and other community members that they are acknowledged, respected, and valued.

Teaching strategies can evolve to become more intentional in the inclusion of linguistically and culturally relevant pedagogy throughout all subject areas across all grade levels. A case in point was designed by a group of preservice high school physics teacher candidates at the University of Toronto. These beginning professionals designed a lesson for a Grade 11 physics class on the properties of light and colour. They adopted the idea of embedding cultural connections whenever possible to interest and engage students and promote interaction. During the physics lesson, students were invited to jot down the words for one colour in their home languages and add some cultural information about the significance of that colour in their home cultures. A gallery walk provided an opportunity for everyone to expand their linguistic and cultural expertise on the topic of colour significance in different cultures.

In another rich example of inclusive instruction, a middle school mathematics teacher demonstrated increased intentionality in making cultural connections when he designed a geometry unit that incorporated learning about the use of geometric shapes in Islamic religious art and decoration. Using an activity downloaded from the Asia Society (2020), his students discovered the basis for construction of traditional Islamic patterns based on geometric shapes and then created their own designs. Having built a significant background, the geometry students were ready to view images of mosques and other buildings to identify the use of similar geometric patterns in the real world.

| FIGURE 1.5 | Physics Venn Diagram Activity I | FIGURE 1.6 | Physics Venn Diagram Activity II |

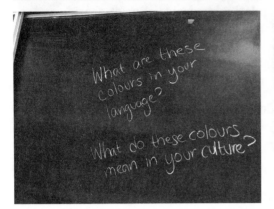

Making It Your Own

Cultivating a culturally responsive ethos that permeates every facet of school life is an ongoing goal that begins with a vision and individual mindful actions. Consider the suggestions listed in Figure 1.7 Culturally Responsive Ethos, that can be demonstrated by various areas of influence and impact within the school. Some suggestions might already be very familiar and well established in your setting. As you survey your school, what visual representations of your students' cultures and languages are incorporated into the environment?

FIGURE 1.7 Culturally Responsive Ethos

AREA OF INFLUENCE OR IMPACT IN THE SCHOOL	ACTIONS FOR CULTIVATING A CULTURALLY RESPONSIVE ETHOS THAT PERMEATES EVERY FACET OF SCHOOL LIFE
Teachers and staff personal level	• Use students' preferred names and pronounce them correctly. Avoid simplifying or changing a student's name. • Learn and use a few words or greetings in students' languages. • Conduct home visits. • Know backgrounds of students and implications for instruction. • Prepare the class in advance to receive newcomers. • Reach out to parents and families. • Pair a buddy or student ambassador with each newcomer. • Other ideas:

AREA OF INFLUENCE OR IMPACT IN THE SCHOOL	ACTIONS FOR CULTIVATING A CULTURALLY RESPONSIVE ETHOS THAT PERMEATES EVERY FACET OF SCHOOL LIFE
Classroom and physical environment	• Display diversity in posters, dual language and multicultural books, poetry, word walls, etc. • Provide a print-rich environment with pictorial support. • Ensure that students see their languages and cultures reflected in a variety of ways (e.g., artifacts, flags, posters, multilingual signage). • Other ideas:
Instruction and assessments	• Consider and respond to student's English language development levels. • Provide scaffolds and support. • Differentiate linguistic expectations based on English Learner-specific data. Interpret results based on differentiated language expectations and other student data. • Teach reading with full understanding of students' language background and developmental language needs. • Incorporate students' home languages routinely, flexibly, and strategically in instruction (translanguaging). • Include historical perspectives, literature, music, contributions, etc., from students' cultures as they relate to the content area (e.g., games from other countries in physical education; international instruments or music in band, orchestra, music, or choral classes, etc.). • Other ideas:
Texts and materials	• Match supplementary materials and supports with English language development levels. • Reflect diverse student experiences, cultures, and languages. • Incorporate differentiated supplementary materials that support content instruction. • Provide bilingual or first language materials as needed. • Ensure that classroom materials reflect diversity of all students (e.g., skin tones in crayons, colored pencils; multiethnic and differently abled dolls and other diverse models and playthings in early years learning centers). • Other ideas:
Extracurricular activities and events	• Ensure equitable participation of English Learners in all aspects of school (e.g., band, chorus, sports teams, school newspaper, clubs, honor society, gifted programming, special education representation, etc.). • Incorporate extracurricular events and clubs reflective of diverse cultural interests. • Incorporate music reflecting students' cultures into school concerts.

(Continued)

FIGURE 1.7 (Continued)

AREA OF INFLUENCE OR IMPACT IN THE SCHOOL	ACTIONS FOR CULTIVATING A CULTURALLY RESPONSIVE ETHOS THAT PERMEATES EVERY FACET OF SCHOOL LIFE
	• Create a "speakers' bureau" of representative student ambassadors for participation and presenting at local conventions, conferences, community meetings, and exchanges with other schools. • Other ideas:
Community participation at school	• Invite community partners to volunteer at school; solicit businesses to partner with school as sponsors; include and explicitly invite parents and families to all school events; involve community volunteers to staff a mentoring program for students or parents; provide childcare, transportation, and food at events for parents; collaborate with local civic groups, places of worship, media, and advocacy groups to expand involvement, support, and communication with students and families. • Other ideas:
Parental communication and outreach	• Ensure that interpreters are available at parent-teacher conferences. • Ensure that interpreters are available for parent-initiated interactions. • Dedicate a phone number allowing parents to report school absences in the home language. • Provide families with written home communication and phone calls in their preferred language. • Offer a family literacy program. • Invite parents to read bilingual books to students at school. • Provide simultaneous interpretation at parent meetings. • Ensure that English Learner parents belong to the school's parent-teacher advisory group. • Offer a parent meeting place at the school that features first language materials, tables and chairs, and other resources to convey welcoming. • Invite parents to volunteer to support teachers in the classroom by cutting, copying, laminating, or other needed activities. • Involve parents as classroom speakers or guests. • Connect students and families with others who speak their language. • Offer English and citizenship classes for parents. • Explore technology that enhances school-home communication, such as reminders about school events. • Other ideas:

AREA OF INFLUENCE OR IMPACT IN THE SCHOOL	ACTIONS FOR CULTIVATING A CULTURALLY RESPONSIVE ETHOS THAT PERMEATES EVERY FACET OF SCHOOL LIFE
Office and school support staff	• Emphasize the important role of every school employee sharing and communicating the school's attitude of welcome and friendliness with students and families.
	• Provide staff training that includes warm greetings in various languages and relevant cultural information.
	• Ensure that the make-up of school staff reflects the diversity of the community.
	• Clarify specific expectations of staff actions.
	• Other ideas:
School nurse or health office	• Become informed about holistic and culturally diverse home medical practices (e.g., the use of various culturally specific home remedies).
	• Learn a few phrases in students' languages to be able to calm or provide comfort.
	• Where possible, obtain glossaries of medical translations (e.g., Erickson Translation (2020) provides a COVID-19 glossary in 18 languages).
	• Ensure that staff have information about the acculturation process, identifying stimuli that can trigger post-traumatic stress and provide information about supportive approaches.
	• Be prepared to advise staff of ways to practice self care to deal with their own stress or fatigue.
	• Ensure availability of bandages for diverse students in various skin tones.
	• Other ideas:

For additional foundational ideas for creating the best possible welcoming environment and atmosphere throughout your school, review the site and roadmap from *The Language Friendly School,* developed in the Netherlands by the Rutu Foundation for Intercultural Multilingual Education (2019). This unique initiative is responding to the fact that worldwide, multilingualism has become the norm rather than the exception. The foundation espouses the belief that all children have the right to an equitable education that respects their cultural identity. The website displays a "road map" that schools can follow to build a school environment that embraces the languages and cultures of all students in the school community. What does being a language friendly school mean to you? Can you use the road map below to see your school's accomplishments and needs? Where is there room for growth and what will you do about it? Beginning with one or two new initiatives is a great start.

FIGURE 1.8 The Language Friendly School

The Language Friendly School

AS LANGUAGE FRIENDLY SCHOOLS WHAT WE DO

As a school

- We develop a language friendly plan together.
- We regularly evaluate our language friendly plan and adapt when necessary.
- We have a Language Coordinator who monitors the implementation of our language friendly plan.
- We encourage making a systematic inventory of students' home languages.
- We give visual representation to students' home languages at school.
- We use language buddies for children who speak the same languages.
- We pay attention to exclusion or bullying around languages, dialects or accents.

- We inform the whole school community about the importance of home languages.
- As teachers, we work together with parents to support the learning of children.
- We facilitate meetings where parents can use their home languages.
- We facilitate multilingual communication with parents.
- We facilitate after school language clubs.
- We ensure that there are books available in various languages.
- Our teachers and staff are aware of language and learning difficulties in relation to multilingualism.

In the classroom

- Our teachers are informed about the role of home languages in learning additional languages.
- We offer regular training and professional development to support our teachers in their multilingual pedagogical approaches.
- We share and regularly reflect on our approaches and the materials we use.
- We reflect on our own values and ideas and are aware of our attitudes towards language, cultural, and ethnic diversity.
- We offer our teachers self-evaluation tools.

- We make room for students' home languages as part of the learning process.
- We encourage all students to develop their whole language repertoire, including dialects and accents.
- We offer where possible instruction in various languages present in school.
- In our classrooms, the home languages of all students are visible.
- We promote written, oral, gestural, and graphic students' communication to promote inclusion.

WHAT WE DON'T DO

- We do not prohibit or discourage the use of other languages at school.
- We do not punish our students for using their home languages at school.
- We do not prohibit or discourage parents to use their own languages at school.
- We do not advise parents to use a different language at home with their children.
- We do not allow exclusion or bullying around languages, dialects, or accents.

LANGUAGE FRIENDLY SCHOOL

De Taalvriendelijke School© is een initiatief van de Rutu Foundation voor intercultureel meertalig onderwijs
www.languagefriendlyschool.org

RUTU Foundation

The Language Friendly School network promotes language friendly learning environments and innovative multilingual pedagogies. Language Friendly Schools commit not to punish and suppress the use of non-dominant languages. A Language Friendly School plan is adapted to the school's own needs and aims at creating an inclusive and language friendly learning environment for all students. The Language Friendly School (www.languagefriendlyschool.org) was founded in 2019 by Ellen-Rose Kambel and Emmanuelle Le Pichon as a programme of the Rutu Foundation for Intercultural Multilingual Education.

Powerful Practice 2: Make connections with
wrap-around support for newcomer students and
their families through education and community partners.

What It Might Look Like

Since newcomer students and families arrive at both Canadian and U.S. schools with a wide-ranging scope of backgrounds and resources, prepared schools must be nimble in identifying and responding to needs that exist within homes and families that could undermine success in school. To increase the capacity for providing meaningful support for both newcomer students and families, experienced school boards and districts in the United States and Canada have forged networks of education and community partners to share and multiply their considerable talents and resources. Schools can access a variety of resources and allies to meet unprecedented needs in their schools by compiling an eclectic list of imaginative education and community partners. The wide-ranging list of potential partners should include representatives from refugee resettlement, faith-based and service organizations; clothing, furniture, and food banks; cultural community sponsors such as a local museum, zoo, or theater; local newspapers and media; colleges and universities; as well as local businesses. Once identified, the entire community can be called upon and involved in making a welcoming and supportive community for everyone.

An elementary school that had just enrolled a large number of young children arriving directly from a refugee camp where they had lived for months provides a great example of wrap-around support. Each of the children had experienced interruptions in education and were beginning to learn in a new language. In response to the needs communicated to the business community by the school, a local car dealership owner dedicated twenty employees to volunteer weekly at the school. Their task was to read stories to the newcomers one-on-one and support literacy development in ways directed by teachers. At the end of the school year, a volunteer celebration with lunch was held honoring and celebrating the faithful volunteers and their contributions to literacy development at the school.

Similarly, a local service organization of retired women extended their support to K–12 newcomers by creating a service project to facilitate their successful start at school. By coordinating lists of grade-level school supplies, they were able to provide each new student an appropriate backpack filled with the necessary tools, setting newcomers up for success in the classroom and also supporting their parents. Distributed to students and families during an initial home visit by school representatives and interpreters, *The Backpack Project* visibly demonstrated a connection with this community organization that extended the school's wrap-around support for newcomers.

Local businesses in the community can follow suit by collaborating with schools as corporate sponsors. In one town, the business consortium provided access to cultural attractions for newcomers and families by supplying admission tickets for the local museum, a community children's theater production, the zoo, and an amusement park. Partnering with these businesses, the schools organized transportation and chaperones for acculturating their newest members to popular but often costly attractions in the community.

Wrap-around services to support newcomer students and families were further extended at another school where teachers themselves noticed that some of their newcomers showed a lack of basic material resources, such as sufficient food to sustain them over the weekend and clothing suitable for cold weather. After soliciting household and clothing donations school-wide and throughout the community, volunteer teachers and staff organized a "garage sale" in the school gymnasium for interested newcomers and families who could take items they needed. The occasion grew to become an annual highlight, now even offering household items and furniture for easing the transition of newcomers and families into an unfamiliar environment as they establish their new homes with a welcoming and appreciated community event.

Partnerships with public library boards bring together another powerful umbrella of services to support newcomer students and their families. Many public library branches stock books, magazines, and electronic resources in a variety of community languages. Programs to support newcomer students and their families abound in many districts. In Calgary, Alberta, Canada, the public library offers a slew of programs and services for newcomer parents, from settlement service counsellors to coffee and conversation clubs, writing clubs, and citizenship exam preparation classes. Parents and caregivers can participate together with their children in a translanguaging-friendly program called *Learn English Storytime*, where adults and children can meet and practice English with others who speak the same home language. The Toronto Public Library system offers online library information for newcomers in forty different languages and a "New to Canada" blog that points the way to information and resources available from the library and around the city for new residents of Canada. In 2016, the Toronto Public Library entered into a partnership with Sun Life Financial to proffer a special museum and arts pass for Syrian refugee families new to the city, giving them free introductory visits to local cultural institutions like the Art Gallery of Ontario and the Ontario Science Centre.

POWERFUL PRACTICES FOR SUPPORTING ENGLISH LEARNERS

In many areas, universities and colleges partner regularly with the middle and high schools by hosting college campus tours and special services for newcomers. Interpreters are arranged in advance, and there is ample time for questions and answers at the university or college. In this way, newcomers can begin to gain a realistic perspective of what is available to them and set future goals for themselves. In addition, collegial and reciprocal relationships allow the school and university to partner in numerous endeavors, including hosting student teacher *practica*, conducting research, and teacher placement after graduation.

Focusing their wrap-around support on healing and family well-being, Toronto's settlement agency, CultureLink, contributes a creative and ongoing way of partnering with schools in easing newcomer transitions. When thousands of Syrian children enrolled in Canadian schools in 2015, the Nai Syrian Children's Choir was soon established. The chorus of children, ranging from six to twelve years old, received formal music education and now, confident and beloved, they serve as ambassadors as they perform their music at many official and community events, including at Canada's federal Parliament buildings in Ottawa.

These examples of education and community partnerships described for enhancing and extending wrap-around services for newcomers and families are but a tiny sampling. With imagination being the only limitation, boundless opportunities exist between schools and potential partners for extending caring and meaningful support to newcomers and families.

Making It Your Own

What examples of wrap-around services and supports for newcomers and families exist in your context? What suggestions do you have for forging relationships and new connections to extend wrap-around support at your school? Have individuals at your school started any initiatives based on student or family needs they have observed or heard about? Are educators and staff aware of where they can access information about available resources and support for newcomers and families?

Powerful Practice 3: Provide professional development for staff that will increase their knowledge, build empathy, and support the inclusion of newcomer students and families in all aspects of school.

One high performing, suburban elementary school of 215 students experienced a sudden transition in enrollment over a two-year time span. As diverse newcomers moved in and others moved out, the enrollment at this neighborhood school stood at 232 students, 104 of whom had recently arrived from various countries and refugee camps in Africa. Teachers who were prepared to teach their students of previous years were now struggling to meet the unfamiliar demands for intensive reading instruction in English, as well as to understand student behaviors, cultural practices, and language differences among their newest students. They felt that their school was in danger of losing its academic distinction, based on standardized assessment results, as a high achieving school. The principal knew that a comprehensive building-wide professional development effort was needed to invest in teachers and empower them with the background knowledge and new tools they were seeking.

At the same time, neighboring residents within the school's attendance boundaries were also struggling with their own misperceptions and fears related to the newcomer families. For example, a police report was made by nervous homeowners one evening with a complaint of several men "walking around the neighborhood." Upon closer examination, newcomer parents who lived in the large apartment complex did, in fact, walk around the neighborhood each evening, often in a small group of three or four friends. This practice was the same as they had done each evening in the refugee camp, conversing as they walked. It had not occurred to them that this practice might induce fear in observers.

In another example of misunderstood intentions, police assistance was sought when children who wandered off the sidewalk on their way to school had stepped into a private yard to pick apples. A resettlement caseworker suggested to the neighbors that children recently arrived from a large refugee camp where food was scarce could understandably be excited at the sight of juicy red apples. In fact, in their new environment, no one had yet explained or demonstrated the purpose or expectation of adhering to sidewalks or the notion of a private yard with privately owned trees or that fruit on trees is not necessarily meant to be picked and eaten without permission. As is true with any assessment, evaluating that which has not been explicitly taught is unfair practice. Further, uninformed assumptions can likely lead to inaccurate conclusions.

The perceptive principal at this small neighborhood school decided to organize and implement an ongoing two-year professional development plan for her staff, calling upon many local resources and community members to assist. Following analysis of a needs assessment, the timeline and elements of the ongoing professional development were conceived, including an embedded professional learning community (PLC) at the school where grade-level teams of teachers could try out and process new learning, share results, and gain support from each other.

To help staff build empathy and understanding of English Learners, teachers were asked to submit a list of their questions to the principal and also to suggest ideas for what was needed to support them. They asked questions such as "How can we improve how we help the community to better understand our new population?" "Could we bring in a panel of parents from different countries and have them explain their education and what their expectations were/are of our education system?" and "What types of after school programs and community involvement should we be offering?" Based on this starting point, The Four-Tiered Model of Professional Development took shape (Figure 1.9). It presented a comprehensive approach to professional development, inclusive of the neighbors and families in the community, by addressing four categories of learning:

1. Build empathy and understanding for students and families by learning about their experiences and realities.

2. Provide training on instructional and assessment strategies that meet the needs of English Learners and culturally and linguistically diverse students.

3. Involve and partner with parents and community members in new learning opportunities and outreach efforts to build community.

4. Highlight and address under-resourced learner issues by creating partnerships with community organizations and businesses.

As one introductory aspect of the professional learning addressing all four tiers of professional development described above, the teacher of English to Speakers of Other Languages (ESOL) designed and organized a cultural exploration activity for her colleagues to support them in better understanding the newest residents in the community. She organized visits to nearby cultural venues to experience firsthand where families shopped, ate, worked, worshipped, and gathered. Teachers reported that they enjoyed this activity immensely since many had driven past the various destinations on multiple occasions, but had not visited them. As they debriefed and discussed their findings, participants seemed energized by their discoveries and reported that they had enjoyed trying an unfamiliar dish, discovering new products to share, or touring the inside of a different place of worship for the first time. Having factual information, combined with newfound appreciation informed by their own personal experiences, helped participants in understanding and creating a more welcoming environment for their newcomer students and families. This engaging and instructive activity was adapted for inclusion in other classes and courses promoting cultural awareness and sensitivity.

FIGURE 1.9 Four Tiered Model of Professional Development

Tier 1

Build empathy for students and families by understanding their experiences and realities.

Desired outcome:

While building background knowledge related to the resettlement process and issues specific to recent refugees from Africa, educators will increase empathy for newcomer students and families.

- Provide background information in the form of simulations, experiences, videos, movies, and speakers ("first person voices") for school staff.
- Involve police officers, local clergy, civic organization representatives, religious representatives, business leaders, neighbors, and other interested community members to build partnership and community.
- Host a community screening of a movie/documentary, followed by guided discussion.
- Provide an overview of the refugee immigration/resettlement process: video clips, group discussion, books authored by refugees themselves.
- Invite immigration attorneys and other guest speakers.
- Invite immigrant parents to tell their stories with an interpreter, if needed.
- Teachers participate in a field trip to visit the most diverse elementary school in the state for ideas of best practice to adopt at their school.
- Participants make a cultural exploration in the community of identified locations and report back.
- Brainstorm and implement ideas to make the school and classroom more welcoming to culturally and linguistically diverse students and families.

Tier 2

Provide training on instructional and assessment strategies that meet the needs of English language learners/ culturally and linguistically diverse students.

Desired outcome:

Staff will adopt and implement strategies to effectively address the instructional and assessment needs of English Learners.

- **Topics of professional learning**
- Differentiation of language demands in assignments and assessments based on student data.
- Sheltered instruction strategies.
- Appropriate reading instruction for English Learners, particularly those at pre-reading levels, regardless of grade level.
- Language acquisition process.
- Accurate interpretation of English Learner data.
- Application of student background information to instructional planning.

Tier 3

Involve and partner with parents and community members in new learning opportunities and outreach efforts.

Desired outcome:

Staff will include community members and parents in activities to build community and promote the success of all students. Parents and community members will feel comfortable and welcomed when entering the school.

- Identify challenges experienced by students and families.
- Build ways to support students outside of school.
- Share resources with teachers on supporting children and families in need.
- Examine lunchroom policies for inclusivity and weekend/summer meal availability for students.
- Examine ways to defray or waive costs of extracurricular participation, uniforms, sports equipment, band instruments, etc., for under-resourced families.
- Explore and develop school offerings: English classes for parents, computer class, family literacy program, Saturday school, summer school, intramural sports, or other.
- Make multicultural and multilingual books for school and home available.
- Conduct home visits with an interpreter; contact the home additionally by phone via interpreter.
- Invite parents as partners into the school to share their skills in various volunteer activities (e.g., reading books in home languages to students).

Tier 4	• Identify needs of under-resourced learners at school.
Highlight and address under-resourced learner needs, creating partnerships with community organizations and businesses to meet needs of students and families.	• Explore the possibility of partnering with community service groups as sponsors of school supplies for students.
	• Consider establishing a food bank or clothes closet at school.
	• Provide clearly marked entrances and signage and a dedicated welcoming area at school for parents.
	• Conduct meaningful home visits.
Desired outcome:	• Hold an event such as school registration at a local venue near where families live, such as a library, for their convenience.
Staff will gain awareness of the impact of intersecting needs that can accompany refugee status and translate their awareness to specific actions to meet student needs.	• Invite adult role models or older students to interact with students (e.g., mentoring, skill building, etc.).
	• Support parents to promote learning for their children, such as suggested tips for literacy development using the family's first language.
	• Open house: invite neighbors, school board members, and community members to meet and hear from new families.
	• Connect with the local Chamber of Commerce to build partnerships and increase support for the entire school population.

Making It Your Own

Become a tourist in your own city! Researching and personally visiting the community to become more familiar with culturally diverse gathering places can facilitate understanding the lives of new students and their families and promote valuable connections. This activity comprised a small part of one district's professional development at multiple school sites and was also a part of annual new teacher orientation at the high school, providing an authentic experience for new teachers to learn about and appreciate their students and families.

Might this type of cultural exploration serve as a useful learning activity for professional development in your context? Referring to Figure 1.10 Cultural Exploration Activity, create your own community exploration based on culturally and linguistically diverse destinations in your school neighborhood. Consider a virtual exploration to expand your geographical boundaries if your school is situated at a distance from culturally and linguistically diverse amenities. Review the menu of potential multicultural venues in the model provided and create a version of your own local destinations that could be explored and experienced. What reflection questions would you like to pose at the end? Who might benefit from participating in such an activity?

FIGURE 1.10 Cultural Exploration Activity

WHERE DO YOUR STUDENTS AND FAMILIES SHOP, WORK, WORSHIP, AND SOCIALIZE?	
NAME OF VENUE	**ADDRESS**

Food Markets

Include a range of different ethnic-specific food markets in the neighborhood.

Restaurants

Include a variety of restaurants from different ethnic backgrounds as well as those featuring different types of service (e.g., formal sit-down service, fast food for take-out, street food, etc.).

Places of Worship

Include a range of venues (e.g., gurdwaras, temples, churches, synagogues, mosques).

Places to Socialize

Include community centers, movie theaters, clubs, libraries, and so forth.

Literacy Opportunities

Notice availability of print in other languages (e.g., environmental print, billboards, street signage, newspapers, magazines, books, bookstores, etc.).

Reflection Questions

- In addition to foods, what other kinds of products are offered?
- Who did you notice at this venue?
- Describe any personal interactions you had while there.
- Would you be able to purchase what you need for a week at this store?
- What products stood out to you?
- Describe an item that is new to you.
- Describe any purchases you made.
- If a restaurant, what are some of the unique ingredients used in the cuisine?
- If you visited a place of worship or a place to socialize, describe any interactions with hosts or others present.
- What impressed you about this venue?
- Can you identify a central belief, practice, or new learning about the religion?
- What is one new general learning that you took away from this exploration activity?

Powerful Practice 4: Prioritize the inclusion of books and resources representing diverse perspectives throughout the school and community.

What It Might Look Like

The American Library Association provides helpful guidance for determining useful resources for inclusion in school collections. By ensuring that all available resources and materials in the school represent the range of diverse perspectives present in the school community, schools can best provide an inclusive and empowering environment for all students. Such an intentional all-embracing approach to school resources encompasses materials in the school library/resource center, individual classroom book collections, artwork, posters, and samples of student work displayed in the school. Striving to develop a school environment that is increasingly linguistically and culturally responsive, the teacher-librarian, supported by the principal, works to ensure that all resources, including electronically accessed resources used by students, represent the entire spectrum of community diversity. The teacher-librarian also advocates for the inclusion of dual language books reflecting the gamut of languages spoken in the school and community, along with accessible books in English and other home languages. Content is sought that equitably mirrors the unique cultural, religious, linguistic, and ethnic backgrounds comprising students' experiences and backgrounds. Such resources are displayed and offered from a prominent location in the library/resource center for all to access.

To further ensure inclusion of all students in appropriate school resources, a school library/resource center must be sensitive to promoting English Learners' literacy development by providing accessibility across the spectrum of reading levels for students at various levels of English proficiency. Frances Ferguson, the teacher-librarian at Greenwood Secondary School, a newcomer high school in Toronto, makes certain that the library's shelves are stocked with an abundance of high-interest, leveled readers that appeal to adolescents, reflecting a variety of student backgrounds and interests. In addition to dual language books, dictionaries, and monolingual books in an array of home languages, Greenwood Secondary School's resource center includes a large collection of children's informational texts covering all curriculum areas. Frances recognizes that students at the beginning levels of English proficiency as well as those with limited or interrupted formal schooling can benefit from using children's nonfiction books with their larger font, less densely written paragraphs, clear definitions, and explanatory visuals. Her inviting resource center also has a section of student-created books for borrowing.

In an inclusive school, individual teachers are also mindful to select resources for their classrooms and courses that demonstrate cultural and linguistic relevance for their students, from texts about scientific discoveries and processes from around the world in the chemistry lab; to posters of diverse artists, musical instruments, and art forms in the music and art rooms; to read-alouds for the elementary classroom where children will see themselves represented.

After becoming familiar with cultural and linguistic backgrounds of students enrolled in his school, one teacher created an array of fourteen posters for highlighting the achievements of role models and trailblazers mirroring students' diverse backgrounds (e.g., Mario Molina, first Mexican-born scientist to receive the Nobel Prize in chemistry; Ellen Ochoa, first Latina astronaut; and Rachelle Jones and Stephanie Grant, Delta copilots and first all-female African American flight crew at Delta Airlines). See two examples following from his set of Diverse Achievers posters created to communicate inclusion and inspire achievement by students able to see their identities highlighted and valued at school (See Figures 1.11A and 1.11B).

Teachers make sure that English Learners have access to print resources that have been adapted for various stages of English language acquisition. They also provide English Learners with access to multilingual and adapted digital resources that support their language learning needs, such as PebbleGo (Capstone, 2020) and Newsela (Newsela, 2020). Developed for elementary students but also useful for adolescent English Learners at the beginning stages of English proficiency, PebbleGo is a digital library of social studies, science, and history topics, providing leveled informational texts and media in both English and Spanish. Newsela, an online source of current events content adapted from a range of trusted news sources, offers elementary and secondary English Learners up-to-date and engaging leveled articles in English and Spanish.

FIGURE 1.11A Franklin R. Chang-Diaz (First U.S. Astronaut of Chinese-Latin American descent)

FIGURE 1.11B John Herrington (First Native American (Chickasaw Nation) U.S. Astronaut)

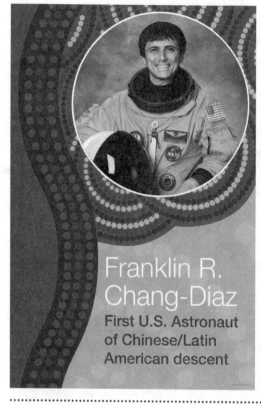

Franklin R. Chang-Diaz

First U.S. Astronaut of Chinese/Latin American descent

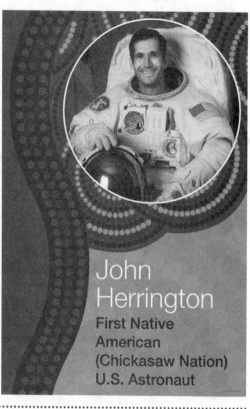

John Herrington

First Native American (Chickasaw Nation) U.S. Astronaut

Poster images provided by Heartland Area Education Agency, https://www.heartlandaea.org/

Photographs of Franklin R. Chang-Díaz and John Herrington are from the NASA Image and Video Library, https://images.nasa.gov/

Reprinted with permission

School populations are also diverse and dissimilar in the ways that students and their families have taken their journeys to where they are now. While some schools may have many immigrant students in their community, other schools may have few or none. No matter what the demographics of a school, reading and thinking critically about the stories of immigrants and refugees is an essential learning experience for children and youth in today's global world, for developing empathy and understanding the challenging life journeys of migrants. Profound books with rich and moving true stories that reveal glimpses into the hearts and minds of refugees and immigrants, reflecting their real-life tragedies and triumphs, abound for readers at all grade levels. Some of the universal issues that flow naturally from such stories include understanding the challenges of a new culture and language that confront newcomers to a new country, walking the tightrope of balancing two cultural and linguistic identities, and empathizing with the demanding and often horrific circumstances that children and their families have had to endure in order to arrive in a safe place. In an age of global human movement, books and resources depicting the myriad of student and family journeys should be an integral part of school and classroom library collections. A selection of recommended books about the experiences of immigrants and refugees is provided in Figure 1.12.

FIGURE 1.12 Recommended Books About Immigrant and Refugee Experiences

Elementary Grades K–3	• Gravel, Elise. (2019). *What Is a Refugee?* New York, NY: Schwartz and Wade. Explains the circumstances of refugees in concepts and language that young children can understand.
	• O'Brien, Anne Sibley.
	○ (2015). *I'm New Here.* Watertown, MA: Charlesbridge.
	○ (2018). *Someone New.* Watertown, MA: Charlesbridge. Companion books portraying the adjustment experiences of elementary children who are newcomers to their school.
	• Ruurs, Margriet. (2016). *Stepping Stones: A Refugee Family's Journey.* Victoria, British Columbia: Orca Book Publishers. A compassionate look at the flight of a Syrian family from their war-torn homeland.
	• Woodson, Jacqueline. (2018). *The Day You Begin.* New York, NY: Nancy Paulsen Books. Elementary school children deal with their feelings of difference and being in new situations.
Elementary Grades 4–6	• Mills, Deborah, & Alva, Alfredo. (2018). *La Frontera: El Viaje Con Papá/My Journey with Papa.* Cambridge, MA: Barefoot Books. Dual language book recounts the story of a father and son who courageously cross into America without documents.
	• Pinkney, Andrea Davis. (2014). *The Red Pencil.* New York: Little, Brown and Company. The experiences of a 12-year-old refugee from the South Darfur region of Sudan, told in free verse.
	• Rauf, Onjali Q. (2018). *The Boy at the Back of the Class.* London, UK: Hachette Children's. When a Kurdish refugee from Syria joins their class, a group of classroom friends make it their mission to help him find his missing family.
	• Skrypuch, Marsha Forchuk. (2016). *Adrift at Sea: A Vietnamese Boy's Story of Survival.* Toronto, ON: Pajama Press. Tells the true story of a Vietnamese family's flight from Vietnam.
Middle School	• Ahn, Angela. (2018). *Krista Kim-Bap.* Toronto, ON: Second Story Press. A Korean-Canadian girl tries to find the balance between her two cultures and languages.
	• Fountain, Ele. (2018). *Refugee 87.* New York: Little, Brown and Company. An African boy embarks on a gruelling journey to freedom across land and sea.
	• Gratz, Alan. (2017). *Refugee.* New York: Scholastic Press. Intertwines stories of three adolescent refugees from different time periods in Nazi Germany, Cuba, and Syria.
	• Nazario, Sonia. (2014) *Enrique's Journey: Young Reader's Edition.* Toronto, Ontario: Ember. The story of a boy's dangerous odyssey across Central America to reunite with his mother in the United States.
	• Tan, Shaun. (2006). *The Arrival.* London, UK: Hodder Children's Books. Wordless graphic novel that recounts the story of an immigrant arriving in an imaginary new land.

POWERFUL PRACTICES FOR SUPPORTING ENGLISH LEARNERS

High School	• Al Rabeeah, Abu Bakr, & Yeung, Winnie. (2018). *Homes*. Calgary, Alberta: Freehand Books. Memoir of a Syrian teenager who flees with his family and settles in Alberta, Canada.
	• Cruz, Angie. (2019). *Dominicana*. The story of an undocumented immigrant from the Dominican Republic navigating teenage marriage and cultural adjustment. New York: Flatiron Books.
	• Vargas, Jose Antonio. (2018). *Dear America: Notes of an Undocumented Citizen*. New York: Dey Street Books. Memoir of an undocumented American from the Philippines who is a Pulitzer Prize winning journalist.
	• Wamariya, Clementine. (2018). *The Girl Who Smiled Beads*. Toronto, ON: Doubleday Canada. A young Rwandan refugee and her sister flee from country to country in Africa and are finally sponsored to come to the United States, where she eventually graduates from Princeton University.

Making It Your Own

Use the following questions to survey the availability of linguistically and culturally relevant materials in different locations that serve your students. Take stock of the books on display in your class and those that you loan to families. Is there a wide depiction of cultural, linguistic, and religious backgrounds; physical abilities; family groupings; sexual orientation; and gender identities in the books and materials available? Research abundant potential additions to create your own display featuring relevant Diverse Achievers posters (e.g., Kamala Harris, U.S. vice-president, Harjit Sajjan, Canadian Minister of National Defence, and Joseph Medicine Crow, recipient of the Presidential Medal of Freedom by Barack Obama in 2009); Browse websites such as Maya's Book Nook (2020), https://mayasbooknook.com/; National Association for Multicultural Education (2020), www.nameorg.org; Read Across America (National Education Association, 2020), www.readacrossamerica.org; Social Justice Books (2020), www.socialjusticebooks.org; and Teaching Tolerance (1991–2020), www.tolerance.org, to discover a wide selection of books, printable posters, and lesson plan suggestions that reflect the unique makeup of your class and beyond. Does your classroom include dual- or home-language books, especially those in the languages spoken by your students? What resources can you provide for colleagues and families that include dual or home-language books (e.g., the International Children's Digital Library)? Do you have a range of informational texts geared for various levels of English proficiency? Are they a good match with the topics and lessons that you will be teaching? Does your school library feature a similarly diverse collection of books and materials? Does your book fair feature books that represent diversity as well as dual-language books, or might you have to advocate for their inclusion? What resources are available at your community library, and how can you partner with librarians to ensure equitable and wide-ranging representation?

FIGURE 1.13 Question B: Overview

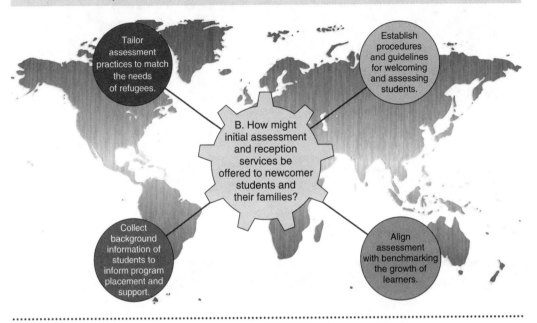

B. HOW MIGHT INITIAL ASSESSMENT AND RECEPTION SERVICES BE OFFERED TO NEWCOMER STUDENTS AND THEIR FAMILIES?

- Powerful Practice 1: Establish clear, supportive, and consistent procedures and guidelines for welcoming and assessing newcomer students.

- Powerful Practice 2: Align initial assessment as part of a larger scheme of benchmarking the growth of English development within jurisdictional requirements.

- Powerful Practice 3: Collect comprehensive background information about newly arrived students to inform the most appropriate program placement and support.

- Powerful Practice 4: Tailor unique assessment practices for refugee students and families who have undergone trauma.

Powerful Practice 1: Establish clear, supportive, and consistent procedures and guidelines for welcoming and assessing newcomer students.

A large North American urban school district such as the TDSB can welcome upwards of 10,000 newcomer students from grades K–12 in a single academic year. Within the TDSB itself, there are more than 440 elementary schools and over 100 secondary schools distributed across the sprawling expanse of the city. Typically, as in many large urban areas, neighbourhoods that contain more multifamily housing tend to receive a lot of newcomer arrivals while other neighbourhoods made up of predominantly single-family homes may receive fewer newcomers.

In a large school district such as in Toronto with so many new arrivals, elementary school-aged children and their families go directly to their local school where they receive immediate welcome, reception, and assessment services from school administrators, teachers, and settlement workers. Secondary school-aged students and their families spend a full day for welcome and assessment at one of two newcomer reception centres strategically placed in the eastern and western halves of the city. Each newcomer reception centre is situated within a larger secondary school building and is located near a subway station for public transport accessibility. Other school districts in Ontario, for example in Ottawa and Mississauga, have chosen to provide central reception and assessment services for both elementary and secondary students. The number of new arrivals, number of schools in the district, size of the district, and transportation feasibility are all factors that will play into the decision of whether to welcome and assess new English Learners at local schools, at a central location, or a combination of the two.

Regardless of the location, the welcome and assessment process should take place in a friendly physical space and be carried out by trained educators who are expert not only in administering and interpreting the assessments but also in understanding and supporting newcomer students and their families in their early days of adjusting to a new country, language, and culture.

In the TDSB, the central venues used for the welcome and assessment of newcomer students are spacious, bright, and cheerful. Separate areas are available for English and mathematics teachers to work with students, as well as a space for the counselling staff, which is large enough for parents to gather with their children for informal interviews. Many newcomer families have young children they will bring to the reception centre, so there is a designated area where families can play, along with some toys and multilingual storybooks. Students may bring food from home, so there is a small microwave oven in a space away from the testing area where students can eat their lunch and relax. The walls in the English and mathematics assessment areas contain multilingual word displays of relevant academic terms, and there is access to several computers. The settlement workers have their own private space to meet with parents and guardians while the students are completing the assessment tasks.

In order to make sure that every student and family will receive the full time needed for assessment and counselling, assessments at the newcomer reception centres take place by appointment only. At the busiest times of the year—August, September, and January—it's vital for students to call ahead to book an appointment. Detailed information about the two newcomer reception centres is easy to find on the school district's webpage, including maps and an overview of everything that will happen during the daylong reception and assessment process. Parents and guardians are strongly encouraged to accompany their teenage children to the reception centre first thing in the morning, so they can participate in helping the reception centre staff get to know the background and needs of the student through an informal interview. Parents also meet with a settlement worker to obtain information about the new school system and to discuss their questions about housing, employment, access for New Canadians to the public healthcare system, and agencies and organizations that support newcomers. Parents are requested to return to the reception centre toward the end of the day, when along with their child they will meet with a guidance counsellor to discuss the assessment and placement recommendations. Reception centre staff are multilingual, and many have lived the experience of being newcomers to our country. There is also access to a real-time interpretation service through an off-site contractor engaged by the school district. Teachers can call in, request an interpreter in a specific language, and are soon connected by speaker phone to someone who can interpret for the family in their language. All staff at the reception centre are sympathetic to the fact that students might not perform to their maximum ability on the day of their initial assessment due to anxiety, lack of familiarity with the Canadian school context, culture shock, and sometimes even jet lag. Students are not rushed through the assessments and may have up to two and a half hours to complete each of the English and mathematics components of the full day assessment.

There are also many English Learners who are not new arrivals, and some new arrivals who are not English Learners. Newcomer students may have received their schooling abroad in an English-medium school context. Other students may have been born in Canada or the United States but have been raised in families and communities where languages other than English are the primary vehicle of communication. Some of these learners may still require English language support for academic success. Other learners may have been born in North America but returned to their country of origin for a period of time, during which they were not exposed to English. Thus classroom teachers need to be attuned to students who might not yet have been identified as English Learners but may be experiencing challenges using English at school. Sometimes a check of the student's official record file may yield a copy of the provincial template for annual tracking of progress in English learning. Other strategies for obtaining further information about students born in Canada include interviewing parents about the child's language use and asking about language use directly from older students. Knowledge of each student's language background, educational experiences, and migration stories can assist in the identification and appropriate placement of students who may benefit from receiving English language support (TESOL, 2020b).

In addition to providing a welcoming environment and a thoughtful procedure for initial reception and assessment in schools, offering a research-based program to enhance parental and family involvement is recommended to meet the changing needs of families (Vera et al., 2012). Schools can provide an authentic context for social and academic integration of students and families as they begin to establish new roots. By creating a pervasive friendly and caring school atmosphere that welcomes and reaches out to parents, schools can best ensure that new students and families consider themselves valued members of the community. In the United States, many schools have relied on the *Newcomers Toolkit* for a comprehensive foundation of useful ideas (U.S. Department of Education, 2017b).

Making It Your Own

Explore the following list of suggestions for communicating with students, parents, and the wider community about your school and district. Would any of them meet the needs of your current context? What would it take to implement new methods of information sharing?

School/district website includes information or links for new arrivals:

- Translations in languages other than English
- Descriptions of English language learning support programs
- Descriptions of bilingual education programs
- Outlines the intake and assessment procedure for new arrivals

School provides

- Orientation information for new students
- Information in languages other than English
- A tour for newly arrived students and parents
- A phased-in reception and orientation program over several days
- Student ambassadors to accompany new students in their early days
- Parent ambassadors to mentor newcomer parents
- Opportunity to meet with a settlement worker

Powerful Practice 2: Align initial assessment as part of a larger scheme of benchmarking the growth of English development within jurisdictional requirements.

It is critical to determine students' initial level of English proficiency so that an informed recommendation can be offered for placement, when indicated, in an appropriate English language support program. This initial English language assessment must be aligned to a larger scheme of benchmarking English language learning progress. Linking initial assessment with English language standards will provide a useful and valid indication of a student's English capabilities relative to the learning expectations and course curricula in the recommended placement (King & Bigelow, 2018; Sinclair & Lau, 2018). Sinclair and Lau (2018) further note that "an assessment based on interviews will have different validity and reliability than one based on a standardized measure" (p. 257). Incorporating an informal interview as part of the language assessment process can enable teachers to learn so much more about each individual student's situation, strengths, and needs.

The initial assessment interview and tasks should include an opportunity for the student to engage in conversation about relevant personal information with the interviewing teacher. A series of age-appropriate questions allows the teacher to determine how well the student can respond to questions on personal and familiar topics. The assessment process can then proceed to tasks that require the student to show proficiency with aspects of academic English, such as reading short texts and answering comprehension questions, which illuminate skills ranging from understanding to making inferences.

The WIDA-APT, a standardized paper and pencil test, is widely used in the United States as an initial screening test for English language proficiency (WIDA English Language Development Standards, 2020c). King and Bigelow (2018) estimate that it ". . . is likely to be administered to hundreds of thousands of students per year" (p. 936). In their extensive review of the initial assessment practices for English Learners in six English-speaking countries, Sinclair and Lau (2018) note that ". . . the U.S. model of EAL identification and placement . . . essentially reduces teachers to test proctors" (p. 274). They further go on to state, "Standardized assessments like those called for in the U.S. are highly decontextualized" (p. 273).

For elementary age newly arrived English Learners, the TDSB has developed a series of brief picture stories that can first be used as prompts for oral conversation and then lead to levelled reading passages on the same stories with accompanying writing tasks. These picture stories and accompanying questions and activities are closely linked with the Ontario Ministry of Education (2015) provincial English language development standards, known as STEP (Steps to English Proficiency). After a student has worked with the picture series and given responses both orally and in writing, the assessing teacher will align the student's responses to descriptors on the STEP continuum, methodically homing in on a recommendation as to the newly arrived learner's initial level on the STEP continuum. The Ontario Ministry of Education also provides a series of online, password-protected initial assessment tasks with visuals and short texts, for both elementary and secondary English Learners.

In addition to students completing the formal English language assessment, best practice in English Learner reception and assessment procedures includes eliciting a short written piece in students' home or dominant languages whenever possible for both elementary and secondary students. Even without a teacher available who can read or understand the student's language, a window of insight into students' literacy skills and prior schooling experience can be opened via the home language writing sample. An experienced and observant teacher will take note of aspects of print literacy as the student composes in the home language, including the ease with which the student holds and manipulates the pencil; the awareness of print conventions such as margins, lines, and punctuation; the ability to smoothly produce letters or characters in the student's language; and the amount of time the student takes to commit to paper a short text on a familiar topic. A first language writing sample can provide a powerful clue for a teacher to ponder whether the student may have limited prior formal schooling, guiding the teacher to inquire into that student's prior schooling experiences. At the TDSB's newcomer reception centres, teachers have prepared several simple writing prompts about students' families and interests, translated into twenty-five different languages. The English language assessment teacher can thus elicit a first language writing sample, even when a student's oral comprehension of English is minimal. Younger students can also be asked to respond to an age-appropriate first language writing prompt or can have a chance to label pictures or write short captions in their first language.

Ontario Ministry of Education policy further mandates that an initial assessment of an incoming student includes assessment of the student's skills and abilities in mathematics. To provide an appropriate starting program for each student, it is as important to gauge their current proficiency in mathematics as in English. The math component of the assessment often supplies instructive information about the student's prior academic background. Students who have had limited or interrupted prior schooling may not have had the opportunity to develop age-appropriate mathematical knowledge and skills. To support the initial assessment of mathematics for incoming students, the Ontario Ministry of Education has developed a series of assessments in simple English, spanning knowledge of the provincial mathematics curriculum in Grades 1 through 12. These assessment materials provide an easily accessed metric for gauging newcomer students' mathematical skills and can flag areas of strength as well as gaps. Considered together, the English language, mathematics assessment, and home language writing sample can paint a holistic picture of a student's current academic skills and thus inform recommendations for initial placement in a program that meets the specific needs of students who have been away from formal schooling for two or more years.

Making It Your Own

What are the initial assessment procedures and tasks at your school? How do they merge with the English language standards that are used by your school district? Are there assessment tasks for both English proficiency and mathematics knowledge? Could you or your district partner with mathematics consultants to produce an initial mathematics assessment that is not heavily dependent on English language knowledge?

Powerful Practice 3: Collect comprehensive background information about newly arrived students to guide the most appropriate program placement and support.

What It Might Look Like

The results of English language placement tests and mathematics knowledge assessments comprise only one aspect of the process of collecting information about English Learners in order to make informed and sensitive decisions about needs and placement for individual students. The welcome and intake process for any newcomer student must also encompass gathering other background information that will illuminate each individual student's unique strengths and next steps. "More holistic assessment policies suggest a broader understanding of the social and emotional demands EAL students face in school" (Sinclair & Lau, 2018, p. 275).

A holistic reception and assessment process emphasizes gathering information about the student related to academic strengths and needs, previous schooling history, possible future goals, languages spoken and written, availability of school records, hobbies, and interests, and any special or exceptional intellectual or physical needs the student may have. Not only does a robust knowledge of the student's background inform initial placement and programming, but it also supports teachers in creating a classroom environment that will be responsive to the linguistic, cultural, and personal diversity of everyone in the class.

The best possible forum for obtaining information on newly arrived students is through a family conversation. Teachers, guidance counsellors, settlement workers or other education-allied workers are all well-placed professionals to orchestrate this informal dialogue with the student and family. Ideally, the interviewer should speak the home language of the family, but if not, a bilingual education worker, professional interpreter, or a bilingual adult member of the student's family can facilitate the flow of accurate information. Whoever may be conducting the interview should keep in mind that families coming from different countries and situations may have varying reactions to answering personal questions posed by school officials in a position of authority. Sensitivity should be shown to reassure family members that the sole purpose of questions is to help find the optimal school program to ensure their child's individual learning needs are met.

Children in different countries begin primary school at different ages depending on the structure of the education system. Children in Finland don't begin formal schooling until the age of seven, whereas children in Ontario can start junior kindergarten at age four. Age-appropriate grade placement is a best practice for newly arrived elementary school children from other countries, even if the grade they completed in their previous country does not align with the grade for their age in their new North American jurisdiction, and even if report cards or records from previous schooling are not available. During the course of the family interview, information about when the child began school, the number of years the child attended school, the child's first language literacy skills, and any interruptions in formal schooling can help to illuminate the path of each child's education journey so far and point the way toward the need for any special programs or interventions to address gaps. Online, World Education News + Reviews (2020), a service of World Education Services, provides education system profiles for many countries, including immediately useful information such as the dates of the country's academic year, the number of grades in primary and secondary school, and the age of children at first school attendance.

Adolescent newcomer students who are in their secondary school years may arrive from other countries with a full set of documents pertaining to their previous schooling, including report cards. Some families have even had the documents translated and notarized prior to their arrival in North America. Other students may present with no documents at all, often because they have left their former countries under conditions of extreme urgency. It's important for every school district to have a process in place to recognize a student's prior academic achievements, even if the school records have not survived the migration route. In the TDSB, a policy was developed for dealing with high school students who lack transcripts of their marks. A panel of educators with experience in ESL teaching, guidance counselling, and school administration worked together to arrive at a policy that was equitable to such students but still required them to demonstrate the academic skills commensurate with the stated grade level of achievement from their previous schooling. When students who arrive without transcripts are placed in the appropriate high school mathematics and science classes according to their initial assessment recommendations, they can be awarded high school diploma credits for their prior learning after they have successfully passed one semester in these subjects.

Making It Your Own

Examine the student intake procedures at your school or district. Is there an intake form to record information about students' background and experiences? If other educators at your school would like information about the new student, is the form available for them to see? Many districts have developed some type of form, sometimes known as a "newcomer profile," which facilitates the gathering of comprehensive information about each newcomer student. As an example of such a form, consider the template below (Figure 1.14) for collecting student data.

FIGURE 1.14 Student Background Brief

Student Name: **D.O.B.:**

Home Language: **Date:**

Proficiency Levels:

Listening   **Speaking**   **Reading**   **Writing**

Student Background Factors

GUIDING QUESTIONS	STUDENT INFORMATION	IMPLICATIONS FOR INSTRUCTION

Home Language

- What is the script of the home language (e.g., Latin, Arabic, character based)?

- How well can the student understand and use the home language?

- How well can the student read and write in any language?

GUIDING QUESTIONS	STUDENT INFORMATION	IMPLICATIONS FOR INSTRUCTION
Age and Grade		
• Is the student the same age as classmates?		
• Is the grade placement age appropriate?		
Family Background		
• With whom does the student live?		
• Who is legally responsible for the student?		
• In what languages are the parents of the student literate?		
Education Background		
• Has there been interruption in formal education?		
• Is there a transcript that can be translated to provide credit for classes taken?		
Living Situation		
• Does the student have safe housing (e.g., caring adults, security, emotional support)?		
• In what language does the student interact at home? Outside of school?		
• What types of language contact and interaction has the student experienced in the past?		
Prior Difficult Experiences		
• Is there a history of difficult experiences or trauma?		
• Is the student under the care of health or mental health professionals?		
• What resources exist to support the student?		
Other Background factors (e.g., interests, personal skills/giftedness, or physical, cognitive, or emotional challenges)		
• What activities does the student enjoy?		
• What would the student like to pursue in the future?		
• Is there evidence of giftedness or special talents in specific areas?		
• Do parents have concerns about the student's growth, development, or special needs?		

SOURCE: Adapted from Fairbairn & Jones-Vo, (2010, p. 34–35), and Fairbairn & Jones-Vo (2016, pp. 110–114). For a detailed description of student background characteristics, see Fairbairn and Jones-Vo (2016, pp. 76–88).

Powerful Practice 4: Tailor unique assessment
practices for refugee students and families
who have undergone trauma.

Students and their families who arrive from war-torn areas, refugee camps, and
other precarious situations will benefit from additional reception and assessment
considerations designed to support their unique needs. To reduce anxiety for both
students and parents and to provide ample time for acclimatization to the new
school context, school districts and schools can consider investing more time in
supporting these newcomers by spreading the welcome, orientation, and
assessment process over a period of several days. A week of compassionate
support, orientation, and assessment is exactly what characterizes the highly
successful reception and assessment program for Syrian newcomers initiated by
the Thames Valley District School Board (TVDSB), located in the mid-sized
university city of London, Ontario, and surrounding area. The school district
temporarily opened its GENTLE Centre (Guided Entry to New Teaching and
Learning Experiences) in January 2016, in response to the sudden influx of Syrian
refugees arriving at many of their schools when Canada mounted an initiative to
admit 25,000 Syrian refugees over a three-month period. Spanning a week of
gradual and supportive orientation and assessment, the GENTLE Centre was
situated in one of the TVDSB's elementary school buildings. During the four
months of its operation, the GENTLE Centre welcomed, assessed, and placed 450
new elementary and secondary Syrian students, simultaneously providing their
families with a safe and supportive environment in which to connect with others
from their community while beginning to think about their own first steps in
learning English and adjusting to Canadian life (Thames Valley District School
Board, 2016). Both students and their parents had the opportunity to complete
English language assessments specific to their age groups during their week
attending the GENTLE Centre. School board transportation was arranged to
convey the children and their families from their temporary hostel and other
accommodations to the GENTLE Centre location. A coffee corner complete with
Arabic and English newspapers was set up where parents and families could
gather while their children were working with the centre's teachers and
counsellors (Dubinski, 2016).

Arabic-speaking support staff helped families to register each student, and
social workers and other professionals were on hand to help families deal
with initial trauma in the short term and then refer them onward for further
psychological support for the longer term. An early childhood educator was

also part of the GENTLE Centre staff to help young children deal with their anxieties and build their comfort level in their new Canadian school environment. Every student received a new backpack, an Arabic/English dictionary, and welcome and information materials in both English and Arabic.

The assessment teachers and counsellors broke down the assessment and orientation process and tasks for the students into smaller chunks spread over several days. The parents also had conversations with the centre's counsellors to learn about the education system in Ontario and were invited to take a tour of the school where the GENTLE Centre was located to get a glimpse of daily life in a Canadian elementary school. Since everyone was initially welcomed at the single GENTLE location, the teachers and counsellors used iPads to show students and parents photos of their new schools and of the various individuals who worked there and who would be present to welcome them the following week. When the Syrian students arrived at their new schools the next week, the assessment teacher and/or counsellor who had established a rapport with them during their GENTLE Centre week made every effort to be on hand as part of the welcome team at the receiving school. Thames Valley's award-winning GENTLE program provides an exemplary model for thoughtful and empathetic reception and assessment of newcomer groups who have travelled difficult paths to finally reach our schools.

In a similar initiative during the winter of 2016, the TDSB and the Toronto Catholic District School Board collaborated on a temporary welcome and assessment initiative for secondary school-aged Syrian refugees. Utilizing several available classrooms in a high school in the city's north end, the two school districts cooperated in providing daily school bus transportation for the newly arrived youth to the school site. A retired ESL teacher taught basic English classes for the group of adolescent refugee students, which grew daily, and English and mathematics assessment teachers and guidance counsellors visited the site on various days to conduct one-on-one assessments with each newly arrived student. Additional support included an Arabic-speaking educational assistant who worked full time every day as an interpreter and supported students with learning and adjustment concerns.

Making It Your Own

Consider your own particular school or district. What specific adaptations to the welcome, orientation, and initial assessment processes have been instituted to respond to the needs of students from refugee backgrounds? What unique features might best support the students with refugee backgrounds who arrive at your school? What ideas do you have to increase a sense of stability for students and families from refugee backgrounds?

FIGURE 1.15 Question C: Overview

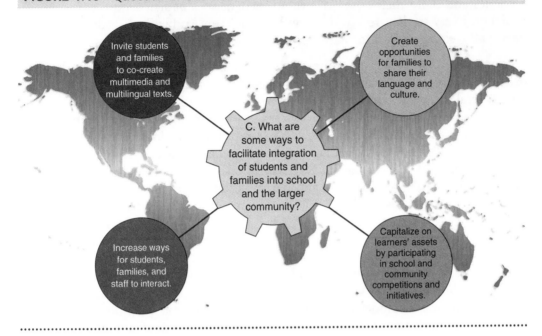

C. WHAT ARE SOME WAYS TO FACILITATE INTEGRATION OF STUDENTS AND FAMILIES INTO SCHOOL AND THE LARGER COMMUNITY?

- Powerful Practice 1: Create opportunities for families to share their diverse and expert linguistic and cultural knowledge.

- Powerful Practice 2: Capitalize on English Learners' assets and perspectives through participation in school and community competitions and initiatives.

- Powerful Practice 3: Increase avenues for interaction between and among students, families, and staff.

- Powerful Practice 4: Invite students and families to co-create multimedia and multilingual texts.

Powerful Practice 1: Create opportunities
for families to share their diverse and expert
linguistic and cultural knowledge.

Educators can embed unlimited creative opportunities for families to use their expertise for academic purposes. One such example is a special project called *Windows Into Our World: A Photography Identity Project for English Learners*. ESL teacher Shannon Hutchison of the Calgary Board of Education in Calgary, Alberta, wanted to use her professional photography skills as a bridge to showcase her students' diverse cultural backgrounds while involving parents and families in the conversation. She was awarded a grant from a local organization, Education Matters, which champions innovative learning projects in Calgary schools. Education Matters recognized the crucial identity sharing and parent engagement involved in this unique project during a time when respect and acceptance for diversity is needed around the world.

Shannon's school in Calgary was able to purchase a number of different cameras, including simple point-and-shoot models, as well as more sophisticated digital single-lens reflex (DSLR) cameras for student use. Shannon provided instruction to the English Learners on how to use the cameras and how to take well-composed and balanced shots. Her English Learners in Grades 1–6 brainstormed their understanding of the word *culture* and shared various cultural traditions and symbols from their diverse communities. Students were given the cameras to document their family life, cultural traditions, and rituals. Families participated by first taking part in a home survey about their cultural traditions and providing rich background information about their traditions, rituals, and symbols. They then helped their children to capture the photographs of cultural traditions for the project. Students wrote captions for their photos, some in English and some in their home languages. All of the photographs were compiled into a huge wall display that now hangs prominently in a main school hallway. The students' writings in both English and home languages about the meaning of culture and its importance to them were digitally overlaid onto an image of the school doors that anchors the wall display.

Laurel Fynes, a kindergarten teacher with the Peel Board of Education just west of Toronto in Mississauga, Ontario, likes to keep in close contact with the parents of her students through various digital platforms. She maintains a private classroom documentation account for class parents and also writes a publicly accessible blog cheekily called *This Kindergarten Life*. Laurel's kindergarten students come from many different cultural and linguistic backgrounds. She wants to instill early in her young students pride for their linguistic heritage and a curiosity about diverse languages. Laurel has made two multilingual identity text videos with her kindergarten children: "Hello, Goodbye" (Fynes, 2014) (https://thiskindylife.blogspot.com/search?q=Hello+Goodbye) and "We Can Count" (Fynes, 2013) (https://thiskindylife.blogspot.com/search?q=We+Can+Count).

Parents became involved with the "Hello, Goodbye" project when Laurel sent a letter home explaining that the children would be sharing the ways they say hello and goodbye in different languages, culminating in a class book and video. Because the videos are posted on a publicly accessible blog, Laurel is careful not to reveal her young students' names or to show their faces. Instead, the camera focuses on their small hands manipulating diverse objects while they count to ten in a slew of different languages or on the words written in both English and the home languages that mean hello and goodbye.

Making It Your Own

Adopting an asset-based perspective in education not only means that the strengths of students and families are recognized, it also encompasses educator skills, aptitudes, and gifts. You might not be a photographer or a media guru. Perhaps you are a master baker, singer, athlete, carpenter, quilter, or gardener. How can you leverage your accomplishments to involve families and students in educational opportunities that draw upon and highlight their expertise? Begin by making a list of your numerous talents and skills and envisioning where you can go from there.

I am talented/skilled at _____, therefore my class can _____.

I am talented/skilled at _____, therefore my class can _____.

I am talented/skilled at _____, therefore my class can _____.

Powerful Practice 2: Capitalize on English Learners' assets and perspectives through participation in school and community competitions and initiatives.

Lunching at McDonald's restaurant one afternoon, Mrs. Patal noticed a colorful flyer on the counter. It described a writing contest for students called the Millennium Dreamer contest, sponsored by the Walt Disney Company and McDonald's Corporation, along with the United Nations Educational, Scientific and Cultural Organization (UNESCO). As an ESOL teacher, Mrs. Patal believed her students could relate to some of the challenging topics (e.g., "What inspires your dream and what obstacles have been a challenge to achieving your dream?" "What does freedom mean to you?"). Always searching for new ways to engage her students in authentic writing experiences, she embedded this writing opportunity in her language arts class.

Mrs. Patal recruited several students to write about their personal responses based on a challenge in their lives. The process of writing and revising, organizing, and editing engaged already motivated students in expressing their personal stories with a strong voice and their unique perspective. To her great delight, one of Mrs. Patal's English Learners was named a national contest winner with her powerful narrative describing heroic action when she saved a life during war before her resettlement in her new country. After winning the contest as part of the prize, both the newly validated English Learner and her proud mother were invited to travel to Orlando, Florida, for a transformative, multi-day leadership event at Disney World, along with other winners and their parents from across the country.

Emboldened by such success, another of Mrs. Patal's ESOL students wrote an essay entitled "Is Freedom Really Free?" for a contest sponsored by the Veterans of Foreign Wars. His essay about the freedom that he and his family had struggled to achieve was so compelling that it garnered both state and national honors and prizes as well, not to mention increased validation and respect among peers. In part, his unique entry provided a first-person perspective written by a refugee who had deep feelings about loss and sacrifice based on his own experiences from resettling in North America. Mrs. Patal expanded her search for other competitive opportunities for her budding writers. She recognized that learning to better express personal thoughts and experiences equips students to better understand their own narratives, advance their communication in writing and speaking skills, and optimally prepares them for future endeavors in careers or academics.

In a similar vein, a number of years ago, elementary ESL teachers in the TDSB noticed that English Learners' contributions were unfortunately being overlooked for publication in the district's annual anthology of student creative writing. To showcase and celebrate the written work and artistic endeavours of elementary English Learners in Grades K through 8, the central ESL department established a special annual magazine just for English Learners. Teachers throughout the district worked with their students on the process of brainstorming, drafting, writing, editing, and polishing their pieces. Children were also encouraged to submit written work in their home language, as well as drawings, cartoons, and paintings. Hundreds of submissions were received from English Learners across the grades. The spring inaugural edition of the magazine, entitled *Canadian Journeys,* was launched with an author's celebration, including parental participation, a storyteller, and a huge congratulatory cake to mark the occasion. Subsequent iterations of the anthology with varying titles (e.g., *Canadian Horizons, Canadian Perspectives*) have made for a popular classroom project with teachers of elementary English Learners in the district, with yearly participation of learners from more than 100 TDSB schools.

Making It Your Own

When developing writing skills, students benefit from frequent opportunities to write for an authentic purpose. Brainstorm a list of possible opportunities to engage in writing for a real purpose. All students can participate in writing when teachers match language expectations to make sure that the task is doable for each student, given their current state of language development. For example, start with list-making using simple words and phrases for beginners, a sure way to develop vocabulary. Teachers can ratchet up the language expectations by requiring lists that start with a verb phrase like "I can . . . " followed by a present tense verb and later possibly a prepositional phrase: "I can buy groceries for my family on the way home from school." Personalizing and contextualizing the task provides motivation and can propel language development using scaffolding, leading to phrases and then sentences. In this way, gradually and consistently, teachers can support increasing the complexity of even biginners' language production within the context of what they know well: their own personal stories and lives.

FIGURE 1.16 Authentic Writing Ideas

CLASSROOM-BASED WRITING IDEAS	COMMUNITY-BASED WRITING IDEAS
Shopping lists for supplies	Various essay contests for students (e.g., Disney Dreamers Academy Essay Contest; Veterans of Foreign Wars: Patriot's Pen Contest, 2020; State Department of Education Essay Contests)
Pen-pal letters	Poster-making and writing contests for various organizations

CLASSROOM-BASED WRITING IDEAS	COMMUNITY-BASED WRITING IDEAS
Letter to principal	Article for local or school newspaper
Planning for school activities	Letters of concern/endorsement to stores, politicians, businesses, and so forth
Journal entry	Letters and cards to those who might be socially isolated in the community (e.g., seniors living alone/retirement homes), those who serve the community (e.g., crosswalk guard, bus drivers/monitors), or veterans in a local Veterans' home/hospital
Class rules or guidelines	
Letters, cards, and notes to school personnel (e.g., teachers, other students, custodians, administrators), for social communication purposes, such as a birthday card, get well, or congratulations card	

Powerful Practice 3: Increase avenues for interaction between and among students, families, and staff.

What It Might Look Like

Innovative ways of engaging both English Learners and families in school are essential to a smooth transition. One energetic ESOL teacher conceptualized a schoolwide plan that connected not only newcomer students and their families but also non-English Learners and their families, in addition to partnering with the student council, the the state's Bureau of Refugee Services, and teachers. His unusual and comprehensive scheme promoted supportive and positive interactions with newcomers from the onset.

Mr. Harkin, an ESOL teacher in a central Iowa school district, was aware of an acute need for refugee sponsors in his state. He knew, because of his personal experience of repeated sponsorship, that becoming a sponsor of a refugee family was indeed a responsibility but that it was not a legal or personal monetary obligation. Knowing the process well, Mr. Harkin first consulted with his principal, who was supportive of his idea to involve the school. Next, he met with a representative from the state's Bureau of Refugee Services for their approval. He proposed that the entire school collaborate to sponsor a family of nine people coming to resettle in their community directly from a refugee camp. Through the student council, he suggested, students in all grades could be involved in preparations to welcome the newcomers: meeting them at the airport; collecting basic furniture for an apartment; cleaning and setting up the new home; providing household items such as pots and pans, bedding, and towels; identifying a crew of able drivers who could take the family to doctor or dental appointments as needed; collecting a supply of food staples for the pantry; acting as mentors for the students who would attend the school; making weekly visits to the parents to check on well-being and needs; and much more. He further proposed that teacher supervisors oversee the planning and student council leaders assume central roles in forming various committees that would be staffed by willing student volunteers. In addition, students and their families already at the school could help to supply the various household needs that a large family would have at the beginning of their resettlement. The Bureau of Refugee Services responded enthusiastically to support the innovative idea.

Mr. Harkin's plan was communicated at the monthly student council meeting and taken back to each homeroom for approval. The votes from students came back unanimously in favor of taking on this unique sponsorship, and the big idea sprang to life. The entire school of 1,000 students had decided that they themselves would sponsor a family of nine refugees in partnership with their own families, the government agency, teachers and administrators, and the student council. The whole school became united in their caring and support of the newcomers in every way possible. Their thoughtful planning fostered a shared ethos of welcoming throughout the school and community. Before the newcomers had even arrived, stakeholders across the community were already informed, committed, and poised to support their newest neighbors in experiencing a smooth transition.

Making It Your Own

In order to routinely expand interactions on a daily basis, consider making intentional connections by matching opportunities with others who have similar language backgrounds through technology. Review a brief video *ESL Innovation Project* (Halton District School Board, 2017, https://youtu.be/XY9YtbkWWys) describing how the Halton District School Board in Ontario, Canada, increased their capacity for providing communication and support for newcomer students and families. Their innovative approach involves students as organizers and planners, connects newcomers with their new teachers, and facilitates the connection of students from similar language backgrounds in different schools via Google Hangouts. What lessons can be learned from their experience?

POWERFUL PRACTICES FOR SUPPORTING ENGLISH LEARNERS

Powerful Practice 4: Invite students and families to co-create multimedia and multilingual texts.

Opportunities abound for involving students and often their families in the creation of learning resources, information displays, art projects, and other initiatives to capitalize on leveraging the linguistic and cultural diversity enriching every school community. Toronto teacher Jennifer Fannin involved both her students and their families in the design and writing of mathematics texts for students at her elementary school (Cummins, Hu, Markus, & Montero, 2015). In the course of a unit on computational problems, students interviewed their family members and used the ages of various relatives to create timelines that represented addition and subtraction statements; they then wrote brief texts explaining the numerical differences in their ages. Families contributed photographs depicting siblings, parents, and grandparents whose ages were used in the math problems. The collected family inquiries were gathered in a printed hardcover book. In another mathematics project, Grade 5 students used their after-school activities to create timelines representing their understanding of elapsed time during the day, a mathematics curriculum expectation for that particular grade. In both of these projects, the lived experiences and home lives of the students and their families became an integral part of their mathematics learning at school. Students shared their identities and their diverse family lives through their study of mathematics concepts.

Another multilingual, multimodal project at this school once again involved Jennifer, this time with her colleague Mike Montanera, and focused on encouraging English Learners to write about their favorite places in the school, as an example of descriptive writing for Grade 3 learners (Ntelioglou, Fannin, Montanera, & Cummins, 2014). After brainstorming, drawing, photographing, and writing about their favorite spots, parents and other family members were invited to be part of the project. The students interviewed their family members about their own experiences in Grade 3 and about their memories of a favorite place or activity at school when they were the age of their young family member. Students, with the participation of their families, could also write up their stories in their home languages as well as in English.

University of Calgary education professor Hetty Roessingh led a professional learning community of preservice teachers from the university's faculty of Education and practicing kindergarten teachers from a local school with a large population of young English Learners. The goal of their project was to engage families and children as they focused together on the universal concept of telling stories about objects of special importance to their family (Roessingh, 2011). An invitation first went out to parents to participate with their children by selecting a special object that had personal or cultural relevance to their family. Parents shared the story behind the item with their child, prompted by a series of background questions supplied by the teacher. The children brought in their objects to share with the class and recounted their special stories, which were transcribed and then illustrated by the young learners and shared digitally. The project culminated in a book launch celebration attended by the children and their families.

Toronto secondary school ESL teacher Janet Jundler launched a collaborative project between her high school English as a second language students and a local Canadian history museum. Youth volunteers at the museum, together with the teenage English Learners, shared stories of their diverse New Year's traditions. Their contributions included descriptions of traditional customs, observations on how old and new rituals are being blended together in their new country, and how family celebrations have changed since moving to Canada. Students and their families contributed many artifacts representing aspects of their New Year's traditions, and the museum mounted a full display that formed part of the winter exhibition at the museum.

Making It Your Own

Lotherington, Paige, and Holland-Spencer (2013) recount their experiences establishing a school professional learning community focused on creating multimodal, multilingual literacy projects. Read their brief article ("Using a Professional Learning Community to Support Multimodal Literacies") and consider the sorts of multimodal work incorporating home languages that you could see happening in your own school context. Could the formation of a professional learning community, with the synergy generated by many teachers' contributions, be the catalyst for promoting multilingual projects in your school?

FIGURE 1.17 Question D Overview

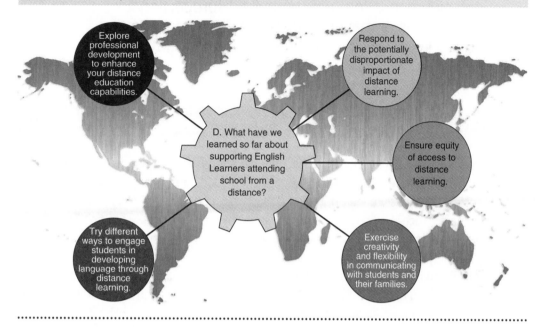

D. WHAT HAVE WE LEARNED SO FAR ABOUT SUPPORTING ENGLISH LEARNERS ATTENDING SCHOOL FROM A DISTANCE?

- Powerful Practice 1: Respond with sensitivity and awareness to the potentially disproportionate impacts the demands of distance learning may exert on the lives of English Learners and their families.

- Powerful Practice 2: Invest resources, initiative, and energy to ensure equity of technological access to distance learning for English Learners.

- Powerful Practice 3: Exercise creativity and flexibility in communicating with students and their families.

- Powerful Practice 4: Try out a wide variety of approaches and strategies to engage English Learners in developing language through distance learning.

- Powerful Practice 5: Explore opportunities for professional learning and teacher support to enhance your distance education capabilities.

Powerful Practice 1: Respond with sensitivity and awareness to the potentially disproportionate impacts the demands of distance learning may exert on the lives of English Learners and their families.

What It Might Look Like

In the spring of 2020, the world faced a situation not seen in a century: a global disease pandemic. The COVID-19 pandemic underscored many inequities in society. Previously underappreciated workers, such as custodians, truck drivers, farmers, grocery workers, caregivers, and delivery personnel, were finally acknowledged as heroes whose hard work keeps society functioning. Many English Learner wage earners are employed as such "frontline" workers, whose jobs often involve increased risk of exposure to the virus and an increased infection and death rate due to COVID-19. The inequitable burdens can be felt not only by adults but also by their English Learner children in schools, making it challenging to learn, particularly through distance learning. Most notably during the transition to distance learning, the foundational need to provide social and emotional support for students and families grew even greater as trusted resources for information and connections with school became less tangible for English Learners and families.

With English Learners, the issue of gaining access to the curriculum becomes additionally complicated because "access" relates both to technology (computers, iPads, Wi-Fi, etc.), as well as the requirement to provide English Learners with access to instruction with rigorous content. In order to thrive and succeed, English Learners and their families also need access to caring educators who respond with sensitivity and awareness to the potentially disproportionate impacts of the pandemic on their lives.

When anticipating the inclusion of English Learners in rigorous learning, awareness and sensitivity to an expanded range of concerns impacting the well-being of students and families must be at the forefront. Schools' and teachers' consideration and humane response to the status of students' and families' physical and psychosocial well-being, particularly in a new era of universal distance learning, is a critical prerequisite condition for English Learners before they can gain access and engage with any curriculum for learning.

Existing challenges for English Learners and families can be exacerbated during the transition to distance learning, such as for those who have limited resources, might have experienced trauma, or may experience job insecurities due to frontline worker positions. In the case of some families living in the United States where healthcare is not universal as it is in Canada, parents may be reluctant to seek medical attention out of fear of deportation, as well as worries about unaffordability. Others may simply delay receiving medical attention due to fear of contracting the virus in medical facilities, which can result in delayed identification of diseases and conditions. These unwelcome intrusions can preclude or limit students' and families' abilities to engage with what is often considered paramount in schools: the curriculum. Clearly, while important, the curriculum must take a back seat, allowing for addressing basic human needs that can enhance outcomes related to student participation and achievement.

FIGURE 1.18 Factors of Successful Distance Learning for English Learners

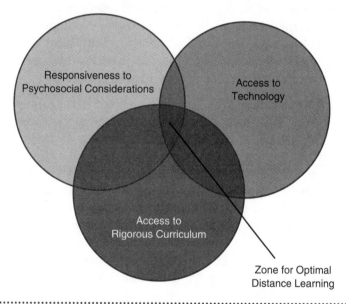

The Rocha family lives in a small town within driving distance to the local meat packing plant. Luis, the father of four children, works there daily to support his family of eight members. His wife, Rosa, and eldest daughter, Guadalupe, work as care providers at a nursing home nearby, and two of the high school-age children, Francisco and Araceli, have jobs after school and on weekends in a fast food restaurant. Together, the family pools their resources to support the entire group that also includes the youngest children, Maria del Carmen, age 9, the baby, Ana, age 2, and Luis's parents who often provide childcare and are beloved and respected grandparents, all living in the home together.

Maria del Carmen is in fourth grade and known by her teachers to be friendly, outgoing, and working very hard in her classes for English Learners. She has a gift for drawing likenesses, and her art teacher encourages and showcases her efforts. Assessment data indicates that Maria del Carmen is making steady progress in English language development. Sometimes, when there is a school assignment that requires the internet, Maria del Carmen asks her father to drive her to the fast food restaurant where her older siblings work. She uses the Wi-Fi there with the family laptop to complete her assignment for the next day.

Rosa and Guadalupe were the first in the family to experience a personal loss due to COVID-19. A close friend who was their coworker and an elderly resident of the care facility both died on the same day due to the virus. This made the pandemic real and personal to them. Considered to be essential workers, the two women still reported to work daily to care for the elderly residents and returned home in the evening. After realizing that the risk of taking the virus home to their family was great, both mother and daughter chose to quit their much-needed jobs to preserve their family's health, despite this causing financial uncertainty for the household.

Next to feel the impact of COVID-19, Luis reported to his family that several of the line workers at the meat processing plant had not shown up for work due to the rapid spread of the virus. Luis's plant reported that over 1,000 workers tested positive for COVID-19. One day, Luis began to feel a headache and a fever. As his condition deteriorated, Rosa knew that he needed medical care. After a call and visit to the local clinic, Luis tested positive for the virus and was advised that he must self-isolate at home for fourteen days until he was no longer contagious to his family or anyone else. This directive was carried out by Rosa and the rest of the family who rearranged the home to create a separate space for Luis, in Maria del Carmen and Ana's bedroom. Now everyone was living, eating, watching television, and doing schoolwork in the same room, while avoiding contact as much as possible with their father who was cloistered in his designated space.

During this time, noticing that Maria del Carmen's assignments had fallen behind, her teacher Ms. Shapiro called to check in with her student. She took the opportunity to reassure the family with the news that the school district had mandated a pandemic assessment policy. No student would receive a final grade lower than that earned before the physical closure of schools, and no student would "lose their year." This was a relief to the older Rocha students in high school who were worried about getting their credits and graduating.

Ms. Shapiro was already apprised of the current family developments since she had begun contacting students by phone for a regular "check in" in the same way she always connected with her students when they were all in the same physical space. She understood that worry about the father's health, the strain of maintaining physical distance protocol in a confined home, and the family financial worries would exact a practical and an emotional toll on Maria del Carmen, impacting her ability to concentrate on schoolwork. She learned of the family's commitment to distance education and how Luis had previously ensured that his daughter had internet service by using public access to Wi-Fi. It was now harder for Maria del Carmen to get homework completed due to lack of internet services in the home. Until dependable internet accessibility could be assured, Ms. Shapiro made plans to deliver some hard copy packets and books for Maria del Carmen that targeted her language proficiency and reading levels so that she could continue her learning. She then investigated potential sources of community Wi-Fi access that might be available for the Rocha family. She delivered a "care package" to Rosa for the family and also informed Rosa of a local food bank in case it might be helpful. Ms. Shapiro would have done these things even before the pandemic because she had cultivated relationships with all of the parents of her students, but her actions were even more important and appreciated now.

Making It Your Own

Drawing from your experiences with English Learners and families in your context while placing well-being and psychosocial concerns at the forefront, consider the following questions about enhancing school-to-home connections:

- What do teachers need to know about each student when they are checking in? Brainstorm a list of appropriate questions related to student and family well-being.

- What do you know about the current family situations of your learners that might impact student engagement and performance?

- In what ways can you support families in addressing their most pressing needs?

- What supports for families exist in your school or community for families?

- Explore the following resources for possible use in your own context. What others would you add?

  - Collins (2020) writes about what the needs of educators teaching through a pandemic in the article *Teaching Through Coronavirus: What Educators*

(Continued)

(Continued)

> *Need Right Now,* https://www.tolerance.org/magazine/teaching-through-coronavirus-what-educators-need-right-now.

- o *My Undocumented Life* outlines resources for those working with undocumented immigrants, https://mydocumentedlife.org/covid-19/.

- o The National Association of School Psychologists (2019) has also provided some resources at https://www.nasponline.org/resources-and-publications/resources-and-podcasts/school-climate-safety-and-crisis/health-crisis-resources/helping-children-cope-with-changes-resulting-from-covid-19.

- o School Mental Health Ontario (2020) has put together information on how to support students and families during COVID-19 in their tip sheets *Educator Conversations with Students and Families during COVID-19 School Closures* available through https://twitter.com/TDSB_Psych/status/1252640472952176640?s=20 and

- o School Mental Health Ontario, *Supporting Student Mental Health During a Pandemic (COVID-19),* available at https://smho-smso.ca/wp-content/uploads/2020/03/InfoSheet-for-Educators-Supporting-Student-MH-During-a-Pandemic.pdf.

Powerful Practice 2: Invest resources, initiative, and energy to ensure equity of technological access to distance learning for English Learners.

What It Might Look Like

School systems around the world faced the rising tide of COVID-19, resulting in the closure of physical buildings in the spring of 2020. As the pandemic began to exact its worldwide toll during the writing of this book, one fact became abundantly clear: instruction delivered by teachers via technology would be universally essential for safely conducting school, perhaps for some time into the future. Teachers everywhere began learning to operationalize a variety of new technologies and a multitude of novel online products in order to teach their students virtually (The World Bank Group, 2020; United Nations Educational, Scientific and Cultural Organization (UNESCO), 2019).

Successful transition to distance learning for all grades requires that the needs of students are the top priority. English Learners need first and foremost a focus on maintenance and strengthening the social and emotional connections between school and English Learners and their families. Second, they need equitable access to technology to engage with and participate in distance learning. Finally, English Learners need continued culturally and linguistically responsive instruction on rigorous content to develop their language proficiency.

To initiate effectively serving English Learners exclusively via distance learning, many schools began by assessing and equalizing the technological reality of students and families to ensure that distance learning could indeed take place universally. It became quite clear that families did not necessarily have the same technological resources. For example, some families shared a single phone or computer among multiple members (including parents who required devices for employment purposes); those in rural communities sometimes struggled without internet service availability; Wi-Fi connectivity was not always reliable in some locations; and some homes were not equipped with Wi-Fi or other hardware. Whatever the reason, each student must be set up for success with equitable academic tools. Access to technology is critical, especially moving forward in a world where distance learning and telepractice is likely to be incorporated as part of everyday life. By conducting a brief needs assessment or survey of parents, schools can identify the most urgent technology needs. For example, one school created a survey that was either e-mailed to parents or conducted via telephone by an interpreter if needed, asking questions such as the following:

1. In your area, is the internet reliably available through a service provider?

2. Does your student have access to a computer during school hours?

3. Are you able to access reliable internet from your home?

Based on responses to questions, schools can target next steps to level the technology playing field for each student. Examples of reported proactive schools' actions for ensuring equitable access to technology include the following:

- Using school, state/province, or other funds to ensure that each student has the necessary equipment, such as a computer, laptop, iPad, or augmentative communication device.

- Providing increased opportunities to enable home Wi-Fi connectivity, such as was done in Chicago, Toronto, and many other locales (City of Toronto, 2020; Hall, 2020).

- Dedicating a school bus to technology that could be driven to various neighborhoods to support internet connectivity for students, as was done in rural North Carolina (Childress, 2020).

- Partnering with a local business to support nearby unconnected students by allowing them to join a business Wi-Fi connection.

- Surveying local internet providers to learn about free supports or resources for schools due to the COVID-19 pandemic, such as free Wi-Fi access or data plans.

- Reserving dedicated parking and seating spots outside school buildings and libraries where students and families can access a Wi-Fi signal outdoors.

- Ensuring that students' families know how to hot-spot an internet connection from their cell phone if they have a phone plan that includes data.

Making It Your Own

No doubt, your school has already done its best to provide technological equity for students in response to the COVID-19 pandemic, during a particularly stressful and uncertain period of time. Many of the solutions may have been temporary, as people, agencies, and technology service providers contributed to the emergency situation. Given that distance learning and telepractice services are likely to continue to be part of our daily life, more reliable, strategic, and permanent interventions might be needed. As access to technology affects all students in a school, you might want to work with some colleagues to reflect on some pertinent questions and to prepare for the future.

1. How does your school determine the technology needs of students in order to position all students for success?

2. What suggestions for ensuring that all students have equitable access to technology has your school implemented? Were these permanent or temporary measures? What is needed to continue to ensure equitable access to technology?

3. As an advocate for English Learners, do you have additional ideas related to using technology to engage English Learners that you would like to explore or recommend?

Powerful Practice 3: Exercise creativity and flexibility in communicating with students and their families.

Establishing and nourishing supportive relationships with students and families will always be a cornerstone of working with English Learners. Good communication has never been more crucial than in a time of distance learning when students and families may be feeling isolated, worried, and overwhelmed by their current situation as well as by the shift to a reliance on remote technology for learning. Educators' shared experiences of several months of distance learning has underscored the importance of making creative and multi-pronged efforts in communicating and collaborating with students and families, including effective ways to connect and build relationships with students and parents, provide communication in home languages, and offer opportunities for families, educators, and the community to make connections and share with each other while remaining at home.

School administrators and leaders need to acknowledge that in a distance learning context, extra time and energy must be invested to establish and maintain regular, supportive communication with students and families, and this time commitment should be recognized and built into teachers' daily and weekly work schedules (Breiseth, 2020a). Locating contact information for some families may take additional time, as they might be in transit, may have recently changed phone numbers, or might not have regular or reliable broadband access to check e-mail correspondence. Spending time tracking down leads for contact information through siblings, school friends, and community organizations can result in success in contacting some hard-to-reach students and their families.

Educators have exercised a high degree of creativity in employing a wide variety of tools to establish and maintain communication and connections with students and parents during learning from a distance, including the following:

- E-mail messages, including screenshots of assignments and classroom information, as needed

- Text messages

- Phone calls

- Social media groups

- Google Classroom announcements

- Telephone trees/chains

- Video chats

- Google forms in English and home languages

- Snail mail letters with enclosed self-addressed, stamped return envelopes

- Home visits using appropriate safety measures, such as physical distancing, remaining outdoors, and wearing face masks

- Education materials pickup at school and/or delivery to students' homes

- School lunch/food pickup/drive-through

- Drive-through library book checkout and drop-off

- Neighborhood caravans

- Video messages of support and caring

- Chalk art messages of unity and encouragement

- Posters and lawn signs of celebratory events such as graduation

The implementation of mass remote learning has shone a spotlight on new education apps and platforms that facilitate communication and community building among educators, families, and students. To be sure, there are pros and cons to each service. For example, some offer virtual chat rooms for group work; some place limits on how many participants can be viewed on screen at a given time; and the security features may vary from platform to platform. Adherence to privacy and confidentiality protocols established in your area, by your employer and/or by your professional regulatory board is crucial at all times. Any platforms or apps used for communication, instruction, or intervention should always conform to your area's requirements for online security and safety. As such, the authors cannot advocate for or endorse any particular technologies for instruction and point out that schools, districts, and states are responsible for making choices about appropriate and applicable technologies and products, bearing in mind security and confidentiality concerns.

There are several school communication platforms that could be explored to determine if their security and communication features meet your specific requirements. One that has really caught on with teachers is ClassDojo. ClassDojo is a free app available across many digital devices that allows teachers to keep parents updated on student progress and classroom news. Its messaging system connects teachers, parents, and students and also empowers students to share photos and videos of their learning and projects. ClassDojo currently also has message translation capability into thirty different languages. Another popular communication app for schools is Remind. Remind enables two-way messaging between teachers and parents and allows teachers to share documents, assignments, and instructional resources with the class and to schedule "office hours" for one-on-one virtual communication. There is even a "read message" receipt feature to help teachers ensure that families are indeed opening and reading important communications.

School districts have introduced a variety of online methods and tools to provide services so that families may receive communication in their home languages during school closures. Some school districts offer a simple digital registration card for any family member to complete and submit in order to request an online interpreter. Many districts have also trained their interpreters in the technology required to provide remote video and online interpretation. Before the adoption of widespread distance learning, some school districts were already providing access to a real-time phone interpretation service that can be accessed by all teachers to use in calls with parents who are more comfortable communicating in their home languages.

During the global pandemic school shutdown, the nonprofit organization Talking Points (2015) was providing free access for high-needs school districts to its well-regarded message translation app. Schoolwide, classroom, and parent messaging are included, and messages can be translated into over 100 languages. In addition, contact letters that explain the use of the app to parents and families are available in over thirty of the app's most widely requested languages. The Talking Points organization was also offering webinars for educators on how to effectively use the app to communicate with families.

Among many concerns in the age of mobile learning is whether students will indeed attend regularly in a distance learning format. The national U.S. nonprofit organization Attendance Works (2018) dedicates its efforts to advancing student success by reducing chronic absenteeism. This concern is tackled in their new publication, *Attendance Playbook: Smart Strategies for Reducing Chronic Absenteeism in the Covid Era* (Jordan, 2020), which presents a range of strategies for messaging and engaging parents, monitoring student attendance, addressing barriers to attendance, and reducing absenteeism in the age of distance learning. One family communication approach that holds promise is the use of "nudging" messages to parents and guardians, which research has shown to improve school attendance. Bergman & Chen (2019) have demonstrated that the use of text-messaging technology for nudging resulted in significantly increased student attendance as well as significantly decreased student failure. The home communication apps described above, as well as regular text messaging, can effectively be used for nudging to increase student attendance and participation in the era of distance learning, as well as in times of in-person classroom learning. Messages about student absences, assignment due dates, learning progress reports, and virtual pats on the back can all contribute to higher student engagement and success.

In their opinion piece on the changes in thinking about education necessitated by the onset of the COVID-19 pandemic, Osmond-Johnson, Campbell, and Pollock (2020) wonder what types of new community/school partnerships will be needed to support families through such unprecedented times. One innovative idea is the virtual parent camp organized by the non-profit ParentCamp (2018). ParentCamp refers to their free offerings as an "un-conference" opportunity for family members, educators, and the community to come together to discuss what works best for children. During times of sheltering at home, they nimbly pivoted from face-to-face gatherings to a virtual model to empower parents, students, and the community to continue to gather together and participate in a shared dialogue about their children's education. Some online sessions are open to participants regardless of their geographical location, while other virtual parent camps can be organized by a specific school district with facilitators provided by ParentCamp in a number of different community languages.

Making It Your Own

What various methods of communication with students and families have you used during a time of distance learning? What do you find to be the advantages and drawbacks to these various communication methods? What ideas do you have to strengthen home-school connections that you would like to implement in the coming school year? Connect with other educators to compare suggestions for classroom communication apps that have worked well in their contexts. Consider creating and curating a list of your favorites to share with others.

Powerful Practice 4: Try out a wide variety of approaches and strategies to engage English Learners in developing language through distance learning.

What It Might Look Like

Mr. Adebayo is an elementary and middle school teacher for a small, mostly rural school district. During a typical week, he travels far and wide to five different elementary and middle schools to provide English language instruction to students in Grades 1 through 8. He supports English Learners in several mainstream classrooms alongside various grade teachers and also works with small groups of recently arrived students at a couple of his assigned schools. When his district abruptly closed schools and shifted to distance learning, Mr. Adebayo's principal immediately convened an online faculty meeting to facilitate the sharing of student and family contact information and to discuss the district's baseline expectations for how many hours of online contact teachers would be expected to have with students.

After establishing contact with all of his English Learners and their families using a variety of communication methods (e-mail, text, telephone, and hand delivered letters), Mr. Adebayo first wanted to check in with all his students to gauge their emotional state during the stressful transition to distance learning. He put together a Google form with some simple questions that could be answered with a few words or an emoji. He was also able to translate the Google form into all his students' home languages. The students' responses opened a door on how they were coping with the new conditions and what additional school and community supports might be beneficial. Mr. Adebayo decided to continue to use the Google form check-in strategy every week during distance learning and also to add several new questions to gauge his students' ongoing learning in the future.

A novice distance learning educator, Mr. Adebayo began to consider how he would provide English language learning support in a remote learning environment. He normally varies his instructional strategies, groupings, and tasks to differentiate for his students' varying levels of English proficiency, learning styles, and needs. He knew he wanted to continue this approach during remote English language support. Just as in face-to-face teaching when he would diversify instructional activities with his students over a class period and full week, so too would he try to create a distance learning schedule that would offer students a broad mix of learning activities and choice in tasks and assignments. Like all educators, Mr. Adebayo also recognized the importance of familiar classroom routines for students, which would provide a predictable and comfortable framework, especially during uncertain times. The school district had mandated that every teacher should either be directly teaching or available online for three hours per day. After consulting with colleagues and doing some research, Mr. Adebayo set up a blended synchronous (the whole class learns online together in real-time) and asynchronous (everyone learns on their own separate time) online teaching schedule with an amalgam of the following: a daily recorded morning message; a combination of short live and recorded lessons; some time every day for whole group learning and discussion in which parents were invited to join for the first few minutes; assignment choice boards geared to various English proficiency levels; small group breakout rooms for the older learners; student presentations, either live or recorded; and one and a half hours daily of individual student instructional support time. He provided feedback through a variety of means: checklists, written notes, and recorded voice feedback clips that students could listen to on their own time. Mr. Adebayo noticed that colleagues were incorporating rotating daily features to engage their students online, such as scavenger hunts for objects, words, and items on news media; blanket fort building; dance challenges and chains; cup stacking competitions; sharing home language words and expressions; and creating visual identity portraits. For Mr. Adebayo's English language teaching purposes, these activities could also be structured with a language objective differentiated for the students' English proficiency levels, such as composing a brief procedural text describing how to build a blanket fort, writing a class patterned sentence book celebrating home language words, or finding a fruit and a vegetable that begins with each letter of the alphabet. He also incorporated home literacy activities that students could do at home with their parents, such as alphabetizing and sorting shopping lists; identifying nutritional values on food packaging; cooking from a recipe; categorizing tools for household maintenance, repairs, and gardening; and even discussion strategies and questions for family television viewing. In this way, Mr. Adebayo supported parents to capitalize on routine daily household activities and chores to build conversational and other literacy skills with their young children, without overwhelming the parents with expectations for home-schooling. He focused on reassuring parents that they can organically support their young children's literacy development in a myriad of practical routine ways by sharing ideas and resources to maximize their interactions.

Mr. Adebayo began learning and experimenting with several digital tools to facilitate his students' online learning contributions. He used Flipgrid (Microsoft, 2020), a web-based educational app that empowers learners to share videos, photos, and texts in a class grouping where members can also reply with feedback to each others' posts. Learners in his middle grade programs wrote and presented one-minute book talks using the Flipgrid platform. Mr. Adebayo's students could each create a book with Book Creator (Tools for Schools Inc., 2011–2019), a tool for students to create digital books in English and other languages, combining text, images, audio, and video. Some of his English Learners in Grades 4 through 6 authored and shared their own dual-language digital books featuring simple machines like levers and pulleys found around their homes, filled with photos, brief texts, and audio readings. He also found out about Seesaw (2020), a digital portfolio app, which would allow students to post and share their work with him, their classmates, and their family members. In the future, Mr. Adebayo is also considering incorporating virtual field trips to an aquarium, zoo, or children's museum in his online instruction program.

When working with middle school students who might have their own or could use a family smartphone or if he were teaching secondary learners, Mr. Adebayo could consider incorporating Kahoot! (Kahoot!, 2020), a free computer crowd-sourcing app that allows teachers to prepare online quizzes for real-time remote student participation. A Kahoot! questionnaire serves as an engaging technology-based anticipation guide to get students to activate their background knowledge when introducing a new content topic, as well as a fun review of concepts covered in a lesson or unit.

Mr. Adebayo also read to his students frequently during their synchronous whole group gatherings. He pointed his students and their families to a number of sources for online story time, both live and recorded, so they could continue to listen to stories of diversity in both English and home languages. A few that he suggested to families were

- Storyline Online (2020) at https://storylineonline.net
- *100+ Free Video Read Alouds* from The Indianapolis Public Library (2020) at https://indypl.org/blog/for-parents/free-video-read-alouds

- Online English and Spanish "StoryTime" on YouTube Channel of The Children's Museum of Houston (2020) at https://www.youtube.com/playlist?list=PLPZCH1CZOF9LmzhhOGbLWId5_DUyuxvzi

- The New York Public Library's (2020) Multilingual Storytimes in Spanish and Japanese at https://www.nypl.org/education/kids/storytime/multilingual-storytimes

- KidTimeStoryTime (2019–2020) for bilingual read-alouds in English and Spanish at https://kidtimestorytime.com

- English-Arabic Storytime: Online storytime from the Arab American National Museum (2020) at https://arabamericanmuseum.org/storytime/

- Moreland Libraries (2020) in Metropolitan Melbourne, Australia, with online stories read in Arabic, Greek, Italian, and Turkish at https://www.youtube.com/channel/UCUAoPvpkSPvg7vRz5f4oYbw/playlists

For those of his students who did not have regular access to a computer or to broadband internet, the central Learning Support department of Mr. Adebayo's school district prepared packets of learning materials containing simplified texts at various English proficiency levels, along with learning activities for reading, writing, and speaking. Mr. Adebayo had a collection of simplified readers, dual language story books, and learner visual dictionaries stored in a bin in his car for his visits to various schools. He combined the learning packets with some simplified readers aligned to each student's individual English reading proficiency level along with some other books and dropped off the materials to students' homes, later to check in with those students via frequent telephone conversations. A colleague also told Mr. Adebayo about a blog hosted by Maria Montroni-Currais, an elementary ESL teacher from New Jersey, called *ESL at Home* (Montroni-Currais, 2020). This blog contains weeks of printable engaging daily activities for English learning that can be accomplished without access to a computer or the internet. The activities have also been translated into over thirty languages and are available at https://eslathome.edublogs.org.

Part of Mr. Adebayo's role as an ESL teacher encompasses supporting classroom teachers in adapting their programs for English Learners. During distance learning, his mainstream classroom colleagues were asking him for suggestions on how to make their instruction and assignments more accessible for the English Learners in their classrooms. Some of the strategies that Mr. Adebayo recommended for scaffolding online learning for English Learners included the following:

- Supplying a word bank for vocabulary that might be unfamiliar

- Searching for video examples in math, science, and social studies to give English Learners additional visual input, and encouraging English Learners to turn on video captions

- Rewriting short texts in simplified English to make them more comprehensible
- Providing translations of instructions in the students' home languages
- Recording audio instructions for tasks
- Creating sentence frames and paragraph scaffolds for writing
- Writing online dialogue journals
- Listening to a story or passage, followed by recording a retelling of the content
- Watching a television show, movie, or cooking demonstration and posting a recorded retell using teacher provided scaffolding

Making It Your Own

Together with colleagues, use a Google Doc or other online shared platform to compile an annotated chart of learning apps, online reading resources, and other materials to use during distance learning. Include also your approaches, strategies, and resources to support students who do not have access to connect online from home.

Powerful Practice 5: Explore opportunities for professional learning and teacher support to enhance your distance education capabilities.

What It Might Look Like

Educators rushing to operationalize their virtual classrooms report that professional learning and support are essential. Simultaneously, they are learning how to effectively use various communication platforms, deliver curriculum, maintain essential caring connections, and maintain and continue language development through content learning. It's no wonder that teachers may feel as if they were "building the plane while flying it." Similarly, other educational professionals such as speech-language pathologists are practicing the administration of online assessment tools using telepractice platforms on their colleagues and sometimes even their colleagues' children.

To be successful in implementing and maintaining robust distance learning for English Learners, educators may need professional learning with technology experts complemented by ongoing collaboration with others focused on the needs of English Learners. In response, schools have instituted multiple ways for professionals to communicate and collaborate virtually with each other while enhancing their distance teaching capabilities. Some of their ideas are to create the following:

- One-on-one helpline at the building or district level, accessible through e-mail or phone calls for questions about technology (e.g., connectivity, how to set up equipment, screen sharing, problem solving, etc.)

- Student-led cadre of technology experts, such as university students, co-op students, middle and high school students, sometimes earning school credits

- Weekly chat to share successes, strategies, and opportunities for improvement

- Social media groups posting successes and problem-solving challenges

Once educators are technologically enabled, they are tasked to design virtual instruction that continues to be culturally and linguistically responsive and that affords English Learners "access to the curriculum," enabling participation in equitable instruction, assessment, reading activities, and so forth, based on their individual data, including proficiency levels. Consider the following suggestions: might any of them be adaptable for use in your context?

1. Institute regular virtual collaboration, such as a professional learning community, for educators and teams related to English Learners and distance learning.

2. Begin to collect and curate your own preferred list of websites, apps, strategies, articles, videos, students' work, and other resources for quick reference and for collaborating with colleagues on improving distance learning for English Learners.

3. Archive all resources for future reference and sharing widely with colleagues at both informal and dedicated collaboration opportunities.

English Learner-focused professional learning via articles, webinars, online courses, and meet-ups are available through organizations such as Californians Together (2020), ¡Colorín colorado! (2019a), edWeb (2020), Teaching Tolerance (1991–2020), TESOL International Association (2020a), WIDA (2020c), and many others. For example, Breiseth (2020b) writes useful advice about distance learning and English Learners through ¡Colorín colorado!. TESOL International Association offers webinars for members, and many publishers offer webinars and book clubs (e.g., Corwin, 2020).

SupportEd offers a number of useful free downloadable tools including a checklist to get educators thinking about student needs when planning for instruction during these uncertain times (SupportEd, 2020).

Educators are discovering new ways to use familiar social media, such as Facebook, Instagram, Twitter, and even Pinterest, for making connections with peers, gleaning creative ideas and strategies, and enhancing their distance learning practices. Teachers looking for ideas to expand their distance learning activities repertoire are participating in such Facebook Groups as Global Educator Collective Network (Facebook, 2020a), Teachers Helping Teachers (Facebook, 2020b), or Trauma Informed Educators Network (Facebook, 2020c). Some educational organizations maintain an Instagram presence, such as Speech-Language Pathology Services at the TDSB (Instagram, 2020), which shares useful resources and materials for educators and parents regarding various communication issues. Danielle Mancinelli (2020) notes that educators are connecting via Twitter during the pandemic and recommends that educators check out hashtags such as #RemoteEd, #DistanceLearning, #QuaranTeaching, and #RemoteLearning. She also suggests participating in regularly scheduled #EdChats via Twitter with a community of teachers who build relationships and pedagogy together, such as how to use various apps and incorporate activities beneficial for English Learners. A sampling of suggested #EdChats for educators include #ELLCHAT, #ELAChat, #2PencilChat, and #EDtechChat. As an example of using Pinterest professionally, one speech-language pathologist posts her "pins" on this social medium to share speech therapy activities, vocabulary, and more.

Making It Your Own

There are currently thousands of apps, platforms, webinars, online workshops, inservices, and other tools vying for educators' attention as they transition to distance learning and telepractice services. While eager to continue refining their technology skills and efficacy, the scope of this challenge can leave educators feeling overwhelmed. You may have already identified some favorites that have supported your transition to universal distance learning. List three influential resources or learning opportunities that you found particularly helpful and informative during the COVID-19 pandemic, as well as why you would recommend these particular sources to a colleague. You may wish to concentrate on those resources with a specific English Learner focus. Ask a colleague (or several) to do the same and then compare your lists. Consider curating a realistic collection of your preferred technology tools, websites, social media, apps, and strategies to reduce the stress of sorting through the onslaught of information. By carefully selecting resources that are specific to your needs and the needs of your students, you can advance your own expertise and continue to meet the needs of English Learners with resounding success via distance learning.

NEXT STEP

In Chapter 1, we explored inspirational Powerful Practices that could be accomplished in the school and community. To make this information your own, please turn to page 255 of this guide. You can now start to label the "School/Community" gear with your preferred ideas, strategies, and suggestions, modified to suit your students, families, and community. When you are ready, Chapter 2 will introduce you to Powerful Practices in the classroom.

FIGURE 2.1 Classroom: Overview

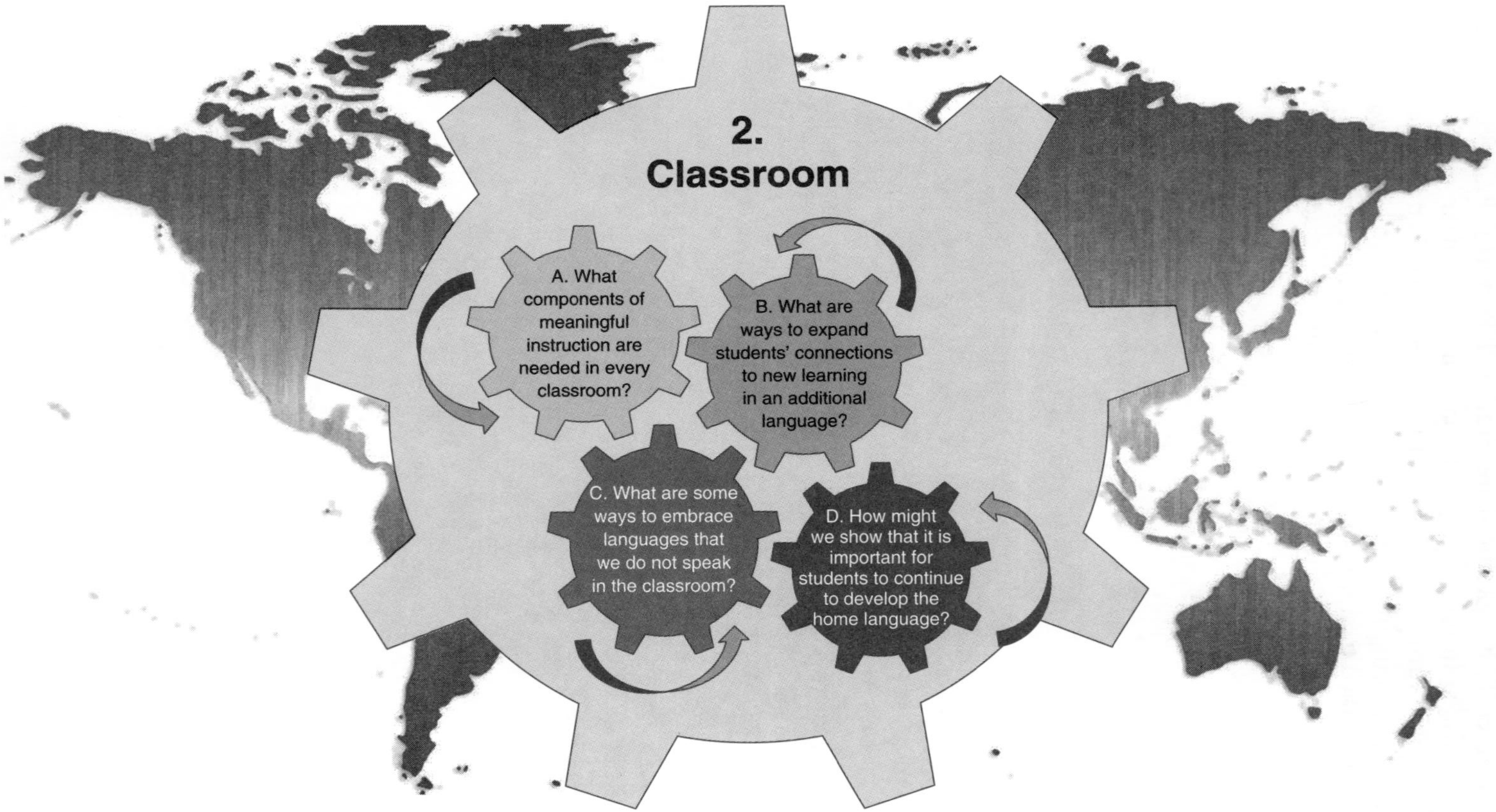

2.
Classroom

A. What components of meaningful instruction are needed in every classroom?

B. What are ways to expand students' connections to new learning in an additional language?

C. What are some ways to embrace languages that we do not speak in the classroom?

D. How might we show that it is important for students to continue to develop the home language?

CHAPTER 2

Classroom

WHAT WE KNOW

Students who do not see their home language or culture authentically appreciated in the classroom and community may become less involved in educational and academic opportunities (Cummins, 1996; Ward Singer, 2018), which can significantly affect academic achievement (Cummins, 1996; Hamayan, Marler, Sánchez-López, & Damico, 2007). Such students may also be more prone to losing connections to the home language and culture (Asgedom & Even, 2017), effecting a decline in home language skills that can result in social, emotional, cognitive, educational, and familial consequences (Wong Fillmore, 2000).

To prevent negative emotional, social, linguistic, and academic consequences, many researchers and educators have strongly advocated for inclusion of students' home language, culture, and prior knowledge into the classroom (e.g., Chumak-Horbatsch, 2012, 2019; Cummins, 1996; Sánchez-López & Young, 2018; Westernoff, Young, & Shimotakahara, 2018). The use of translanguaging pedagogy is an example of incorporating the authentic use of multiple languages into the classroom and is gaining traction in linguistically diverse classrooms. Translanguaging pedagogy is intended to mirror the fluid use of languages by bilingual and multilingual speakers in real communication (García & Lin, 2016). Translanguaging strategically and purposefully moves across all of students' language repertoires and modalities (García, 2020) for teaching and learning purposes rather than focusing exclusively on the use of English (García & Seltzer, 2015). As such, the many languages of the classroom would be heard and seen seamlessly in a classroom (Chumak-Horbatsch, 2019; Menken & Sánchez, 2019). Many of the powerful practices in Chapter 2 reflect a translanguaging perspective, such as reading dual language books in both languages or having small group discussions in more than one language. Celic and Seltzer (2013) provide a comprehensive guide for educators seeking to incorporate translanguaging practices into their classrooms.

Educators who make an effort to incorporate home languages into the classroom and who actively demonstrate the value of the home language and culture through their words and actions can have a profound effect on students and families (Sánchez-López & Young, 2018). Academic engagement, achievement, and feelings of self-worth and pride are enhanced when students see that their home language and culture are of importance. Integration of powerful practices that show students, their families, cultures, and languages reflected in school life also has the potential to reduce students' "affective filter" (Krashen, 2009). With a lowered affective filter, students feel less self-conscious about their learning efforts and more willing to take linguistic risks. This can assist in accelerating their language learning, as well as promoting their inclusion and participation in classroom and school activities.

The impact of a teacher demonstrating respect for languages and cultures is not lost on parents either, some of whom may not be focused on the retention of the home language, but rather on the mastery of English language proficiency and literacy. Parents who receive the same positive message regarding the importance of home language and culture may have a greater understanding of how and why they can support their children's development of the home language and ultimately their children's English language development and academic achievement.

The importance of incorporating culturally and linguistically responsive practices into education has been formally recognized at the governmental level. Few comprehensive programs articulate the expectations or benefits of cultural and linguistic responsiveness as succinctly as the guidance set forth by The Early Head Start National Resource Center in a document entitled *Revisiting and Updating the Multicultural Principles for Head Start Programs Serving Children Ages Birth to Five* (2008).

In 1991, the United States Federal Office of Head Start (OHS) first recognized the need to respond to changing demographics of children and families. By 2008, the need to respond systemically had become paramount when nine out of ten families served by Head Start programming spoke a language other than English at home. Head Start asserted the following:

> "For Head Start programs, it is absolutely necessary to respect and incorporate families' cultures into the systems and services provided. Program management should actively promote the development of a positive cultural and individual identity for all children. In addition, as program staff are also members of cultural groups, programs must find ways to identify and include cultural information from program staff." (Early Head Start National Resource Center, 2008, p. 14)

Similarly strong sentiments are expressed by the Ontario Ministry of Education in various curriculum documents advocating that students see their experiences reflected in the learning environment (Ontario Ministry of Education, 2007, 2008, 2016b).

"Students who see their previously developed language skills acknowledged by their teachers and parents are more likely to feel confident and take the risks involved in learning a new language. They are able to view English as an addition to their first language, rather than as a substitution for it. There are numerous positive outcomes that result from continuing to promote the ongoing use and development of ELLs' [English Language Learners'] first languages. Respect and use of the first language contribute both to the building of a confident learner and to the efficient learning of additional languages and academic achievement." (Ontario Ministry of Education, 2008, p. 8)

In this chapter, we explore strategies within the classroom as we answer the following key questions:

A. What components of meaningful instruction are needed to support English Learners in every classroom?

B. What are some ways to expand students' connections to new learning in an additional language?

C. What are some ways to embrace languages that we do not speak in the classroom?

D. How might we show that it is important for students to continue to develop the home language?

FIGURE 2.2 Question A: Overview

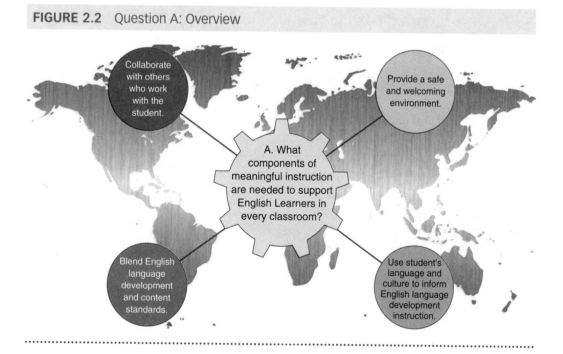

A. WHAT COMPONENTS OF MEANINGFUL INSTRUCTION ARE NEEDED TO SUPPORT ENGLISH LEARNERS IN EVERY CLASSROOM?

- Powerful Practice 1: Ground academic instruction in an environment of acceptance and welcome, with opportunities for positive interactions.

- Powerful Practice 2: Use the student's language background to inform English language development instruction.

- Powerful Practice 3: Blend English language development standards with content standards for instruction.

- Powerful Practice 4: Collaborate with other professionals involved in the care of the student.

Powerful Practice 1: Ground academic instruction in an environment of acceptance and welcome, with opportunities for positive interactions.

What It Might Look Like

Mrs. Sheridan taught at a suburban school where there was limited cultural and linguistic diversity in the student population. When she learned that she would be receiving a student from South Sudan, she wondered how to support Kariem, the new English Learner who would be the only student who spoke Nuer and Arabic, as well as the only student of color in her class. She also realized that all of Kariem's teachers would need to operationalize their responsibility of being the language teacher for everyone in their classrooms, including the new student.

In addition to the social and emotional aspects of welcoming a new student from an unfamiliar background, she worried about how she would be able to meet the student's educational requirements. She realized that every English Learner arrives with a unique set of background characteristics (e.g., features of the home language, literacy development, English language experience, school experience, possible traumatic experiences), all of which carry instructional implications. For example, the student with limited formal education will likely need a far greater emphasis on developing pre-reading skills in English than the student who is already reading at grade-level in the home language. Similarly, a student whose first language is written using other than the Latin script will require specific instruction in forming letters and handwriting, regardless of age or grade. Mrs. Sheridan wondered how to provide focused instruction to fill in learning gaps and provide a strong literacy foundation in English. She recognized the need to attend carefully to the student's background data to understand the student's circumstances and then layer elements of his essential instructional requirements into daily instruction (Fairbairn & Jones-Vo, 2016). To do so, she focused on four components essential for meaningful instruction in her classroom: providing a safe and welcoming environment, using the student's language background to inform English language development, blending content and English language learning, and collaborating with others in the building who might also be working with Kariem, thereby extending his language learning throughout all classes.

Mrs. Sheridan's greatest concern revolved around helping others understand and welcome the new student so he would feel safe and at ease. Feeling emotionally comfortable is foundational for learning in a new environment, in a new language, and with new classmates. She recognized that preparing her class in advance to receive and befriend Kariem would support such relationship-building. Many students volunteered as "ambassadors" to make sure that Kariem would become familiar with school directions and locations and enjoy dining buddies in the lunchroom. The entire class learned about geography in South Sudan, traditions and customs, and the dozens of languages spoken there to better understand their new friend's background. This new learning fueled their artwork, which decorated the classroom as a welcoming gesture.

Since Kariem would be interacting with multiple teachers in his new school, Mrs. Sheridan realized that her colleagues could also likely benefit from learning more about Kariem. Anticipating the staff's need for information, she created flyers about the new student's culture and first language background and distributed them accordingly. The helpful materials included a map of Africa highlighting South Sudan, a picture of the country's new flag, some facts about Kariem's two home languages, essential key words in both Nuer and Arabic (e.g., greetings, washroom or bathroom), and a transliteration of the student's name so that every teacher could pronounce it correctly. Mrs. Sheridan added a link to a website providing an opportunity for teachers to take a pledge to pronounce students' names correctly in order to foster their sense of belonging and to build positive relationships from the first day of school (Santa Clara County Office of Education, 2016, https://www.mynamemyidentity.org).

In taking on the role of cultural broker for her colleagues, Mrs. Sheridan supported Kariem's teachers to build relevant background that could help them design appropriate instruction and assessments for him. Sensing that her colleagues might need support to adapt both content and language development standards for a student with unique background characteristics, Mrs. Sheridan sought the support of her school leaders to allow her to provide staff development around English for Speakers of Other Languages (ESOL) topics, delivered weekly during a dedicated staff development time. She began to assume the role of the school's "go-to" cultural informant and ESOL teacher leader, learning along with her colleagues.

Making It Your Own

Putting students at ease in a new and unfamiliar environment is essential before new learning can take place. What steps have you taken in the past to pave the way for newcomers in your classroom community? What worked especially well? What might be modified to improve for future use? What additional ideas do you have for supporting your current students to welcome newcomers? Consider using the chart in Figure 2.3 to reflect on classroom practices that contribute to creating a safe learning environment. Add additional ideas as you collaborate with others.

WIDA (2020d) asserts that, "A welcoming classroom is about community and equity. By keeping these two ideas in mind, you can create an environment where students feel safe, visible and valued and where they are provided access to rigorous curriculum that engages and challenges them in meaningful ways." To engage students in creating such a safe learning space, you might ask them to imagine what life could be like if they arrived in a distant country where they did not know the language. How would they feel? What would they need? What things might help them feel respected, comfortable, and ready to interact with others? What would they like to see displayed in such a classroom to make them feel at home? Guide your students in co-creating a list of welcoming ideas and behaviors that they themselves can implement in their classroom.

FIGURE 2.3 Checklist of Co-created Practices for Welcoming Students in Classrooms and School

CLASSROOM FEATURES	PRESENT ✓	COMMENTS/ NEEDS
Teachers and staff learn students' names and correct pronunciation.		
Classmates are prepared in advance to welcome newcomers and introduce themselves.		
Classrooms are labeled with teachers' name, photo, and grade level/class/subject.		
Students' and families' languages and cultures are visually represented in a variety of ways in hallways and classrooms (e.g., student work, posters, artifacts, flags, maps, art, etc.).		
Fiction and nonfiction books are available in students' languages or dual languages; library resources are inclusive of different languages, cultures, and reading levels represented in the school.		
New students are assigned a peer buddy or student ambassador for orientation (e.g., lunch time, moving to a new classroom, getting on the bus).		
Cooperative learning is used to promote interaction among classmates for learning language.		
School objects are labeled in various languages of students.		
Food choices in the lunchroom are labeled in different languages; culturally diverse food choices are available.		
Holiday and cultural displays reflect the diversity of the community.		
Classroom rules and expectations are explained and supplemented with visual support.		
A bilingual liaison representative/interpreter is available to welcome families and to help families and schools connect throughout the year (e.g., home visits, telephone calls, relating important information regarding upcoming events and deadlines, parent meetings, school functions, etc.).		
Other:		

Powerful Practice 2: Use the student's language background to inform English language development instruction.

Mrs. Sheridan reflected on the skills that her native English speaking students brought into the classroom and how this might differ from the language learning background of her new student. While speakers of English as a home language have typically spent the first five years of life playing with sounds, singing, rhyming, and developing vocabulary that matches the school curriculum in English, other students arrive at school with a different linguistic repertoire. Educators often take for granted or even expect that the students in their classrooms possess a well-stocked treasure chest of significantly developed English skills. The language treasure chests of newcomers, on the other hand, rich and appropriate for learning their first languages, vary widely among students. Comprising a bounty of skills in various home languages, each student's treasures likely include fewer jewels in English, given each individual's differences in contact and experience with languages. Some students may have been exposed only to English media; others may have had informal English lessons; while some may have received formal English language instruction. There may be some students who have not been exposed to English before appearing in your classroom. Some students may be multilingual in a variety of languages while others may be multiliterate. Each student's treasure chest merits careful unpacking and analysis in order to leverage and optimize their English language development instruction.

Searching for clues to best inform her instruction and assessment, Mrs. Sheridan reviewed what she knew about her new student's language experiences, gleaning some of his instructional strengths as well as needs. In order to provide meaningful and comprehensible instruction, she reviewed what she knew about her new student:

- Kariem's first and home language is Nuer, which his family reported to be orally well developed for social and everyday purposes. As such, Kariem possesses many linguistic attributes in his home language that could be incorporated into classroom instructional practices, including useful vocabulary in Nuer.

- Kariem's second language is Arabic, which is at a beginning level. He reportedly understands some spoken Arabic and is able to use certain words and formulaic language (e.g., How are you?).

- Since Kariem has had no significant exposure to English before arriving in North America, he will benefit from oral language development including English vocabulary and social phrases for daily life. Mrs. Sheridan will design her instructional strategies rooted in comprehension and meaning, avoiding decontextualized skill drills lacking visual support, such as those applied in certain reading development interventions designed for non-English Learners, in order to optimize Kariem's language learning.

- Since Kariem has not yet received formal education in either Nuer or in Arabic, his formal educational experience will begin in his new setting. Mrs. Sheridan projected that arriving at school must feel unnerving, if not frightening, for her new student. As a result, Mrs. Sheridan planned for her class to make a special effort to welcome Kariem and support him becoming familiar with routines, behaviors, and expectations in the new education system starting on his first day.

- Apart from being able to write his name in Arabic by copying, Kariem is essentially pre-literate. As such, he has not yet developed a literacy schema to access or draw upon, which would support him in applying a similar systematic approach to reading in English. Students who, unlike Kariem, are literate in their home language generally are able to apply the basic underlying processes of learning to read intuitively to their new language, subconsciously relying on relevant cues from their existing linguistic repertoire. For example, given that Arabic is read and written from right to left, teachers would need to reorient Kariem to the opposite directionality of print in English, as they might reasonably expect that he would rely on his first-learned process of reading right to left. As Kariem is at the pre-reading level in English, collaboration with expert reading teachers who are familiar with the language acquisition process, as well as embedding foundational steps upon which to build his literacy in English, are essential. Kariem will benefit greatly from reading instruction in English that considers his unique status as a beginning English Learner, emphasizing the same pre-reading skills and continuous oral language development upon which non-English learners have based their budding reading ability. Due to being nine years of age and unfamiliar with Latin script, Kariem's learning to read in English from the very beginning stages is of utmost importance. His instruction is not to be considered remedial reading, since he has never received initial reading instruction. Rather, reading instruction for Kariem requires the applied reading expertise of his reading teachers, vocabulary and oral development in English, scope and sequence in content, measurable objectives, and imaginative visual supports and scaffolds. Intentional reading development instruction for Kariem must be purposeful, intentional, and sustained as it is for younger students in earlier grades and preschool when pre-reading skills and reading instruction commences.

Making It Your Own

While students arrive with widely varying levels of background in English language development, they also bring a variety of home language assets to build upon. Knowing essential language background information is key in identifying each student's instructional needs and gifts, with particular implications for teaching reading in English. Use the Instructional Reading Inventory for Newcomer Students (Figure 2.4) to analyze a student's language background in your classroom. Based on responses to the questions, determine what essential instruction is needed to develop literacy skills in English. Compare your ideas with a colleague who also knows the student. Add your own suggestions and professional ideas. Note: students with limited or interrupted formal education (SLIFE) is a topic addressed in more detail in Chapter 4.

FIGURE 2.4 Instructional Reading Inventory for Newcomer Students

---

Student Name: **Grade:**   **Age:**

Home Language: **Date of Arrival:**

Relevant Background Information: **English Language Development Levels:**

L _____ S _____ R _____ W _____

Use information about the student's previous language experience in the home language(s) and English, as well as relevant background information to anticipate instructional needs in reading.

1. What language-related assets are in the student's "treasure chest"?

   _____

2. What language learning or exposure to language(s) has the student had in both oral and written forms?

   Oral: _____

   Written: _____

3. What are some specific characteristics or features of the home language(s) that are the same/different from English, and how might these features be used to facilitate English reading instruction?

   _____

4. What is the student's educational background and history?

   _____

---

5. What was the language used in previous education? What was the language of literacy?

_____

6. What is the script used in the student's home language?

_____

7. Can the student write in another language?

_____

8. Is the student able to form letters of the Latin alphabet and write in English?

_____

9. Is there a specific teacher who has responsibility for teaching handwriting and pre-reading skills in English? Who can serve as collaborators to ensure daily support?

_____

10. Is there a plan and schedule for putting reading development in place that supports students who have interrupted education and have not yet received reading instruction in English?

_____

11. Are reading teachers with both beginning literacy background and language learning experience providing essential reading instruction for newcomers and SLIFE students?

_____

12. Does your school have a plan for teaching reading to older students to ensure their reading instruction matches their instructional needs?

_____

13. Are classroom teachers in your school routinely prepared to provide English Learners with accessible supplementary materials that support content areas?

_____

Based on responses to these questions, what recommendations might you have for the reading instruction of this student?

A. _____

B. _____

C. _____

D. _____

E. _____

Powerful Practice 3: Blend English language development standards with content standards for instruction.

In different locales, such as in U.S. consortia with multi-state membership or in some individual states in the United States and most provinces in Canada, schools base instruction on state or provincially mandated content standards. When English Learners are in the mix, all teachers must then also be familiar with their local English language development standards, as well as their local content standards. Responsible for teaching both language and content, teachers weave elements of both sets of standards together instructionally, thereby enabling students to experience English language development propelled and driven by the course content. By providing explicit language development contextualized by content learning, teachers can meet the language development needs of all students in their class very efficiently.

In the Canadian province of Ontario, Steps to English Proficiency (STEP) provides a useful frame-work for identifying English Learners' literacy and language acquisition capabilities at each level of development across the Ontario Curriculum (Ontario Ministry of Education, 2015, http://www.edugains.ca/resourcesELL/Assessment/STEP/STEPUserGuide_November2015.pdf).

In the United States, a majority of states are part of the WIDA consortium (formerly known as World-Class Instructional Design and Assessment), which provides English language development standards for teachers' reference and guidance. Further, for instructional purposes, the WIDA (2020a) Can Do Descriptors detail linguistic expectations for teachers to apply to their English Learners at various levels, enabling all students, regardless of language level, to engage in the curriculum (https://wida.wisc.edu/teach/can-do/descriptors). Some states such as Texas, New York, approach English language development standards independently or in smaller consortia.

With Kariem in mind, Mrs. Sheridan was well aware of the need to teach her local content standards, as well as to embed English language development standards. Having explicit guidelines for both content and for English language development helps teachers to achieve this dual outcome simultaneously: increasing English language proficiency as well as increasing content knowledge, skills, and abilities, based on a student's individual data. Mrs. Sheridan plans to consider the data available and the background information she has about her new student in order to customize and differentiate instructional materials, scaffolds, and particularly her language expectations of Kariem within the context of her grade-level curriculum. While his reading skills do not yet mirror those of his new age-level peers, Mrs. Sheridan knows that with instruction and supplementary accessible materials that correspond with his starting points, Kariem will be able to make significant gains essential for his academic and workplace future.

Making It Your Own

Various consortia, states, school boards, and districts in Canada and the United States rely on a variety of independently developed sets of content standards and English language development standards. We now invite you to try out this blending of standards practice in your context by identifying which standards you are utilizing in your area. To weave language standards together with content standards, follow these steps with a specific student in mind:

1. List a specific English Learner from your context, along with their English language development levels or STEP levels in listening, speaking, reading, and writing.

2. Using a resource related to English language development standards recommended or required in your area, such as the WIDA Can Do Descriptors or STEP or others; familiarize yourself with what your local English Learner can be expected to be able to do with language at each of the reported levels of language development (listening, speaking, reading, and writing).

3. Think of a specific lesson you are planning, with your selected English Learner in mind. What do the Can Do Descriptors or STEP tell you that your student, at that specific level, could be expected to do with language? (Note that if you are targeting writing, you will focus on the student's writing level, matching the data-informed description of what that student is able to do at a specific level with your expectations of language production in writing.) Bear in mind the need to provide instruction that pushes the student to the next linguistic level. This process metaphorically resembles climbing a set of stairs, reaching the top after a sustained effort of many small advances. Differentiating expectations and gradually increasing them, based on student data, requires vigilance and awareness of how language develops over time.

4. Identify the content standard of your specific lesson. Begin to think about how you can provide scaffolds and supports for your English Learner, based on their English language development data, to make it more accessible or understandable and the tasks more doable for a student at that specific level. In other words, to differentiate for English Learners at various levels of development, adjust your linguistic expectations for classroom assignments

(Continued)

(Continued)

or assessments in order to match the proficiency descriptions of an English Learner at their specific levels in each domain of listening, speaking, reading, and writing. Based on English language development data available to teachers, such as an annual WIDA ACCESS assessment or perhaps a portfolio that notes oral proficiency and classroom performance providing each student's placement on the STEP continuum, make sure that you have a clear idea of what to expect linguistically from your student. You are preparing to design and differentiate instruction to include your specific student in classroom learning. Whether the student engages or is overwhelmed by the expectations depends upon the teacher matching doable activities to their range of current capabilities in English.

5. Next, locate and familiarize yourself with the English language development standards in your area. Locate where your student fits on this continuum and infuse your instruction with those expectations for that student. Consider writing a language objective for each lesson that ensures English language development in your classroom embodies general English language development standards and that it provides comprehensive progression over time.

6. Finally, weaving the appropriate English language development standards together with your particular content standards, make a conscious effort to include activities that focus explicitly on academic language development. By adjusting and gradually increasing your expectations of what students are able to produce linguistically, based on their individual background data of all kinds, you can best engage English Learners in classroom learning. Providing level-appropriate instruction and activities and adjusting language expectations to match current levels of student proficiency, make the content accessible. English Learners are able to participate in classroom learning when the instruction is comprehensible, relevant, and doable, while higher expectations are applied incrementally.

Powerful Practice 4: Collaborate with other professionals involved in the care of the student.

What It Might Look Like

Based on her knowledge of Kariem's background, Mrs. Sheridan realized that his needs might extend beyond her educational training as a content area teacher. Besides learning English as an additional language, Kariem had experienced civil unrest, food insecurity, and considerable trauma while living in a refugee camp. The rest of his background and how it might impact social and academic achievement was yet unknown. Mrs. Sheridan thought that she would best be able to serve her newest student if she collaborated with other specially trained school consultants with additional expertise. She considered the members of the school support team: the principal, counselor, special education consultant, speech-language pathologist, social worker, and school psychologist. An informal chat with the school psychologist, counselor, and social worker might prove helpful in anticipating Kariem's needs. To do so, Mrs. Sheridan would again need administrative support. Mrs. Sheridan advocated to form an entire team of experts who could meet regularly, brainstorming appropriate responses for newcomers.

After gaining the support of the principal, Mrs. Sheridan scheduled the first meeting of the team. Armed with fresh coffee from a local shop and her concerns itemized in her mind, Mrs. Sheridan was prepared to discuss Kariem's strengths and needs, to identify some realistic goals, and learn some strategies to reach those goals from her colleagues. She used the following worksheet to guide her discussion with other school professionals.

FIGURE 2.5 Collaborative Consultation Plan

Identifying Information:

Student Name: _____ DOB: _____ Student #: _____

School: _____ Teacher: _____ Grade: _____

Team Members: _____ Date: _____

Home Language(s) _____ Date of Arrival: _____

Diagnosis: _____ Other: _____

STUDENT STRENGTHS/RESOURCES	STUDENT NEEDS

(Continued)

FIGURE 2.5 (Continued)

Target Goal(s)

1. _____

2. _____

3. _____

PLAN OF ACTION

TARGET GOAL	WHAT	WHO	WHEN	OUTCOME	NEXT STEPS
1					
2					
3					

SOURCE: Adapted from: Speech-Language Pathology Services. (2006). *Collaborative Consultation Action Planning Worksheet.* Toronto, ON: Toronto District School Board.

Making It Your Own

Think about the various school support staff who serve your school. What are their respective areas of expertise? Have you had the opportunity to work collaboratively with them to attend to the needs of a particular student, group of students, or an entire class? Do you need the input of multiple professionals for a particular student? How can you coordinate your work? Each school district or board of education allocates support services differently, with its own set of rules, regulations, and guidelines. Are you familiar with how those work in your jurisdiction? Your voice as an educator brings specific and much needed expertise to the collaborative table. Decisions made by school teams on behalf of English Learners can be best informed by including the insight, perspective, and expertise of all team members.

FIGURE 2.6 Question B: Overview

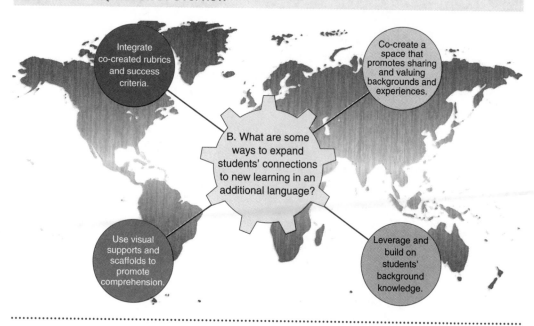

B. WHAT ARE SOME WAYS TO EXPAND STUDENTS' CONNECTIONS TO NEW LEARNING IN AN ADDITIONAL LANGUAGE?

- Powerful Practice 1: Lead the co-creation of a safe space that promotes sharing and valuing of backgrounds and experiences.

- Powerful Practice 2: Leverage and build on students' background knowledge.

- Powerful Practice 3: Use visual supports and scaffolds to promote comprehension.

- Powerful Practice 4: Integrate the use of co-created rubrics and success criteria.

Powerful Practice 1: Lead the co-creation of a safe space that promotes sharing and valuing of all backgrounds and experiences.

The entire social studies teaching staff was meeting to discuss the seventh grade social studies curriculum in the first year of a new textbook adoption. Ms. Djuric, a social studies teacher whose students encompassed a wide, dynamic range of linguistic and cultural diversity, suggested that the newly designed course could be reconfigured to highlight the many countries and backgrounds represented by English Learners and others in the school in new and inclusive ways. She recognized that her English Learners might be reticent, but insisted that if the expectations were consistent and clear, participation and learning of all students could be enhanced through the creation of a safe space to share and learn about a range of cultural behaviors, beliefs, and values. First, she suggested that teams of student "experts," including English Learners from the various regions to be studied, would collaborate on their learning. Ms. Djuric projected that these English Learner cultural experts could incorporate authentic, first-hand facts and relevant knowledge about their backgrounds that would not otherwise come to light without this inclusive, contributory framework. These teams, including "first person voices," could choose to present their relevant information in a variety of ways, creating a classroom where all students felt more comfortable sharing information and ideas from their diverse backgrounds.

As part of a small group presentation format, each student would be expected to research and present an aspect of the assigned country. In addition to basic facts, such as geography (e.g., climate, location, physical features), people (e.g., demographics, languages, religions), and economics (e.g., currency, primary industries, natural resources), Ms. Djuric expanded students' opportunities to experience the richness and depth of cultural diversity across different countries and regions, and so the list of possible student contributions grew longer:

- Instruction of a mini-language lesson by expert students where classmates learned useful social language in another language they could use daily with peers

- An inquiry into the education systems in various countries, including the educational opportunities available for women and girls and minority groups

- A survey of culture-specific gender roles in relation to different contexts, such as the home and the workplace

- An inquiry into aspects of social etiquette in family relations and wider society, such as the use of honorifics in addressing elders, conversational norms with family or strangers, and views about the importance of time and punctuality

- A look at a culture's relationship to animals, both domestic and agricultural

- An overview of home medical practices and remedies in case of simple ailments or injuries

- Creation of a model of a place of worship and description of various religious artifacts and observances

- A cooking lesson, where students prepared a favorite dish from their home country using authentic ingredients, followed by a tasting of samples

- A lesson on how to create a hand-crafted item, such as demonstrating the art of *hekla* or hand-crocheted table placemats from Bosnia or applying a beautiful temporary tattoo on a hand, as in *mehndi* for an Indian wedding

- Demonstration of a national folk dance followed by presenters teaching the audience how to perform the dance

Ms. Djuric saw that English Learners sharing personal input as experts with peers can both inspire student motivation and catapult their language development while laying the groundwork for a classroom environment that makes everyone feel safe and valued. Students began to feel greater ownership and belonging in the classroom and more comfortable in expressing themselves freely. Ms. Djuric also had each of her students set up a "Cultural Awareness Log" (Thier, 2013), in which they could record descriptions, details, and observations about various cultural practices, values, and beliefs. Students also journaled their reflections on initial inferences about various cultures, as well as their changing and deepening understandings of various cultures during the project, which served as a basis for rich classroom discussion leading to a widening of viewpoints among many students.

Over time, Ms. Djuric noticed that her students arrived more frequently in her classroom before school hours and free periods to meet other students. She considered her conscious role in creating and supporting this environment of respectful and inclusive sharing, caring, and laughter among students and realized that she herself felt at home there, as well.

Observing her students' increasing interactions and exchanges, Ms. Djuric knew that the accepting and collegial social environment inside her classroom now better supported diverse students developing English skills and new learning. As a result, she developed ways to extend the message of welcome to all students, regardless of national origin, age, race, language, gender, sexual orientation, religion, class, political beliefs, or physical ability. For example, Ms. Djuric invited her students to design signs for her classroom door, as well as the doors of other interested teachers, that served as a signal to all students that this classroom takes a proactive stance in welcoming and respecting all students.

Making It Your Own

Establishing a shared sense of belonging and welcoming in the classroom has the potential to transform students' school experience, motivate their engagement in learning, and accelerate English language development. The strategy of positioning English Learners as experts to share their own information, described in the preceding section, promotes English Learners themselves highlighting their cultural and linguistic backgrounds and establishes a schoolwide norm for the inclusion and valuing of all students. When such practice is consistent, all students benefit from learning from each other, including non-English Learners learning concepts about other cultures to which they might not otherwise be exposed. This strategy is among the most foundational and important when considering the well-being and social integration of newcomers and other English Learners.

Think about and discuss your responses to the following questions:

1. In your context, what might you have done already to create a safe and comfortable space that promotes sharing and valuing of backgrounds and experiences?

2. In what ways have you involved students in co-creating a safe and familiar environment that they enjoy?

3. What other ideas do you have to expand this type of positive environment in your classroom?

4. How could you gather student input for ideas about what they might like to see or experience in the classroom?

Next, using Figure 2.7 as a starting point, brainstorm ways that colleagues from other academic areas could expand the inclusion of English Learner expertise in their content areas, including possible ways to connect student backgrounds to content and to offer potential benefits for all students. Compare your results with those of colleagues to establish a consistent expectation of highlighting the assets and cultures of English Learners throughout the school.

FIGURE 2.7 Ensuring Cultural Connections to Content

SUBJECT AREA	TOPIC OF STUDY	IDEAS TO INCORPORATE RELEVANT BACKGROUND INFORMATION OF ENGLISH LEARNERS	BENEFITS OF MAKING EXPLICIT CONNECTIONS TO SUBJECT AREA CONTENT
Social studies or history	World Regions; presentation on background knowledge about aspects of a country, culture, or other relevant idea	Assign ELs as experts from a certain country to join a small group. Invite students to share cultural knowledge, practices, customs, etc. Allow for student choice.	**English Learner**: able to show expertise on assigned country, impact on sense of self (*funds of identity*), garners respect from classmates, contributes specific knowledge not readily available in texts, able to participate more fully in the learning **Non-English Learners**: the opportunity to witness capabilities of English Learners, build understanding and respect for each other, construct understanding of individuals for building relationships
Music class or band			
Math			
Reading or language arts			
Science			
Art			
Other			

Powerful Practice 2: Leverage and build on students' background knowledge.

What It Might Look Like

Mrs. Looker's High School Health and Home Sciences class was learning about nutrition recommended in daily meals by the United States Department of Agriculture initiative *Choose My Plate*. Her upcoming lesson relied on the MyPlate icon and the agency's website material in multiple languages (https://www .choosemyplate.gov/other-languages). She also found multilingual support, information, and images on the Government of Canada webpage Canada's Food Guide (2020) (https://food-guide.canada.ca/en/), and the website of the Food and Agriculture Organization of the United Nations (2020) highlighting food-based dietary guidelines from around the world (http://www.fao.org/home/search/).

By supplementing her lesson with material in students' home languages, Mrs. Looker hoped to enable her English Learners whose foods at home did not easily match foods depicted in some visuals to participate in the activity. English Learners were asked to illustrate a well-balanced, wholesome meal visually on a paper plate using craft materials, grocery flyers, magazines, and online access to free images and then to describe the meal to the class. This grade-level assignment meets grade-level curricular expectations and also scaffolds language to promote development in English by enabling all students to draw from their background knowledge.

Mrs. Looker noticed that some of her students who spoke English as a home language were preparing plates with spaghetti and meatballs, mashed potatoes, hamburgers, and pizza. She recognized a stellar opportunity to include the cuisine of her newest English Learners. She encouraged all of her students to include their favorite home-cooked foods, appropriately labeled, thereby completing the paper plate assignment with international flair. Mrs. Looker's English Learners rose to the task, preparing visual meals featuring *kesra* (flatbread from Algeria), *bún thịt nướng* (grilled pork with rice stick noodles and fresh herbs from Vietnam), *empanadas* (pastry stuffed with pumpkin, meats, or sweets from Mexico), *korma* (lamb stew with vegetables from Afghanistan), *ćevapi* (small grilled sausages from Bosnia), *arepa* (stuffed white corn cakes from Venezuela), and many others. Learning from one another, all of Mrs. Looker's students enriched their knowledge on the topic of international nutrition, sparking continued interest to learn more about preparing and tasting various multicultural delicacies. Embedding such cultural exploration and relishing the riches of diversity in their midst is part of the joy for teachers with English Learners.

Mrs. Looker extended her multicultural lesson on nutrition by assigning the creation of narrated cooking demonstrations of a favorite dish. Focusing on oral language development while holding students accountable for using sequencing words provides a powerful opportunity for authentic communication while blending English language development standards. Further building on this experience, Mrs. Looker collected favorite recipes from students, teachers, families, and school staff to compile a multicultural school cookbook. This extension of the nutrition lesson targeted organizational and writing skills and even math conversion skills for measurements. Everyone in the school, including the principal, custodial staff, parents of English Learners, parents of non-English learners, teachers, and paraprofessionals contributed their treasured family favorites and memorable holiday dishes to this special project. This schoolwide project supported everyone in the school in making connections to new learning and with each other, resulting in a collection of 850 recipes from fifty-four different countries. The bound volume, with a shiny cover featuring dozens of international flags, served as a lasting artifact of their useful and innovative school involvement.

Making It Your Own

Think about your own classroom learning environment. Brainstorm ways that you have already supported your students to access and leverage their own backgrounds and languages in the classroom. In what ways have you accessed first languages as a support in learning English? For example, do you routinely share relevant cognates? What first language news sites might you recommend for students? Brainstorm authentic resources, such as multilingual websites, first language newspapers, and newscasts that could enrich English Learners' understanding. Compile with colleagues a list of resources that classroom teachers currently use to engage and accelerate the learning of English Learners, and add to it as others become familiar. What additional ideas do you have for building on students' diverse backgrounds in your classroom?

Powerful Practice 3: Use visual supports and scaffolds to promote comprehension.

What It Might Look Like

Ms. Chau was preparing her students for a social studies assessment and worrying about the English Learners who had joined her class late in the school year. She knew they had extensive background knowledge, but the reading, writing, and speaking in English were still more challenging for these newer second graders. Ms. Chau recognized that important content learning was taking place, yet the assessment results would likely not accurately reflect what her newer students knew and could do since the medium for assessing itself amounted to a "test of English" rather than a pure test of social studies content.

For this reason, Ms. Chau herself relied on visual supports and a variety of other scaffolds that could help her students comprehend and demonstrate their knowledge while working toward full English proficiency. She had already observed how her English Learners were able to demonstrate knowledge in content areas while developing language, particularly when supports, such as a Venn diagram or a sequence map, were utilized. Ms. Chau used a variety of visual aids to incorporate critical language development into her instruction and posted these supports within the classroom for her students' future reference. Importantly, she held students accountable to demonstrate these structures in their speaking and writing assignments, such as in one of her favorite lessons, examining and contrasting features of the community.

Ms. Chau's students were engaged in answering the curricular question, "What are the built features and natural features in our community?" First, they conducted an exploration that included a walk in the community, online research, and watching a video. After activating background knowledge and adding new ideas, students were asked to draw images of various community features on sticky note paper. They then had to decide if their drawing was a *built* or a *natural feature* of the community and add their ideas where appropriate to a large, wall-sized Venn diagram.

Ms. Chau then scaffolded their oral descriptions using posted sentence frames, formulaic sentences that communicated the results of the jointly constructed Venn diagram. Observing the sentence frames decorating her classroom walls, she appreciated that they had been used many times since that activity to scaffold additional conversations and writings. The students seemed very pleased to produce such academic sentences as "One place that features both _____ and _____ is _____." and "Based on the diagram, there are as many _____ as _____ in our community."

Because Ms. Chau supported her students making meaningful and comprehensible connections to the curriculum while providing contextualized language instruction, she was able to teach her students both content and language simultaneously. In addition, they were able to transfer and apply the new sentence constructions to other topics and classes.

Making It Your Own

Looking back over the lesson on community features, multiple visual supports have been used in an effort to maximize students' comprehension. For example, the students took a walk in the neighborhood where they observed realia; they watched a relevant video; they drew sketches of community features they saw learning vocabulary; they were held accountable to speak and write using sentence frames posted for visual reference; and finally, a Venn diagram relied on pictures and words to assist comprehension for the purpose of comparison. It is well-established that students at earlier levels of language development require more extensive scaffolds. For English Learners' instruction and assessment, visual support is essential and must be routinely provided.

Think of a lesson that you have recently taught.

1. Make a list of the visual supports and scaffolds that were used.

2. Which one do you think is the most effective? Do you feel that you provided enough visual supports?

3. If you were to include additional scaffolds to your list, what might you like to add?

4. Do you routinely incorporate visual supports in classroom assessments as well as in instructional materials?

Powerful Practice 4: Integrate the use of co-created rubrics and success criteria.

At the beginning of the school year, Miss Nguyen learned that her classroom had twenty-seven English Learners, representing thirteen different languages. Some of the students were beginners in learning English and had also experienced interrupted formal education. Miss Nguyen was struggling to learn the names of the many new students and was not yet familiar with their backgrounds, which she deemed essential to informing her lesson planning. In addition, her students did not yet know one another.

Miss Nguyen decided to have students create pictorially supported posters to introduce themselves. The poster activity would serve as an excellent entrée for getting acquainted with students while providing the opportunity for development of the vocabulary and oral communication skills foundational to reading and writing. With her instruction and modeling of the assignment, students could practice basic presentation skills that would serve them well in other classes across the curriculum.

Miss Nguyen especially appreciated that the poster format could engage students at all levels of English proficiency in making connections to new learning. Newcomers as well as intermediate or advanced English Learners could all draw upon their previous knowledge to successfully complete the academic requirements using available supports, such as pictures, word banks, time lines, modeling, demonstrations, illustrations, sentence frames, exemplars, and so forth. However, one cannot assume that all students have experience with such a request as talking about themselves in class or experience with or even access to various media. Careful step-by-step explanation, vocabulary development, demonstration, and modeling will support newcomers in becoming acquainted with different approaches to education than what they might have experienced in the past.

Miss Nguyen designed a detailed plan for her poster strategy where all students, regardless of their English language development levels, would be able to earn full marks for their assignment. She planned to co-create the success criteria for the self-introduction poster along with her students. Her purpose for integrating the use of a co-created rubric was multifold: to put her students at ease, to informally assess her students' language output, to teach language and classroom procedures, to clarify achievement expectations for students, and to demystify grading. Her steps for lesson design included the following:

1. Along with students, co-create a rubric for what will be included in the self-introduction activity. Students can suggest familiar topics, such as

family, hobbies, and so forth. The co-creation step is essential for English Learners whose backgrounds vary greatly, especially those who might be unfamiliar with North American education. Discussions can help clarify what students are actually going to produce and provide the added benefits of hearing English modeled in context several times and practicing using new English structures before they are used for evaluation purposes. In addition, during co-creating, the teacher can informally assess student language levels by listening to their verbal contributions.

The teacher will provide information for the rubric that describes how students at different English language development levels could achieve full credit for meeting adjusted language expectations. Adjusting language expectations ensures English Learners' access to and participation in the curriculum. In addition, using a rubric (Figure 2.8) with adjusted language expectations empowers all students to earn high marks for demonstrating their knowledge and comprehension of the curricular topic to the extent that, as indicated by all of their individual and background data, they are able.

FIGURE 2.8 Success Criteria

SCORE (POINTS)	PURPOSE	USE OF VISUAL SUPPORT	USE OF ORAL PRESENTATION SKILLS	OVERALL FEEDBACK BASED ON RUBRIC EXPECTATIONS RELEVANT TO LEVEL OF ENGLISH LANGUAGE DEVELOPMENT
	Introduce yourself to the class using a poster. *Include:* 1. Name 2. Parents 3. Siblings 4. Home country 5. Language 6. Hobby 7. Food 8. Clothing 9. Celebration 10. Other	Use photos from free web sites, magazines, personal photos, drawings, etc. Describe your poster using sentence frames, vocabulary, or labels posted in the classroom. Use some words from your first language.	1. Strong vocal volume 2. Good eye contact with audience 3. Stand still 4. Point to appropriate image(s) 5. Practice in advance	• The poster describes you. • You present the poster with oral language. • You use a variety of relevant photo and image sources. • The poster contains relevant information. • Your poster shares some words from your home language. • The poster is ready to be displayed in the classroom. • The poster reflects your best effort to display your current level of English development. • Other

SCORE (POINTS)	PURPOSE	USE OF VISUAL SUPPORT	USE OF ORAL PRESENTATION SKILLS	OVERALL FEEDBACK BASED ON RUBRIC EXPECTATIONS RELEVANT TO LEVEL OF ENGLISH LANGUAGE DEVELOPMENT
		Assessment Rubric		
5	8–10 facts	Relevant images from 5 sources	All five presentation skills	The class now has a great idea of who you are!
4	6–7 facts	Relevant images from 4 sources	Four presentation skills	We know some interesting facts about you, but would like to know even more!
3	4–5 facts	Relevant images from 3 sources	Three presentation skills	Your poster is well on the way to introducing you!
2	3 facts	Relevant images from 2 sources	Two presentation skills	Your poster is making progress!
1	1–2 facts	Relevant images from 1 source	One presentation skill	We look forward to knowing more!

2. Identify and pre-teach essential vocabulary needed for the content of the presentation. Add new words underlined supported by pictures to an ongoing classroom or individual word bank. Word banks provide a record of vocabulary that can be consulted for clarification, reference, and more throughout the school year. An alternate form could be producing word cards (English and home language) or those with picture definitions on the flip side.

3. Post sentence starters throughout the classroom for student reference. Sentence starters contain words needed to begin to talk about a topic. They are particularly helpful for students at earlier stages of English language development. Academic sentence frames of increasing complexity can also effectively support advancing English Learners. Sentence starters can be used as scaffolds when practicing and presenting the self-introduction poster. For advanced students, academic sentence frames can be used to articulate more complex and advanced ways to compare, analyze, summarize, and so forth. The sentence frames that follow might work for newcomers.

- My name is _____.

- My parents/guardians are _____ and _____.

- My siblings are _____ and _____.

- My home country is _____.

- I speak _____.

- My favorite hobby to enjoy is _____.

- My favorite food from my home country is called_____.

- I like to wear _____.

- A big celebration in my culture is _____.

- I choose to share about _____.

4. Provide poster-making materials, including magazines, scissors, glue, markers, and poster board or cardboard. Specify additional resources that students could use for their creation, such as clip art, free online images (e.g., Pixabay (2020) www.pixabay.com; Public Domain Pictures (2007–2020), www.publicdomainpictures.net; and Unsplash Photos for Everyone, www.unsplash.com), as well as personal photographs or drawings.

5. Create an exemplar poster of yourself. For students who have never produced such a poster, a visual image depicting a final product that meets high expectations is extremely beneficial. Include words in your first language (Vietnamese, in the case of Miss Nguyen) for labeling some items on the poster and presenting to the class.

6. Model presenting the self-introduction presentation to the class, referring to your poster for visual support. Modeling is essential for English Learners who might be unfamiliar with a rubric or who are not familiar with the language of self-introduction.

7. Display both the poster and the rubric for evaluation in the classroom, as useful references to teach students how a rubric informs what they are expected to do in order to achieve full credit.

8. Invite the class to evaluate the teacher's poster presentation based on the rubric and discuss the feedback and final grade. This demonstrates how to use and interpret a rubric effectively to meet teacher expectations with predictable and positive results.

9. Students create posters in class. Encourage students to incorporate words from their home languages and in English. The end result will likely reflect a cornucopia of posters featuring varying amounts of English and home languages. This translanguaging supports newcomers in making sense of new content and feeling comfortable in the new environment as well as instructs other students' new learning.

10. Students practice presenting their posters orally to a partner to receive feedback, using the posted sentence starters, as needed. The teacher could provide reusable bookmarks printed with feedback comments based on the rubric expectations (e.g., Your eye contact was good; Your volume was not strong; Your body language needed gestures).

11. Students present their posters to the class. Take notes during the students' self-introductions to incorporate new vocabulary from other languages into future interactions with your students. Keep a running list of new words in a variety of languages, posted for all to see and use.

12. Provide students with feedback on their presentations. Based on differentiated language expectations, all students should be able to earn credit for demonstration of their content knowledge, as described by the rubric.

13. Prominently display the completed student posters. Upon entering the classroom, other teachers, students, and parents immediately see evidence of valued student identities and languages.

14. Reflect on the results of making and sharing the self-introduction poster, noting potential adjustments for next time.

Making It Your Own

The effectiveness of co-created rubrics is realized during both the instruction and assessment phases. For the instruction phase, the teacher activates students' background knowledge by asking their ideas and input based on what they know. Since students already know much about themselves, they are readily more able to become engaged in language learning, classroom conversations, and suggesting ideas for inclusion in the rubric. For the assessment phase, students can also contribute ideas for the rubric that clearly describes what a product must include across English language proficiency levels, since the work produced by a student at Level 1 is different than work by a student at Level 4. Recognizing that all students, regardless of their levels, are able to engage with the content to the extent individually possible, teachers use a rubric to lay out the appropriate language expectations and plan for appropriate scaffolds in classroom assignments and assessments. When language expectations are matched to English language proficiency levels, teachers can demystify the grading process for language learners.

Using the rubric template that follows (Figure 2.9), adapt the poster activity to an upcoming topic or lesson in your class. Practice co-creating the success criteria with your students. Be sure to specify each requirement in any task for earning full credit or high marks and to adjust language expectations to match various levels of English language development.

Some states, provinces, and consortia of states define a varying number of language proficiency levels for English Learners, which could be incorporated into your specific rubric. Think about which supports and scaffolds could be incorporated into the rubric. The adjustments in language expectations that you make will render the assignment or assessment "doable" for students who have not yet reached full English proficiency. Rather than "watering down," this linguistic differentiation based on student data recognizes that English Learners can engage in content to the extent of their current language development levels while simultaneously learning English while teachers refine instruction pushing them ever higher.

FIGURE 2.9 Sample Rubric Template for Teacher Use

SCORE IN POINTS	PURPOSE	USE OF VISUAL SUPPORT	USE OF ORAL PRESENTATION SKILLS	OVERALL FEEDBACK BASED ON RUBRIC EXPECTATIONS
5				
4				
3				
2				
1				

FIGURE 2.10 Question C: Overview

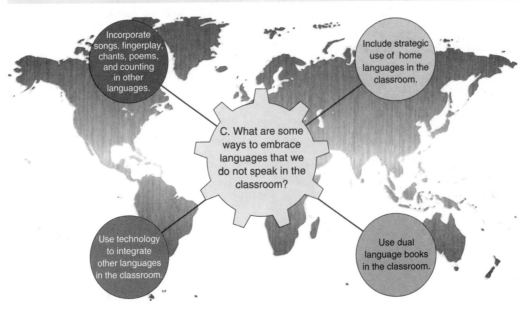

C. WHAT ARE SOME WAYS TO EMBRACE LANGUAGES THAT WE DO NOT SPEAK IN THE CLASSROOM?

- Powerful Practice 1: Include strategic use of students' home languages in the classroom.

- Powerful Practice 2: Use dual language books in the classroom.

- Powerful Practice 3: Use technology that supports the integration of other languages in the classroom.

- Powerful Practice 4: Incorporate songs, fingerplay, chants, poems, and counting in other languages.

Powerful Practice 1: Include strategic use of students' home languages in the classroom.

What It Might Look Like

The languages of students can be used authentically in the classroom for both social and academic purposes, providing opportunities for the teacher to engage in translanguaging pedagogy. Socially, when educators learn even one word in a different language, they send a very powerful message to students (Asgedom & Even, 2017; Cummins, 1996). It demonstrates that students' languages are important, models openness to learning, shows how to take risks, and provides the opportunity for English Learners to be experts in the classroom. There are many easy ways to use words in other languages throughout the day for real-life interactional purposes.

- Threshold greetings, those done at the doorway entrance to the class, provide a meaningful way to connect with students (Asgedom & Even, 2017; Linton Howard, 2017). Greeting your students with "Good morning," (English), "Guten Morgen" (German), "Bom Dia" (Portuguese), or "Dobro jutro" (Croatian) can help them feel safe, connected, and valued, making it easier to engage in the learning

(Continued)

(Continued)

process (Ward Singer, 2018). Greeting students in a different language is not a new idea (e.g., Chumak-Horbatsch, 2012; Kottler, Kottler, & Street, 2008; Linton Howard, 2017; Sánchez-López & Young, 2018), but it remains an excellent one. There are many commercial and personal books, posters, and wall displays that provide greetings in multiple languages.

- Another idea is to use home languages when praising students. Instead of repeating "Well done" and "Good," you could offer "bien," (French), "buono" (Italian), or "zoo" (Hmong). Create a word web of praise with the help of your class, online translation sources and/or other native speakers of different languages. Be sure to verify online translations for accuracy and appropriateness with a native speaker.

- Encourage students to teach you words in other languages. Identify a word of the day that could be used authentically and practically in the classroom. It might be a word from an upcoming lesson or an item in the classroom. Have a native speaker write the word in their language and then provide a transliteration (how you would say it) as a guide to pronunciation (Figure 2.11). Put the word on the board each day for easy reference. Attempt to use the word functionally several times during the day or, better yet, on a subsequent day. Dual language dictionaries, such as the *Oxford Picture Dictionary* (Adelson-Goldstein & Shapiro, 2016) and the *Dorling Kindersley (DK) Bilingual Visual Dictionary Series* (Penguin Random House, 2020) can be used as resource material.

The use of the home language is a powerful cognitive support for learning English in an academic setting. A robust body of research confirms that when their home languages are used as a tool to help students transfer knowledge and understanding into English, students will learn English more effectively and achieve greater success in school (Goldenberg, 2008; Cummins and Early, 2015). Many strategies can support English Learners in using their home language to bridge their understanding and build their English proficiency while at the same time sending a clear message that all languages are recognized and valued in the classroom. The teacher need not be a speaker of the student's home language to employ any of the following classroom translanguaging strategies.

- Pair newly arrived students with a classroom buddy who speaks the same home language. The buddy serves as a valuable resource for the new student in grasping classroom talk and concepts in the early period of English language learning.

- Let beginning students know that they are welcome to compose dialogue journal entries in their home language as they slowly transition to writing in English. You could also work with bilingual students, parents, and staff to compile a stock of multilingual journal prompts. As writing proficiency in English grows, students should still feel comfortable to insert words in the home language that they don't yet know in English. Dialogue journal prompts and exchanges with the teacher will often point the way to the English words that the student needs.

- Give students, individually or in small groups, the opportunity to brainstorm concepts about a topic in their home language before beginning a classroom lesson on the topic. Provide a similar opportunity for home language preview by supplying background reading on a topic in home languages before starting that topic with the whole class.

- Turn on the closed captioning feature in other languages when showing a video.

- Allow students to write an outline or rough draft of a piece of writing in their home language before tackling the composition in English.

- Invite learners to write captions for images and artwork in English as well as their home language.

- Provide links to multilingual subject glossaries, such as those available at https://research.steinhardt.nyu.edu/metrocenter/resources/glossaries (The Metropolitan Center for Research on Equity and the Transformation of Schools. NYU/Steinhardt, 2020). These academic language glossaries cover multiple topics in mathematics, science, and social studies and are available in over forty different languages from Albanian to Wolof.

- Point out and discuss cognates between English and your students' home languages. Keep cognate charts visible in the classroom for reference.

- Search out and display popular chapter books and novels that are available in multiple language editions for the classroom/school library. Current and popular titles for children and adolescents are sometimes available in a number of different languages and at various levels of accessibility. Students can choose in which language they want to read during independent reading time.

- Broaden word webs that help students learn more academic vocabulary to include multilingual verbs related to physical education activities or adjectives that describe the taste of a special snack.

- Affix labels to classroom areas, furniture, and supplies in languages of your classroom community. Students, their families, and online searches can all be used as resources in finding words.

FIGURE 2.11 Chart With Transliterations

ENGLISH	HOME LANGUAGE	SOUNDS LIKE . . .
Santa	Mikulás (Hungarian)	Mekolash
move	Intaqqil انتقل (Arabic)	nahkolat
rice	riza (Slovak)	reeja
branch	עֲנָף (Hebrew)	anaf

Making It Your Own

How can you keep track of all the multilingual words used throughout the school year? Would a class-made multilingual dictionary be better suited to documenting all the new words learned by your students and yourself? What could a multilingual word wall look like in your classroom? Which translanguaging strategy might you try with a content class in science or mathematics?

Powerful Practice 2: Use dual language books in the classroom.

What It Might Look Like

Dual language books, those written in English and a different language (and sometimes more than one additional language) are particularly interesting and useful. Incorporating a translanguaging perspective by using dual language books has an impact on all learners in general, as well as specific benefits for those who understand that particular language. Words in print carry a certain amount of power and prestige. Therefore seeing different languages in the pages of a book can help elevate the status of languages. Furthermore, experience with a variety of print expands everyone's world knowledge. For example, learning that not all alphabets are the same and that some print can be written from left to right (e.g., English, French, Spanish), right to left (e.g., Arabic, Hebrew, Urdu), or optionally from top to bottom (e.g., Chinese, Japanese, Korean) are all eye-opening revelations.

Using dual language books is an easy and powerful way to reflect diversity, even if you do not speak the language. The most basic format, reading the English portion and discussing the other language on the page, shows great appreciation and respect. Be sure to name the other language and talk about the font so that everyone gets a chance to learn something new. There may even be an expert in your class who could provide some assistance to your efforts. *The Pet Dragon: A Story About Adventure, Friendship, and Chinese Characters* by Niemann (2008) provides an ideal way to talk about Chinese characters, which are creatively embedded into the pictures in the book.

Celebrate your own multilingual skills and impress your students by reading both languages of the book yourself. Or partner with an invited guest reader (live or electronically) and take turns reading the story in both languages, either page by page or sequentially. You could also invite multiple guest readers and have the story read in different languages simultaneously around the room (or school!) or host multilingual story time over lunch, when students can listen to tales in the home language while they munch. Technology can lend a voice and help you read a story in more than one language. There are many websites that provide culturally relevant stories in English and/or other languages. Some of these websites are animated, narrated, student created, or are read aloud by a celebrity. These websites are worth exploring, as they provide access to stories for both teachers and families.

FIGURE 2.12 Multicultural, Multilingual Story Websites

African Storybook, (2015–2019). https://africanstorybook.org/

Bloom: Let's Grow a Library—Book Library. (2020). https://bloomlibrary.org/browse

Books for Friends (BFF) Gallery. https://sites.google.com/tdsb.on.ca/bffgallery/home

Dolly Parton's Imagination Library. *Good Night With Dolly*. https://imaginationlibrary.com/

Global Storybooks Portal. https://globalstorybooks.net/

International Children's Digital Library. http://en.childrenslibrary.org/

Open Culture. (2006–2020). www.openculture.com/freeaudiobooks

Somali Book Project. https://mnhum.org/stories-and-culture/somali-bilingual-book-project/

Storybooks Canada. www.storybookscanada.ca

Storyline Online. www.storylineonline.net/library/

Tar Heel Reader. https://tarheelreader.org

Unite for Literacy. (2014). www.uniteforliteracy.com

Write our World. (2016–2020). https://writeourworld.org

Worlds of Words. (2006–2020). https://wowlit.org/

Worldstories. https://www.worldstories.org.uk

Electronic resources also make excellent additions to listening stations, where students can use headphones to listen to stories in the home language. Students who recognize their home language in classroom books will be particularly thrilled, even if they have yet to develop the literacy skills needed to read the book themselves. The fact that the teacher has selected a book featuring their language instills pride, confidence, and can encourage students to maintain and continue to develop their home language.

Making It Your Own

Brainstorm different ways to use dual language books and write down all ideas, without judgement or censorship. An idea that seems far fetched today might need just a little tweaking to be useful next month or even next year. Decide on a reasonable action that is within your comfort zone, something that will meet the needs of your students and still be manageable. Who might you need or want to include? There may be some valuable multilingual speakers right in your building. The principal, lunch supervisor, student teacher, or even older students might be willing to show off their literacy skills in the home language. Once you start taking achievable steps, you will quickly find that what you originally thought was beyond your reach is far more obtainable.

Powerful Practice 3: Use technology that supports the incorporation of other languages in the classroom.

What It Might Look Like

There are numerous technology tools available for the classroom today that allow educators to nurture a translanguaging classroom stance and incorporate the use of other languages into daily classroom activities, as well as in learning academic subjects.

One engaging example described by Dagenais, Toohey, Bennett Fox, and Singh (2017) is the application called Scribjab (www.scribjab.com), developed at Simon Fraser University in British Columbia, with the support of the Canadian government. Scribjab is an app that can be downloaded onto a mobile device by teachers, parents, and students. Using the app, students can create their own bilingual stories in English and another language. The app has a drawing function that supports students in adding their own colorful artwork to the stories they write. Students are also able to include audio readings of their stories in their Scribjab literary creations. Teachers may choose to upload students' work to the site, which can then be read by other Scribjab users around the world.

Binogi Canada (www.binogi.ca) offers another rich online resource for supporting middle and high school students in learning mathematics and science concepts through content in their home languages. Binogi Canada currently provides free online animated lessons in nine different languages. Students view animated videos in English on topics such as multiplication of decimals, food chains and food webs, or the periodic table of elements, along with subtitles in the language of their choice. Alternatively, they can view the animated video in their home language first and then in English. These multi-language viewing processes allow students to first access the science and math ideas in their home language for initial conceptual understanding, leading the way to greater understanding of the subject material in English. Each lesson is accompanied by a full written transcript of the animated film, as well as several quizzes on the material in the lesson.

Khan Academy (2020) (www.khanacademy.org) is another educational resource for subject learning that is available in a variety of languages. This nonprofit organization based in Mountain View, California, provides an encyclopedic range of video lessons in all areas of the curriculum and at all grade levels. Students can view lessons in English or choose from twelve other available languages. Subtitles are also available for many of the English lessons on the Khan Academy platform.

A dynamic educational technology tool that can be used in real time with an entire class of learners is Mentimeter (www.mentimeter.com). This digital tool allows teachers to create interactive presentations to involve learners in class activities such as polls, quizzes, and surveys. Using their smartphones, students can contribute to a class-generated word cloud by providing words in their home languages, simply by typing on their home language keyboards installed on their phones. Mentimeter is a wonderful aid for engaging students in comparative vocabulary study, as they contribute and discuss words and expressions in a variety of languages.

Vocaroo (2007–2020, https://vocaroo.com/) is a web-based tool for creating audio recordings that will also generate a matching QR code for the recording. Using this app allows students, teachers, parents, and volunteers to record their voices on recordable QR codes that can be mounted in books. The app can play back and/or record customised audio in any language. Another app with a similar capability is Cloud QR Generator. Findings from a dual-language reading study with preschool children using a similar QR-capable technology indicated that children experienced enhanced opportunities to practice social, cognitive, and multilingual literacy skills through the use of this type of engaging technology (McGlynn-Stewart, Murphy, Pinto, Mogyorodi, & Nguyen, 2019).

Google offers a powerful collection of tools to support English language learners and provide translations in a myriad of other languages. Extending beyond the familiar Google Translate feature to translate words, phrases, and sentences into other languages, Google Docs contains a built-in tool that can translate an entire document into another language. The site https://translate.google.com provides additional tools and translation options, including the ability to translate typed or pasted texts, spoken words, uploaded files, and even entire URL websites. Google expert Eric Curts (2018) provides a handy tutorial, *Google Tools for English Language Learners* on the website Control Alt Achieve (https://www.controlaltachieve.com/2018/08/google-ell.html).

Finally, middle and secondary school students who are learning about the world's climate crisis and how they might make their daily effects on the planet more sustainable can calculate their own carbon footprints in English and thirteen other languages, including Chinese, French, Russian, and Spanish at Carbon Footprint (www.carbonfootprint.com/calculator.aspx). This online carbon footprint calculator takes the reader through a series of questions about their use and habits in driving, flying, and heating their homes as well as other activities that contribute to greenhouse gas emissions.

Making It Your Own

The technology tools mentioned are just a few examples of the many online resources available for supporting English Learners and incorporating multiple languages in the classroom. Plan a brainstorming session with colleagues to pool your collective knowledge and experience with technology applications and online tools that facilitate the integration of other languages in the classroom or that in other ways support English Learners.

Powerful Practice 4: Incorporate songs, fingerplay, chants, poems, counting, and math concepts in other languages.

What It Might Look Like

Teachers of young students routinely incorporate songs with accompanying actions in the classroom. Children delight in moving their fingers to imitate the crawling of an itsy bitsy spider, the ears of a hopping bunny, or rounding their arms above their heads to represent the sun rising above the earth. It is easy enough to sing a song in another language—just think about how many times the

French tunes "Frére Jacques" or "Alouette" have been sung in an English classroom! A quick jaunt into www.YouTube.com reveals a plethora of songs in a multitude of languages that could easily be incorporated into a classroom. For example, Ella Jenkins, American singer and actor, is well known for her multilingual children's songs (Jenkins, 2020, https://www.youtube.com/playlist?list=OLAK5uy_mEuG2Qc5fT5ealCppg2W09z731RlA4mN0).

Older students might appreciate more complex songs or those that are commercially familiar as well as chants, raps, and poems in the home language. The YouTube video *Frozen Song—Let it Go, Sang [sic] in 25 Languages* (Anderson-Lopez & Lopez, 2013a, www.youtube.com/watch?v=v7G-B4l881Es) provides an impressive and diverse rendition of the Disney song, with lines sung in twenty-five different languages by singers from around the world, all labeled for easy identification. Students paying close attention might recognize that multilingual singers are featured more than once because of their linguistic talents. Equally impressive is the version by Travys Kim (Anderson-Lopez & Lopez, 2013b), a man who sings the same song in twenty-five languages, all on his own (www.youtube.com/watch?v=X_dcTc3CPxU&list=RDX_dcTc3CPxU&start_radio=1&t=210).

Young children engage in oral counting for many reasons, to find out how many students are present, the number of sunny or rainy days in a month, how many ducklings are on a story book page, and the number of snacks needed to share with friends. While learning to count to 100 and skip counting are common activities in the early grades, it might not be realistic to learn to do so in multiple languages. Counting to ten in different languages may provide an easier way to incorporate home languages. Numbers and counting material in other languages can be easily found on YouTube, with many clips lasting only one minute in length. Multilingual counting books and posters are also commercially available. For example, Far Eastern Books (fareasternbooks.com/search.php?search_query=numbers&x=0&y=0, 1975–2008) offers number posters in Arabic, English, Gujarati, Panjabi, and Urdu. Chumak-Horbatsch (2012) describes a lovely dual language activity called "My Numbers" booklet. Young children are given a booklet of ten pages, in which they draw and number familiar items—one on the first page, two on the second, and so on (p. 121). This activity allows students' counting skills to be highlighted in one or more languages. As such, all students, regardless of English language proficiency, can participate in the classroom activity (with relatively little linguistic stress on the teacher).

Older students might benefit more from learning key math terms in the home language (e.g., *addition, subtraction, sum*) and relevant math concepts (e.g., radius, diameter, area). A poster with translation of key math terms in multiple languages might prove to be especially helpful.

Making It Your Own

Gathering a list of songs, poems, and math terms in multiple languages may require some investment of time, but a repertoire of high quality materials can be used over and over again. In addition, partnering with another educator can cut the work in half. Decide on the languages you might need and then the material that matches a theme or class lesson. Working with meaningful themes is an effective teaching tool (Kottler et al., 2008), allowing students to build on prior knowledge and providing authentic opportunities to hear and use key vocabulary numerous times to promote depth of understanding. By using thematically relevant material in different languages, students can learn key vocabulary in the home language, which will facilitate learning the words in English. In addition, songs, chants, and poems that include rhymes have the added benefit of effortlessly focusing on phonological awareness, a key skill in learning to read. Let the search begin! Look for videos, posters, and books. What materials are already available in your class, school library, or community library? What material might you need to supplement your growing library? What materials would be easy for you, parents, or students to cocreate?

FIGURE 2.13 Question D: Overview

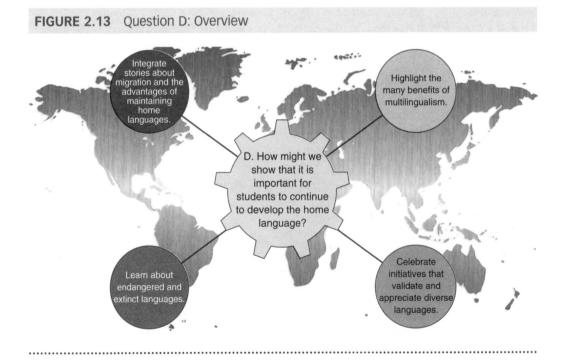

Integrate stories about migration and the advantages of maintaining home languages.

Highlight the many benefits of multilingualism.

D. How might we show that it is important for students to continue to develop the home language?

Learn about endangered and extinct languages.

Celebrate initiatives that validate and appreciate diverse languages.

D. HOW MIGHT WE SHOW THAT IT IS IMPORTANT FOR STUDENTS TO CONTINUE TO DEVELOP THE HOME LANGUAGE?

- Powerful Practice 1: Highlight the many benefits of multilingualism.

- Powerful Practice 2: Celebrate initiatives that demonstrate validation and appreciation of diverse languages.

- Powerful Practice 3: Learn about endangered languages and what happens when they become extinct.

- Powerful Practice 4: Integrate stories about migration and the advantages of maintaining home languages.

Powerful Practice 1: Highlight the many benefits of multilingualism.

What It Might Look Like

Everyone agrees that it is great to know more than one language, but Ms. Mohammed was unsure of actual research benefits. She had recently seen a television commercial depicting an engaging and playful example of adult multilingualism in action (Global Beer Fridge Extended—Molson Canadian, 2015, www.youtube.com/watch?v=CfpatqyujM0) but wanted to know more. The benefits of multilingualism must extend beyond merely being able to talk to more people. Ms. Mohammed reasoned that if she were familiar with the many advantages of multilingualism, she might be able to use them in discussions with parents, who sometimes focused exclusively on English language development as the sole measure of their child's success.

Based on her research readings, she knew that those who spoke more than one language experienced cognitive benefits including the potential to delay the onset of age-related dementia for up to four years (Bialystok, Craik, & Freedman, 2007), a significant and desirable outcome. In addition, she recognized that those who spoke more than one language would have a significant advantage over monolinguals when seeking employment. Inspired by a recent tweet from John McCrae Public School in the TDSB (2019) (twitter.com/John_McCraePS/status/1184449679662206976), she decided to engage her students in exploring the benefits of knowing more than one language. Their research and related artwork could inspire others in the classroom and school. Armed with their new knowledge, her students might become ambassadors for multilingualism at home and in the community.

Making It Your Own

Working with your class, decide on a visual representation for this research project (e.g., map of the world, illustration of the brain, use of speech bubbles, etc.). Allow students to work in small groups to research potential benefits of speaking more than one language. Can the benefits be grouped together in categories (e.g., cognitive, familial, educational)? How will these benefits be added to the visual model being used for this group presentation? How will students be able to share their contributions?

Powerful Practice 2: Celebrate initiatives that demonstrate validation and appreciation of diverse languages.

What It Might Look Like

If students are to continue to develop their home language, their communities (social, educational, personal, local, global) all need to show that the language is valuable and relevant. As validation, the importance of home languages has been recognized worldwide by the United Nations, which celebrates International Mother Language Day on February 21. Join in the celebrations by visiting the website for more information and ideas (https://www.un.org/en/observances/mother-language-day).

Mr. Egorov, a middle school teacher, was perusing the International Mother Language Day website, when an activity caught his attention. There was a call to submit favorite proverbs on select topics in various languages. The use of proverbs and idioms often presents some confusion for English Learners (Kottler et al., 2008; Sousa, 2011). Although the deadline for submission of entries was long passed, Mr. Egorov thought that this would make for a wonderful class project examining literal versus figurative uses of language across cultures. He would incorporate language arts and media into the project by asking students to illustrate the literal interpretation and provide a written explanation of the figurative meaning in a "billboard" that could be displayed in the school. He even thought about adding a role-play activity to highlight the use of the proverbs. He anticipated seeing a picture of a cat escaping from a sack, alongside a description of "telling a secret" to depict the English proverb "letting the cat out of the bag." His middle school students would have great fun with the activities. Mr. Egorov was hoping that by displaying the billboards, other teachers would be encouraged to participate in similar activities to celebrate International Mother Language Day the following year.

Making It Your Own

Create two 1-hour lesson plans. The first plan will teach the concept of literal versus figurative language through the use of proverbs. Use large group instruction and small group discussions, as well as think-pair-share or partner work, to help students deepen their understanding. The second plan will allow students to create their own billboards depicting proverbs in various languages. How will you showcase the work of your students? How can you extend the activity to a third lesson plan to allow students to role-play use of the proverbs (perhaps both literally and figuratively)?

FIGURE 2.14 Proverb Lesson Plan

Lesson Plan: Proverbs

Learning Objectives:

(1) To define the concepts of *literal* and *figurative* language

(2) To define the term *proverb*

(3) To use art/media and writing to demonstrate this knowledge (English or home language) by creating billboards

Length of Time: <u>2 one-hour classes</u>

Key Vocabulary: <u>literal, figurative, proverb</u>

Lesson 1: <u>Understanding the concept of "proverb"</u>

(Continued)

FIGURE 2.14 (Continued)

Material (e.g., books on proverbs, English examples):

_____

_____

Large Group Instructions (e.g., how to access background knowledge on proverbs):

_____

_____

Think-Pair-Share Discussion (e.g., topic, questions):

_____

_____

Small Group Activity:

_____

_____

Lesson 2: Using art, media, and writing to create billboards to demonstrate understanding and use of proverbs

Materials:

_____

_____

Large Group Instructions:

_____

_____

Written Language Expectations (English and/or home language):

_____

_____

Oral Language Expectations (English and/or home language):

_____

_____

Model and Instruction Modifications (e.g., sample billboard, sentence starters, model presentation):

_____

_____

Individual Work:

_____

_____

Group Share: Presentation and Discussion of Billboards:

_____

_____

Lesson 3: Extension: Drama activity

Materials:

_____

_____

Large Group Instructions:

_____

_____

Small Group Activity:

_____

_____

Group Share: Presentation:

_____

_____

Powerful Practice 3: Learn about endangered languages and what happens when they become extinct.

Another fact from the International Mother Language Day website caught Mr. Egorov's attention. He was astounded to read that a language disappears every two weeks, along with its cultural and intellectual heritage. He was surprised at this rapid rate of extinction and wondered which languages had already been affected, which were now in jeopardy, and which still had a chance of survival. He reasoned that this would be a great topic to study in a lesson on social justice, with students doing research in a small group reciprocal teaching format. Mr. Egorov was familiar with the four roles for individual group members:

1. The summarizer—identifies three key ideas about a topic

2. The questioner—identifies three key questions based on the material

3. The connector—makes text-to-text, text-to-world, and text-to-life connections about the material

4. The predictor—forecasts what might occur next (Kottler et al., 2008; Soto, 2012)

Mr. Egorov set about gathering a range of reading materials and multimedia resources on why languages are endangered/become extinct, examples of endangered/extinct languages, the consequences of extinct languages, and what could be done to preserve languages. He was particularly excited by stories that made the news headlines regarding efforts to preserve languages, such as the Welsh language, as well as the international interest of an Inuit delegation to learn from their successes in order to preserve Inuit languages in Canada (Semple, 2016). In small groups, Mr. Egorov's students assumed one of the four roles and collectively gathered information and insights from their inquiry. Their findings were later shared in a whole class seminar.

Mr. Egorov's colleagues from the community high school English department could approach the topic of language loss and extinction through the vehicle of Linda Christensen's "Language and Power Tea Party," an empathy-heightening role-play designed for secondary school students (Christensen, 2009). In this engaging role-play, students adopt the personae of historical figures hailing from various nations and language backgrounds who have suffered the indignities of language suppression and loss due to colonization and prejudice. Christensen provides role cards for eighteen different individuals. Teachers can create additional historical scenarios based on their own community demographics. For example, we have created roles to reflect the experiences of Canadian indigenous peoples, those of Basque heritage, the precipitous decline in Yiddish speakers worldwide, and Japanese Americans and Canadians interned during the Second World War.

Making It Your Own

Provide students with information on endangered/extinct languages in a large group lesson. Key topics include (1) defining what is an endangered language and what is an extinct language, (2) providing examples of each, (3) explaining why languages become endangered/extinct, and (4) highlighting preservation efforts. This information could be further supplemented by individual or group research. Soto's (2012) *Reciprocal Teaching Organizer* (p. 129–133) provides an excellent vehicle for students to participate in a small group format to deepen their understanding and leadership regarding this topic. What instructional modifications will best help students use this model of investigation? Or perhaps you might want to host your own version of Christensen's "Language and Power Tea Party."

Powerful Practice 4: Integrate stories about migration and the advantages of maintaining home languages.

What It Might Look Like

Mr. Vellikanthan, a Grade 1 teacher, uses read-alouds for early primary children to engage his young multilingual students in thinking about the advantages of using and developing their home languages side by side with English. *Mango, Abuela and Me* (Medina, 2017) tells the story of how Mia and her grandmother help each other to learn English and Spanish and together find that communication across the generations comes in many forms. *Grandfather Counts* (Cheng, 2000) is another evocative children's story that provides a springboard to considering how knowing more than one language can benefit children and their families. *The Name Jar* (Choi, 2001) serves as a catalyst for young children to think about how names in other languages are part of one's unique identity.

While Mr. Vellikanthan's early primary class is discussing the benefits of knowing more than one language, down the hall in Ms. Carol's middle school class, the students are engaged in a classroom literature study of the Young Reader's edition of *The Distance Between Us* (Grande, 2016). In this compelling memoir, Reyna Grande recounts the story of her family's migration from Mexico to the United States and shares her experiences of becoming a successful bilingual and bicultural author, while balancing her allegiance to both Spanish and English. Parent groups in some U.S. schools have also used the Spanish edition of Grande's account, *La Distancia Entre Nosotros* (Grande, 2013a), as a reading group selection to facilitate dialogue and problem-solving about the challenges children face in a new country, culture, and school environment.

Meanwhile, in the nearby local high school, English teacher Mr. Ruiz has included the powerful novel *Girl in Translation* (Kwok, 2010) and *The Namesake* (Lahiri, 2003), as well as *We Have Always Been Here* (Habib, 2019) and the adult reader's edition of *The Distance Between Us* (Grande, 2013b), as four of the selections from which his eleventh-grade students may choose for their memoir study project. Mr. Ruiz aims to incorporate critical discussion on the theme of being pulled by two languages and cultures as one aspect of the memoir study unit.

Making It Your Own

Begin by selecting an appropriate story to be read aloud or for independent reading. Is the story available in other languages? Perhaps you have selected a story such as *My Name Is Sangoel* by Williams and Khadra (2009), a tale about a Sudanese boy whose Dinka name is difficult for some people to pronounce, or *Zakery's Bridge: Children's Journeys From Around the World to Iowa* by Fenton Smith and Spaulding (2011), which recounts the stories of twelve immigrant children now living in central Iowa. What themes are identified? Have you selected books and stories that both mirror and extend the cultures represented in your classroom and school? How could you further broaden the themes to a group or class discussion activity, a writing task or age-appropriate research inquiry task?

POWERFUL PRACTICES FOR SUPPORTING ENGLISH LEARNERS

NEXT STEP

Chapter 2 has been filled with creative and practical Powerful Practices, including those reflecting a translanguaging perspective. To integrate the information into your own context, please turn to page 255 of this guide. Begin to label the "Classroom" gear with ideas, strategies, and suggestions that have resonated with you. Once this gear is completed, you are ready to begin Chapter 3, exploring aspects specific to families of English Learners.

FIGURE 3.1 Family: Overview

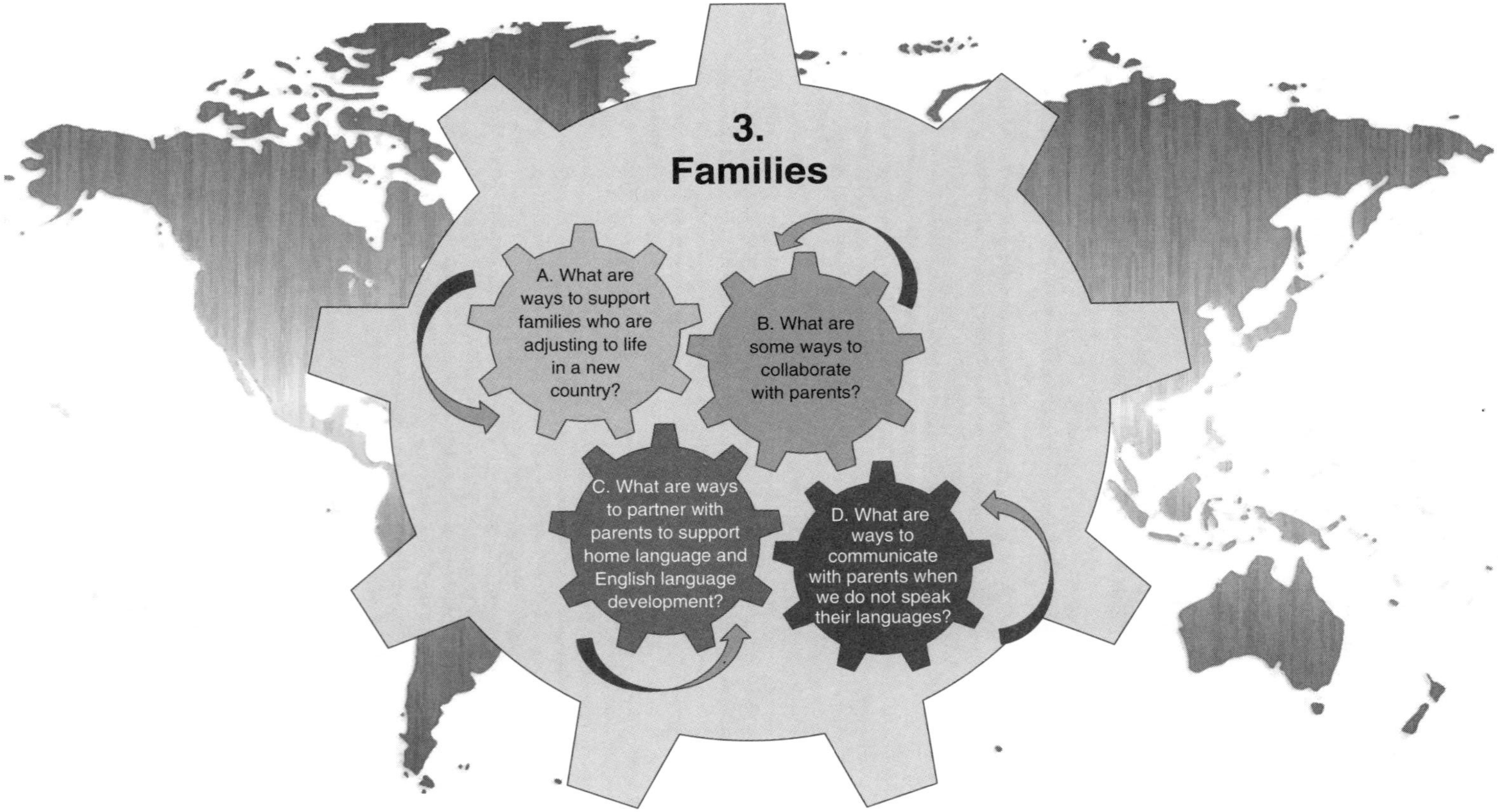

3.
Families

A. What are ways to support families who are adjusting to life in a new country?

B. What are some ways to collaborate with parents?

C. What are ways to partner with parents to support home language and English language development?

D. What are ways to communicate with parents when we do not speak their languages?

CHAPTER 3

Families

WHAT WE KNOW

The importance of parents in the education of their children is undeniable. Students do best when their parents are involved in their education, regardless of the home language or whether or not the family speaks the language of the school (Cummins, 1996; Hamayan et al., 2007; Staehr Fenner, 2014). Government initiatives in both the United States and Canada have formally recognized the impact of parental involvement in education.

In the United States, parent involvement was first named and required in the 1965 passage of the Elementary and Secondary Education Act (ESEA). Reauthorized in 2002 and renamed the Every Student Succeeds Act (ESSA), this federal law also introduced the term "parent and family engagement" while setting requirements and funding for school districts. As a result, parental resources have been developed and are readily available online. The United States Department of Health and Human Services and the U.S. Department of Education (2016a) have jointly issued a policy statement on family engagement from the early years to the early elementary grades. The Head Start Early Childhood Learning and Knowledge Center (ECLKC) website offers a range of guidance focused on diverse and multicultural families and parents of dual language learners, with valuable resources for addressing involvement and engagement of diverse families. By incorporating multilingual and multicultural considerations into all aspects of programming, such as staffing, classroom considerations, and professional strategies, the documents serve as a cornerstone for planning fully inclusive of diverse families.

The importance of parental engagement is also well recognized in Canada (e.g., Government of Canada, 2017; Ontario Ministry of Education, 2010, 2016b). Provinces have invested in the involvement of families from diverse backgrounds. For example, the Ontario Ministry of Education (2019) provides translated versions of important information for parents on their website in a section entitled *Parents: Important information in many languages*. Manitoba Education, Citizenship and Youth (2006) provides an online, culturally informed resource book entitled *Helping Your Child*

Succeed at School: A Guide for Parents and Families of Aboriginal Students, describing parental involvement across the school years.

There are many reasons why any parent might seem less involved in school life, including poverty, transportation barriers, work or family obligations, linguistic barriers, and medical constraints. Some families might not be very involved in schools because they are familiar with education systems that consider the teacher as the "expert" who manages all school-related activities and decisions. As such, they might be unaware that North American educators expect to partner with families to support students. There also exist some myths surrounding second language learning that can dissuade parents from participation in educational matters.

A common myth held by some parents might be the belief that their lack of facility in English limits their ability to help their children academically. However, those who ensure that their children attend school regularly and on time, are well nourished, well rested, appropriately clothed for the weather conditions, with completed homework and administrative forms, are doing wonders to prepare their children for a day of learning. The benefits of these efforts cannot be understated. Showing an interest in school-work and school life has a considerable impact on academic outcomes and can be achieved in any language and at any age. In the words of Mawi Asgedom, who commends his parents for helping him succeed from a refugee camp to Harvard, "No one succeeds on their own" (Asgedom & Even, 2017, p. 70).

Some students are pressed to learn English at the expense of their home language, resulting in language attrition or language loss. In Wong Fillmore's seminal work (1991), she concluded that when parents and children do not have a shared proficient language for communication, parents' ability to socialize their children, to impart shared values, beliefs, and notions of responsibility, may be weakened, impacting families in negative ways. Demonstrating respect for and appreciation of all languages can go a long way to encourage continued development and use of home languages, thereby helping to maintain the bonds between family members.

Just as each English Learner arrives at school at a specific point in learning the language, so does each family arrive at their own stage in their unfolding story of adjustment to a new country and its school system. As educators, awareness of the needs of different families, depending on where they are in this process of orientation and acculturation to their new country and education context, can prove helpful. Han and Love (2015) propose a useful model of four stages of immigrant parent involvement: cultural survivors, cultural learners, cultural connectors, and cultural leaders. Recognizing and understanding these stages can better equip teachers and schools to respond appropriately to the needs of various newcomer families. While parents at the cultural survivor stage may not yet possess either the English language proficiency or the cultural comprehension to comfortably participate in curriculum night, they may begin to develop their connection to the school through special orientation events offered with interpretation in their home language. At the other end of the immigrant parent involvement continuum, parents at the cultural connector and leader stages may gain a sense of empowerment and a voice for their community through participation in local school councils. Han and Love (2015) caution that "it is imperative to understand that a one-size-fits-all outreach model or program does not meet the needs of all immigrant parents" (p. 25).

Research strongly supports the development of home oral language skills as foundational to the development of literacy skills, as well as other languages (Ijalba, 2015). Sousa (2011) explains that proficiency in the home language impacts brain development by building robust language networks and mental lexicon. Children with weak abilities understanding and/or using spoken language (English or otherwise) often experience challenges learning to read and write (Paradis, Genesee, & Crago, 2011; Sánchez-López & Young, 2018). Speech-language pathologists routinely share their knowledge regarding the link between oral and written language. They advocate for, coach, and deliver a range of opportunities and strategies to help children develop strong oral language skills, for both preventative and remedial purposes.

While children need a sufficient amount of exposure to learn language, the quality of that language plays a significant role in language and literacy success. Children need rich language stimulation to develop depth and breadth of language. This includes complex language, shared reading, rhymes, and songs (Wong Fillmore, 2000). Another bonus for the English Learner is research that shows children who received considerable home language stimulation did better in English language acquisition (in Paradis et al., 2011).

In addition to providing the foundation for literacy and language development, the home language can be used to "bootstrap" English language development. Skills in the home language can be used to advance the skills in another (Paradis et al., 2011). Research shows that knowledge transfers between languages and that students who learn concepts and vocabulary in the home language learn the equivalent in English faster than those who do not (in Hamayan et al., 2007; Ijalba, 2015). Unfortunately, bilingual bootstrapping is an often overlooked and underused strategy to support linguistic and academic development of English Learners. Creating partnerships with families who can support home language development is therefore critical.

Educators are aware that families come in all sizes, configurations, and backgrounds. Today's families are more diverse than ever. There are split families due to divorce, as well as single-parent families by choice or due to a death. There are same-sex parents, foster families, blended families, interracial, interfaith, and intercultural families, legal guardians, and both local and international adoptive parents. Many families live in extended family contexts, with grandparents or others taking the lead in daily caregiving roles. Some students may be in the country unaccompanied or in the care of a stranger or distant relative. Working effectively with families requires that we understand particular family dynamics and identify key partners—for example, including grandparents who might be in an ideal position to support the home language simply due to the amount of time they provide childcare. Throughout this guide, we will use the terms "parents" and "family" interchangeably to represent all the loving biological, nonbiological, and extended nurturers who are raising students.

Cummins and Early (2011) describe societal powers in the classroom that contribute to relationships that either disable or empower students. The same could be said of relationships between educators and parents. How we interact with parents contributes to an interpersonal space where parents become empowered or uninvolved in their child's education. We want our families to be empowered. To do so, we need to collaborate and share power with parents. Part of changing the power relationship might be to dispel some of the myths around language learning. Parents might be unaware of how the first language can promote English language learning or even that educators support home language development. They may have been advised by well-meaning professionals to promote English at all costs, including forfeiting the home language.

Empowered parents have access to the necessary school information required to make informed educational decisions. Sometimes there is a mismatch between the expectations within education and the experiences of our parents. For example, while we expect children to come to school during the winter months when it is snowing, some parents may feel that young children should not be exposed to such extreme weather conditions. We cannot assume that our expectations have universal application, and so we may have to make our implicit understandings very explicit. For instance, we may need to advise parents that children should attend school even when it is snowing and where they might look for cancellations due to weather conditions. We may also need to help parents access information through the use of translation and interpretation.

In this chapter, we explore powerful practices involving the family, as we answer the following key questions:

A. What are some ways to support families who are adjusting to life in a new country?

B. What are some ways to collaborate with parents?

C. What are some ways to partner with parents to support both the home language and English language development?

D. What are some ways to communicate with parents when we do not speak their languages?

FIGURE 3.2 Question A: Overview

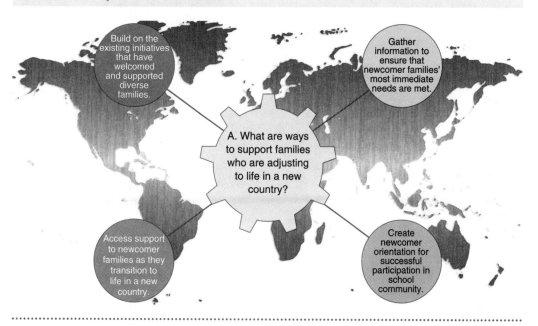

A. WHAT ARE SOME WAYS TO SUPPORT FAMILIES WHO ARE ADJUSTING TO LIFE IN A NEW COUNTRY?

- Powerful Practice 1: Gather information about newcomers and families to ensure that their most immediate basic needs are met.

- Powerful Practice 2: Create welcoming and supportive opportunities for newcomer parents, families, and students to experience orientation needed for successful participation in their new school community.

- Powerful Practice 3: Access the necessary support to newcomer families as they transition to life in a new country.

- Powerful Practice 4: Build on the existing initiatives of others who have welcomed and supported diverse children and families.

Powerful Practice 1: Gather information about newcomers and families to ensure that their most immediate basic needs are met.

What It Might Look Like

Newcomers arrive with varying degrees of readiness for life in a new country. Some arrive with useful shipments from home, while many others begin their new lives with very few belongings or possessions. Many families arrive without the basic necessities of life. A delegation of sponsors from one school came to this understanding through a heartbreaking realization. Twenty-three students, two ESOL teachers, an interpreter, and a handful of other volunteers traveled to the Des Moines International Airport to greet the family of refugees being sponsored through their school. The student sponsors, all of whom had been refugees themselves, included students from the elementary grades, as well as middle school and high school levels. There was great excitement as the new family descended the concourse escalator and approached the cheering welcome committee, waving their handmade welcome banners aloft. The interpreter stepped forward, expressing the collective "Welcome to Iowa" message to the parents. Meanwhile, the excited students escorted their new peers around the corner toward the baggage carousel. After waiting some time, the young sponsors seemed perplexed as the baggage carousel seemed to have no more luggage. Confusion and concern set in; someone suggested that maybe the luggage was lost! What should they do next? To whom should they report this unfortunate and inconvenient event?

With the help of the interpreter, the details emerged that the family, in fact, did not own any luggage. The newly arrived family traveled from thousands of miles away with only the clothes they were wearing as material possessions. What a stunning moment of learning for the young sponsors!

Making It Your Own

Each newcomer is deserving of consideration to ensure they have what is needed to feel safe and welcome. Supporting basic needs for physical and emotional well-being upon arrival will help students and families feel comfortable enough to engage in new learning and experience success.

Look through the English Learner (EL) lens (Fairbairn & Jones-Vo, 2016) using a role-playing perspective to anticipate newcomers' most pressing needs. The EL lens allows viewers to place themselves in the situation of another by applying cultural and other relevant information to determine a close interpretation of immediate needs. Ask yourself, "If I were in the same situation in a distant and unfamiliar environment, what would be top priorities needed for me to feel at home?" Consider Figure 3.3, Checklist for Supporting Basic Needs of Newcomers, in anticipation of the arrival of a family from Bhutan. The checklist has been partially completed based on known factors before the family arrived. With a proactive mind-set, think about what is most essential for this particular family, as well as what sponsors and educators can do to provide for immediate needs in their new community. Brainstorm additional ideas with a colleague and add them to complete Figure 3.3. When a real-life opportunity to support a family's resettlement necessities arises, anticipating predictable needs can help you and your team enact a comprehensive personalized response that communicates welcome, safety, and comfort, and sets families up for success at the outset.

FIGURE 3.3 Checklist for Supporting Basic Needs of Newcomers

WHO

Parents and two school age children from Bhutan, ages 6 and 8; Hindu religion; speak Nepali at home, have been exposed to English in the refugee camp in Nepal where they lived for six years. The father, Tulsi, earned a degree from India and has strong skills in English. The mother, Bima, has limited formal education and will benefit from interpreter support.

WHAT DO I KNOW? ➡	POSSIBLE IMMEDIATE NEEDS
Housing: two bedroom apartment (preferable)	• Address:
	• Expenses:
	• Landlord's name and contact information:
	• Beds, bedding, towels
	• Cookware and utensils
	• Furniture (sofa, table, chairs, coffee table, lamp, etc.)
Food	• Familiar foods (e.g., red or white rice, chicken, turmeric, tomatoes)
Communication	• Nepali interpreter's name and contact information:
	• Mobile phone number for family:
Transportation	• Housing close to public transportation
	• Training for family on using public transportation
	• School bus for children

(Continued)

FIGURE 3.3 (Continued)

WHAT DO I KNOW? ➡️	POSSIBLE IMMEDIATE NEEDS
Income	• Will receive government assistance for up to six months, then family then needs secure income
Community connections	• Where to buy preferred foods, where to worship, and so forth • Complete address and family mobile phone number written on cards for each family member
Sponsor	• Name and contact information:
Skills for employment	• Father is interested in work as a tutor in schools • Studied architecture
Health considerations	• Health concerns: • Dental clinics: • Health clinics: • Hospital: • Other
Education	• Name, address, and contact information for local school: • Name, address, and contact information for adult English classes:

Other potential areas of support

Powerful Practice 2: Create welcoming and supportive opportunities for newcomer parents, families, and students to experience orientation needed for successful participation in their new school community.

What It Might Look Like

There are many successful educational orientation opportunities for newcomers. For example, federally funded settlement organizations across the province of Ontario in Canada offer two valuable annual orientation events for newcomer students who are beginning school for the first time. Newcomer students starting school in the middle grades can attend a one-day event called Welcome and Information for Newcomers (WIN), together with their parents. Students who will be going to high school have the opportunity to attend a four-day intensive program at local high schools called NOW, Newcomer Orientation Week. A central tenet of the NOW program is the involvement of secondary school-aged peer leaders, former newcomer adolescents living in Canada for several years, who serve as role models on the adjustment to life in a new culture and school. During the four days of the program, which takes place before school begins in September, newcomer students participate in ice-breaker activities together with their peer leaders. They view *New Moves: An Orientation Video for Newcomer Students* (Ontario Council of Agencies Serving Immigrants, 2005), a video available in twelve languages, in which adolescent newcomers share their experiences starting school in Canada. Peer leaders then offer reflections of their own newcomer school experiences and facilitate a discussion on new students' expectations about beginning school in an unfamiliar country. Finally, the newcomer students brainstorm and share strategies for dealing with their feelings and concerns about their new venture. On succeeding days, the newcomer students participate in a scavenger hunt of locations in the school, using a specially prepared "passport" to be stamped at each location. Requirements might include the following: meet a variety of school administrators and staff members, participate in and create original skits about adjustment to new school life, visit the local library and/or community centre to learn about available programs and services, and move around the high school on a day's simulated timetable to increase their comfort level with the physical environment of the school and the pace of the school day.

Many schools have created a parent centre near the front office or in the school library/resource centre. In addition to information and parenting resources in English, an inclusive and welcoming parent corner can include newspapers, magazines, and resources and information in a variety of languages represented in the school community. The Ontario Ministry of Education (2019) publishes a range of brochures and documents in multiple languages, such as *Reading and Writing With Your Child K–6, A Parent's Guide; A Parent's Guide to Financial Literacy in Ontario Schools, Grades 4–12; Bullying: We Can All Help Stop It*; and *Parents Matter*, a strategy guide for parent involvement. The entire selection of available translated materials is available online (http://www.edu.gov.on.ca/eng/parents/multi Languages.html).

The work of the multilingual staff at Thorncliffe Park Public School in Toronto provides another example of how orientation efforts can help new-comers adjust to life in a new country. The diversity of the students and staff is well highlighted in the CBC News segment Welcome to Our World (2013) (https://youtu.be/BSA_7jQqNec). The staff at this elementary school has prepared a series of welcome booklets in a variety of languages to illustrate various locations in the school, along with the staff who work there. With a large number of newcomer students arriving each week, Thorncliffe Park

Public School has designed a weekly orientation and intake process to ease the transition for newly arrived students and their families. At the beginning of the week, new families are welcomed by the intake team, complete all necessary paperwork, and take a tour of the school with an introduction to school life in various languages. On succeeding days, the ESL teacher completes an initial assessment of the incoming students' English and mathematics skills, and when appropriate, has the children compose a writing sample in their home language. Children will be introduced to their classroom and teacher and spend some time acclimatizing to the new class environment. While their children are in the classroom, the parents will meet for a discussion group led by the school settlement worker. By the end of the orientation week, newcomer children will feel more comfortable to attend school full-time on the following Monday, and parents will feel more knowledgeable about the school routines and expectations.

Making It Your Own

Reflect on how your jurisdiction and school helps newcomer families and supports their diverse needs. Which of the following does your district or school offer? How could you begin to implement one or more of these strategies in your school or district?

- Orientation/intake program for newly arrived students

- Orientation and/or settlement services for newcomer families

- Translation and interpretation services

- Translated materials and resources in print and online

- School welcome/orientation materials

- Multilingual signage

- Multilingual parent centre

- Relationships with organizations supporting immigrants and refugees

- Culturally responsive and inclusive gatherings for parents

- School council with diverse representation from many communities, including newcomer parents

Powerful Practice 3: Access the necessary support to newcomer families as they transition to life in a new country.

Newcomer families face a range of challenges to navigate in order to successfully transition to a new country. Finding appropriate housing, initiating an employment search, accessing health care services, achieving economic stability, and learning a new language all compete for the time and energy of newcomer families in their journey of adjustment to a new country and culture. These transition needs are less immediate than the basic needs required for human survival. Transition needs tend to be more intricate, requiring planning and preparation, involving people and agencies, and often taking longer to satisfy. These needs tend to be interdependent and may change over time. For example, securing permanent housing may necessitate a switch in schools, or getting a full-time job may result in a housing change.

Accessing trained, multilingual professionals to assist in the transition process can make the adjustment period smoother. A number of Canadian provinces have implemented a valuable resource program for newcomer families who have children in the school system through funding received from the federal Ministry of Immigration, Refugees and Citizenship. In the province of Ontario, this program is called Settlement Workers in Schools. Approximately 200 settlement workers in Ontario schools, very often Canadians who were once new arrivals themselves, provide information, counseling, and referrals for newcomer parents in both elementary and high schools in more than twenty different school boards across the province. Proactive in identifying and connecting with newcomer students and parents so they can offer information, assistance, and support with all aspects of the newcomer adjustment process, settlement workers can provide resource material in a variety of languages as well as referrals to diverse community support organizations.

Settlement workers frequently organize group information and learning sessions and other programs for parents in schools, often in conjunction with school staff. They act as an important resource for educators about the diverse settlement needs of newcomer families and provide office hours in public libraries across the province so that any newcomer who visits the library can access the available information and referral services.

Settlement Workers in Schools utilize many useful publications to support newcomer families in gaining familiarity with the Ontario school system, such as The *Elementary School Guide for Newcomers to Ontario* (Centre Ontarien de Prévention des Agressions [COPA] [2018a] https://www.cin-ric .ca/PDFs/resources/Guide-Elementary-School.pdf) and the *Secondary School Guide for Newcomers to Ontario* (Centre Ontarien de Prévention des

Agressions [COPA] [2018b] https://www.cin-ric.ca/PDFs/resources/Guide-Secondary-School.pdf). These resources present information on how Ontario schools are organized, aspects of the curriculum, the rhythm of daily school life, how parents can become involved in their children's school community, a glossary of school-related vocabulary, and much more. The guides can be accessed online in English and French. Some sections of the guides have also been translated into multiple languages by various nonprofit community agencies. For example, a range of educational issues are shared through *Multilingual Tip Sheets for Parents* and are available in a variety of languages from People for Education (2020) (https://peopleforeducation.ca/topics/parent-involvement/). Settlement.org (2016) provides information for parents new to Canada on how to make sure their young children are warmly dressed for a cold, Canadian winter. Ontario school settlement workers have prepared an entertaining short video introducing all the elements for dressing for a winter day in a Canadian schoolyard (https://settlement.org/ontario/education/elementary-and-secondary-school/general-information/dressing-for-winter/). There is even a downloadable handout for learning the vocabulary of all the items in the winter clothing repertoire, like mittens and snowsuit.

Community efforts also go a long way to help newcomers transition to their new life. Staff at an Iowa elementary school united to support an influx of newcomer families who expressed an interest in learning English. After polling parents on their availability, teachers and supporters quickly set up a Family Literacy Program at their school in the evening. Elementary reading teachers were particularly well-positioned to teach the newcomers reading in English. Partnering with school leaders and the Parent Teacher Organization (PTO), the adult literacy classes provided childcare with literacy activities for children, refreshments, and transportation when needed. Field trips were organized to further support newcomer learning. The Family Literacy program culminated with parents and their children attending a children's production at the local community theater.

Making It Your Own

What are some of the transition needs of newcomer families in your community? Are parents in need of learning English and are there local opportunities available? What benefits might be realized from establishing a family language/literacy program at your school? What other ideas do you have to support families in learning English? Brainstorm a list of ideas that could be incorporated into such a program in your context. Build on the ideas below:

- Volunteers to teach reading

- Joint reading by parents and children (in the home language)

- Interpreters and/or translators

- Childcare staff (older students?) with literacy activities

- Support of organizations, such as a Parent Teacher Organization or Parent Council

- Transportation, as needed

- Field trips

- Authentic culminating activity for parents and children rooted in literacy

- Refreshments or a light meal for participants (consider donations by local grocery stores or restaurants)

Powerful Practice 4: Build on the existing initiatives of others who have welcomed and supported diverse children and families.

What It Might Look Like

Current federal policies and politics have at least temporarily curtailed not only the admission of refugees to the United States but also the funding that is needed to support resettlement efforts. The Pew Research Center (Radford & Connor, 2019) reports that the United States resettled millions more refugees than the rest of the world's countries combined until 2017. However, in 2018, Canada resettled more refugees than the United States, marking the first time the United States did not lead the world in this measure since 1980.

Decades of successful experience in welcoming and resettling refugees has contributed a wealth of practical and creative ideas. For example, a tradition of welcoming newcomers in Iowa, a Midwest agricultural state, was formalized following the Vietnam War in 1975 to assist and resettle Southeast Asian refugees who had experienced traumatic events and unfathomable losses. The governor of Iowa was responsible for establishing his state's response to the needs of refugees from around the world (Iowa Public Television, 1995–2020) in an endeavor that saw Iowa embrace the status of being the only state of fifty to dedicate a government agency to the needs of new refugees (Grey, 2006). Governor Robert D. Ray's vision transformed his state, as described in a moving documentary produced by Iowa Public

Television and the Commission on the Status of Iowans of Asian and Pacific Islander Heritage, *A Promise Called Iowa* (Iowa Public Television, 2007).

The Iowa Bureau of Refugee Services (BRS) addressed the basic needs of newcomers first by providing case workers, job training, and English classes. However, they went one step further to help the enterprise succeed, by enlisting volunteer refugee sponsors, private citizens who provided personal caring connections. As a clearinghouse of services and volunteers, the BRS connected churches with sponsored refugee families and took care of the immediate needs of newcomers, such as meeting them at the airport upon arrival from camps and setting up new living quarters. Private Iowa families, organizations, and individuals who connected with the BRS were able to sponsor families, individuals, groups of individuals, and unaccompanied refugee minors. Expanding the idea of community involvement, schools were also able to participate in the welcoming and resettlement process by involving students in sponsoring and supporting newcomers (Iowa Department of Human Services, 2020). This successful model of private citizen sponsorship guided by an organized state infrastructure experienced unparalleled success for decades due to compassionate and energetic volunteers. The purposeful innovative model resulted in enhancing the state's economy, enriching its culture, and in the words of Governor Robert Ray, "It was the right thing to do."

Canadian examples of responding to newcomers in need of welcoming are plentiful and ongoing. In the four months between December 2015 and March 2016, Canada welcomed over twenty-five thousand refugees from the war in Syria to large metropolitan areas, as well as smaller, rural communities all over the country. Prime Minister Justin Trudeau modeled the Canadian approach to welcoming newcomers by personally greeting the first Syrian refugees to arrive at the Toronto airport, welcoming them to their new home, and bestowing warm coats to ward off the winter cold (BBC News, 2015). Toronto's municipal government established a Newcomer Settlement Roundtable with participation from organizations in the settlement services, education, health, and employment sectors. Meeting on a monthly basis for two years, the roundtable shared information and facilitated the establishment of partnerships to best deliver support to the wave of newcomers. Several underused Toronto hotels were conscripted to house hundreds of refugee families, with onsite settlement services offices and survival English classes set up on the premises, as well as halal food prepared in the hotel kitchens. The TDSB took a lead in establishing partnerships with a number of settlement agencies in the city, pooling their ideas and resources for assisting the Syrian newcomers. Education representatives accompanied by Arabic-speaking interpreters visited the hotels and presented sessions for parents about the school system in Ontario. The school board was intentional about involving refugee sponsors, who provided caring personal connections and were well informed about the education system and opportunities for newcomer students. Buses transported children to half-day reception ESL classes set up in various schools around the city until their families found permanent housing, and each class had an Arabic-speaking educational assistant to assist in the children's adjustment.

Inspirational stories of how everyday people provided extraordinary support for the successful settlement of Syrian refugees flooded the media. National welcoming, personal sponsorship (Kantor & Einhorn, 2016), employment opportunities (Cecco & Sakkab, 2017), provisions for academic success, and more, helped newcomers feel an immediate sense of belonging and safety in Canada.

Making It Your Own

Educators are very familiar with K-W-L graphic organizers, which require students to reflect on what they already *know* about a topic, what they *want* to learn about the topic, and what they *learned* about the topic. But it has probably been a long time since most educators actually completed such a graph for their own personal or professional reasons. Well, that's about to change. This modified graphic organizer K-W-A-R, based on the familiar K-W-L chart, allows you to review *knowledge* of what others have initiated to welcome newcomers, identify *which* of the initiatives might be a good match for those new to your community, determine *actions* to welcome newcomers, and then *reflect* on the outcome as a learning experience.

FIGURE 3.4 KWAR Chart

K WHAT DO I KNOW ABOUT EXISTING COMMUNITY NEWCOMER SUPPORTS?	W WHICH INITIATIVE MATCHES MY COMMUNITY'S NEEDS?	A WHAT ACTION CAN I TAKE?	R WHAT ARE MY REFLECTIONS AND THOUGHTS ABOUT THIS EXPERIENCE?

FIGURE 3.5 Question B: Overview

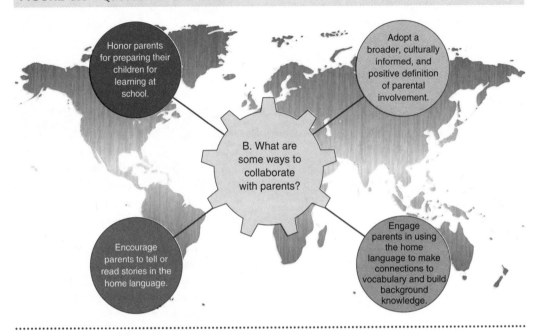

B. WHAT ARE SOME WAYS TO COLLABORATE WITH PARENTS?

- Powerful Practice 1: Adopt a broader, culturally informed, and positive definition of parental involvement in education.

- Powerful Practice 2: Engage parents in making connections to key vocabulary and concepts and building relevant background knowledge in the home language.

- Powerful Practice 3: Encourage parents to tell or read stories to their children in the home language.

- Powerful Practice 4: Honor parents for their contributions in preparing their children for learning at school.

Powerful Practice 1: Adopt a broader, culturally informed, and positive definition of parental involvement in education.

North American educators tend to have a particular set of behaviors in mind when they think of parental involvement in their child's education. The traditional scenario representing an involved parent includes regular attendance at parent-teacher meetings, curriculum nights, and other school events. It also encompasses helping with homework and advocating directly with the teacher and school for their child's educational needs. Many newcomer families come from cultures that take a different approach to the concept of parents' involvement and engagement in their children's schooling, one that is often manifested in parental involvement behaviors occurring outside of the school (Poza, Brooks, & Valdés, 2014). Goldsmith and Robinson Kurpius (2018) note that the Mexican immigrant parents interviewed for their study often exhibited their caring involvement in their child's education through home-based behaviors, such as instilling discipline and setting limits, maintaining high expectations for their children, and drawing on the support and strength of the entire family to contribute to the child's growth and success. In their research with Korean immigrant parents, Kim, An, Kim, and Kim (2018) observed frequent out-of-school parental involvement behaviors, such as giving children life advice, modeling character development, supporting children's interests, and being attentive to their needs. Educators need to appreciate that our expectations of parental engagement are culturally influenced and that there is a diversity of valuable ways in which newcomer parents demonstrate involvement in their child's schooling depending on their cultural background. Poza et al. (2014) also observed that some immigrant parents felt uncomfortable visiting their child's school due to language barriers and perceptions of bias. We need to work together to minimize these feelings of discomfort for newcomer families so that all parents will feel comfortable and welcome in our schools. Instead of educators always making the decisions about what newcomer parents need to know, working together also means asking parents and families what they feel they need to learn about their children's school and facilitating opportunities for teachers, families, and community members to learn together.

The work at Crescent Town Elementary School in Toronto provides an excellent example of expanding understanding of parental involvement. The school holds a community *iftar* event, the meal that breaks the fast each night during Ramadan. In a predominantly Muslim school community, this potluck *iftar* evening in the school gym provides an opportunity for families and educators to gather together for a meaningful occasion on which the parents are the experts rather than the teachers. Over two hundred members of the school community have a chance to learn about each other outside of the traditional school meeting format. In this context, educators are witness to parents visibly demonstrating their engagement with their child's school and education in a culturally responsive setting.

In another example of embracing cultural diversity by incorporating a broader definition of traditional parent involvement in the education of children, Grace Chung, a teacher of English as a second language (ESL) in Toronto, Ontario, arranged an after-school "ESL Café" for newcomer students and their families. A different food theme was chosen each week, such as pancakes, fruits, or pizza. Ms. Chung selected one or two picture books on the theme to share with the students and families, taking care to also include bilingual books such as *Salsa: Un Poema Para Cocinar/A Cooking Poem* (Argueta, 2015), *Hiromi's Hands*, a story about sushi (Barasch, 2007), and *Yum Yum Dim Sum* (Wilson Sanger, 2003). In the school staff kitchen, the entire group then prepared a dish on the theme using a simple recipe, often provided by one of the parents, and everyone enjoyed the finished treats together at a communal table. The ESL Café provided a forum for parents to participate on an equal footing with the teacher in a school literacy program where everyone was learning together and from each other.

Making It Your Own

Use the following chart to provide some practice expanding how you might interpret behavior that is representative of parental involvement in their child's education. Figure 3.6 contains a list of deficit-based behavioral interpretations in Column A. Column B has a different interpretation of those same behaviors. Draw a line to match interpretations in Column A to alternate possible interpretations in Column B. Then, in the space provided, indicate how, if needed, you might offer assistance. An example is included as a model. Please note that there are no right or wrong answers in this activity. There can be many different interpretations of the deficit behaviors listed in Column A. In fact, completing this exercise with colleagues might lead to some interesting discussions!

FIGURE 3.6 Interpretation of Parental Behaviors

COLUMN A DEFICIT INTERPRETATION	COLUMN B ALTERNATIVE INTERPRETATION → WHAT CAN I DO?	
These parents never come to after school meetings.	They are trying to get their child to school on time.	
The parents always arrive late to our meetings.	They are dressing to impress the teacher.	
The parents don't seem to care about what is happening in school. They never return any papers.	They have to walk a great distance to get to the school.	
This family is so poor. The parents always wear the same clothes when they come to school.	They work the evening shift.	Ask parents when it would be best to connect with them (day of the week, times, specific date). Offer telephone or video conferencing options for meetings. See if the family is available for early morning meetings.
These parents coddle their child. They walk the kindergarten student to school in a stroller.	They read their home language, but they don't read English.	

Powerful Practice 2: Engage parents in making connections to key vocabulary and concepts and building relevant background knowledge in the home language.

What It Might Look Like

Research shows that information transfers from one language to another and that words and concepts are learned more easily in a second language when they are known in the first language (in Hamayan et al., 2007; Ijalba, 2015). It is also well accepted that learning takes place by integrating new information into prior knowledge. It is especially important to harness English Learners' prior knowledge to facilitate learning or to build the necessary background knowledge, if needed (Cummins, 1996). Imagine for a moment, a kindergarten teacher reading the story of *Goldilocks and the Three Bears* (e.g., Marshall, 1998). Students who have already heard the tale will have a distinct advantage answering story questions and engaging in story discussions. Those who have never heard the story but who understand that *porridge* is a type of cereal served warmed, that a *rocking chair* is a seat that moves, and "just right" means satisfactory, will be well positioned to understand the story. Those unfamiliar with the concept of fairy tales may be completely baffled by the notion of bears living in a house with human comforts. Inviting parents to pre-teach key vocabulary and concepts and to build relevant background knowledge prepares students for the learning that will take place in the English classroom.

Home Programming Suggestions is a simple form developed by Speech-Language Pathology Services at the TDSB. The goal of this form is to help teachers connect with families so they can pre-teach key vocabulary and provide related conversations and experiences in the home language as preparation for an upcoming lesson. The form has since been translated into twelve languages and included in the multilingual book bag program, the Home Oral Language Activities (HOLA) Program (to be discussed ahead). The form itself can and is being used independently of the HOLA Program. Similarly, educators can use more high-tech options to communicate this information with parents, such as outgoing telephone or text messages, brief video, or posting information on their class websites. For example, before a unit on animals, parents can be asked to brainstorm a list of different kinds of animals with their children, discuss personal experiences with various animals and the unique characteristics of specific animals. As such, students will be better prepared to participate in class when the information is presented.

Making It Your Own

Consider the most efficient way for you to connect with parents on a regular basis so they can preview key vocabulary and build background knowledge. Can you use low-tech options (e.g., paper, telephone tree hosted by parent volunteers) or high-tech options (e.g., outgoing telephone messages, social media, class website) to communicate? What are key vocabulary words needed for a particular lesson, and how can they be highlighted for parents (e.g., English, pictorially, with definitions, translated)? What are some related activities needed to build necessary background knowledge (e.g., reading the story that will be read in class or a story on the same theme; watching a video clip; participating in a community experience, family conversation on the topic)? The job becomes easier when educators use the same mode and format of communication regularly and routinely. Families become familiar with the request and expect it on a certain day and can therefore plan it into their schedule more effectively. Consistency also helps educators, especially on those very busy days, who can routinely include all needed information.

Powerful Practice 3: Encourage parents to tell or read stories to their children in the home language.

What It Might Look Like

All children benefit from listening to a range of stories in their home language, even when we might think them to be too old for traditional "story time." The national campaign Read Aloud 15 Minutes stresses the importance of reading to your child for fifteen minutes daily, setting this as the new standard in child care. Their website (https://readaloud.org/) documents the many benefits of reading aloud to children—including language, literacy, and brain development—and provides some impressive resources for families. Telling and reading stories is wonderful entertainment, providing enjoyment for all members of the family. Exposure to stories at a younger age can promote a life-long passion for reading for pleasure. Older children in the home could be reading stories to younger siblings or enjoying books independently. With linguistic, literacy, mental health, and social advantages, the benefits of reading for pleasure are just beginning to be realized (Clark & Rumbold, 2006).

There is a whole world of stories available in a variety of formats. Large books, small books, pop-up books, electronic versions, animated tales, cloth books, the list goes on and on. Some important stories have never been put to paper. These oral stories include tales handed down from generation to generation, those that recount past events and family happenings, or those that are newly created, specially personalized, or imagined. A photo album or household item can be used as a jumping point to a story—how a particular item came to be in the family, for example. Older students might be especially keen to hear these stories and to be able to share them with younger family members. Other stories are in printed formats, such as a handwritten journal or a book. Written stories can be read aloud to children, or the tale can be told by paraphrasing or "reading the pictures" instead of decoding every single word of the text.

Sharing stories can be used to build necessary background knowledge while also facilitating English language development. It's just a matter of matching the story in the home language to what will be read or taught in the classroom. The ideal match would be to use the same story in the home language before it is read aloud in English in the classroom. If a match cannot be found (or made), the next best option is to use a story in the home language on the same topic or theme as that which will be read or covered in English in the classroom. This allows for priming of new vocabulary and concepts but perhaps not the actual story content. For example, the story of *The Very Hungry Caterpillar* (Carle, 1969), available in multiple languages, could be read at home before an English lesson on nutrition. Sending dual-language books home to be read in the home language before they are read aloud in English in the classroom will impress parents with your commitment to helping students continue to develop the home language, bootstrap their linguistic skills, and involve parents in the education of their children.

The HOLA Program is a multilingual book bag program, developed inter-professionally at the TDSB by three departments: Speech-Language Pathology, Early Years, and English as a Second Language (Toronto District School Board, 2010). This program was designed to help teachers connect with parents to use the home language to develop vocabulary, content, and background knowledge in authentic communication interactions, in preparation for successful participation in classroom activities. The HOLA Program consists of teacher materials and a manual, as well as six different story bags containing a story book (mostly dual language), accompanied by related activity materials (e.g., toys, manipulatives, sorting cards) and a parent manual translated into twelve languages (Arabic, Bengali, Chinese, English, Farsi, Gujarati, Korean, Somali, Spanish, Tamil, Urdu, and Vietnamese). The parent manual provides suggestions for home use that are related to the kindergarten curriculum and are easy and enjoyable to implement into the daily lives of busy families. Teachers are encouraged to read the stories and engage in some of the activities in class. Story bags are on loan to families for a week at a time. Use of the HOLA Program was piloted and evaluated in a Grade 1 class and two kindergarten classes. The results indicate that the HOLA Program was well received by teachers, parents, and students and that it has merit as an initiative that involves parents in the education of their young children (Westernoff, 2014).

The importance of having access to books as an essential component of literacy development is being recognized through many different initiatives. The Little Free Library Network (2009–2020) has recognized the importance of having access to books, especially in areas where books are scarce. This nonprofit organization supports the establishment, stewardship, and promotion of neighborhood book-sharing boxes. These mini libraries allow neighbors to borrow, read, enjoy, and share books. A group of students and educators in Sunrise, Florida, recently celebrated the grand opening of five new Little Free Library book-sharing boxes containing multilingual books (Megan, 2009–2020, https://littlefreelibrary.org/students-create-little-free-library-network-stocked-with-multilingual-books/). Likewise, Dolly Parton's Imagination Library mails free, high-quality books to many enrolled children around the world on a monthly basis from birth until they begin school (Dolly Parton's Imagination Library, 2020, https://imaginationlibrary.com/about-us/).

Making It Your Own

There are many different ways to partner with parents to read dual-language books at home. To ensure success, it is best to match resources to classroom content and to set clear parental expectations. Both take a bit of planning.

1. Resources: Identify the topic, theme, or book that will be used in an upcoming lesson. Then look at available dual-language books that are the closest match to the lesson. Can they be sent home with the student, or are they available on a free online library? Is reading the book sufficient, or do you want to add an activity or discussion for home completion? Adding a well-adhered note to a book with a simple suggestion (e.g., "Talk about healthy snacks" in the book *The Very Hungry Caterpillar* [Carle, 1969]) can go a long way to deepen comprehension of concepts.

2. What are your expectations for parents, and are they aware of these expectations? You might need to make expectations explicit. For example, parents may not understand how reading to their children in Tagalog, Polish, or Farsi will help them succeed in English. They might need to know that concept knowledge crosses linguistic borders.

Powerful Practice 4: Honor parents for their contributions in preparing their children for learning at school.

Parenting in a new country can be quite complex. In addition to attending to their own worries about security and family obligations, parents try to make life safe and comfortable for their children. It would be easy to overlook what it takes to be prepared for a full day of learning at school. When physical and emotional needs are not being satisfied, then learning is inefficient. As adults, we can often mitigate our physical or emotional discomfort, at least for a short time. We can still concentrate well enough to drive home, even when we are very hungry. We can still schedule a doctor's appointment when we are gripped by fear regarding a potential medical problem. Many children cannot easily negotiate the social and academic demands of the classroom while under less than optimal physical and emotional conditions. Firstly, they may not even recognize or be able to name bodily sensations of fatigue, hunger, worry, or fear at any given moment in time. Or they may not know how to advocate for satisfaction in the short term, and long-term solutions are often beyond their control (e.g., food security). Sadly, educators have witnessed capable children who cannot concentrate due to poor nutrition, illness, exhaustion, concern, and stress.

Families do their very best for their children. With many competing economic and social demands, parents may not be thinking about or aware of expectations that can help prepare children for optimal learning (e.g., medical, vision, hearing check-ups). Similarly, they may not realize just how much their herculean efforts to get their children prepared for school actually contribute to a successful day of learning. Resources such as *Raising Young Children in a New Country: Supporting Early Learning and Healthy Development,* a joint project by Bridging Refugee Youth and Children's Services, The National Center on Cultural and Linguistic Responsiveness, and the U.S. Department of Health and Human Services, can be very helpful in opening up discussions.

Ms. Kumar was just finishing a parent interview with Mrs. Ramasundaran, the mother of one of her Grade 4 students, Lakshmi. Ms. Kumar was happy to be able to converse directly with Mrs. Ramasundaran in her home language of Tamil. Ms. Kumar was even happier to report that Lakshmi was progressing well and proving to be a hard working, responsible, and successful member of the class. Mrs. Ramasundaran confided that she wished she could do more for Lakshmi but was unable since she did not speak much English. Ms. Kumar felt puzzled by what she was hearing, knowing that the family seemingly did everything needed to help Lakshmi succeed. Using the gift of their shared home language, Ms. Kumar proceeded to review how students need to be "ready to learn" every day, a responsibility that the Ramasundaran family was completing regularly and very well. Ms. Kumar explained that by ensuring regular school attendance and punctuality, their actions had enabled Lakshmi to be available and receptive to school lessons and announcements. In addition, Ms. Kumar detailed that Lakshmi brought sufficient healthy food and drinks to school, so she was well nourished and hydrated throughout the day and therefore energized to concentrate and participate in all activities. She appeared well rested and primed to learn. Furthermore, Ms. Kumar pointed out that the family took responsibility in ensuring that all forms, library books, and assignments were returned on time, which no doubt contributed to Lakshmi's sense of responsibility, belonging, and success. Finally, at home, by discussing school activities and the school day with Lakshmi, the family was actively showing their interest and support for school life and academics while continuing to develop their shared home language. Ms. Kumar concluded by praising the Ramasundaran family for being great partners whose essential contributions are highly valuable in Lakshmi's education.

Making It Your Own

What do your students need to be physically and emotionally primed for learning? List the advantages of the following achievements, so you have ideas ready to discuss with families. Be sure to highlight every accomplishment. What resources are available to help families who might be struggling with a particular expectation? Keep in mind that children should be increasingly independent in some of these activities as they get older. How can you help parents support their child's independence in age-appropriate responsibilities?

- Attending school regularly _____

- Arriving at/leaving school on time _____

- Being well nourished/bringing healthy food/fluids to school _____

- Being well rested _____

- Being clothed appropriately for the weather _____

- Returning forms, fees, library books, assignments on time _____

- Showing an interest in school work _____

(Continued)

(Continued)

- Showing an interest in daily activities of school life _____

- Encouraging participation in extracurricular activities _____

- Regularly wearing glasses/hearing aids/braces in good working order
  (as needed) _____

- Attending regular medical and dental appointments _____

- Establishing efficient routines at home (e.g., bedtime, homework) _____

- Completing self-care tasks (e.g., dressing, physical and dental hygiene) _____

- Participating in regular physical and social activities _____

- Other _____

FIGURE 3.7 Question C: Overview

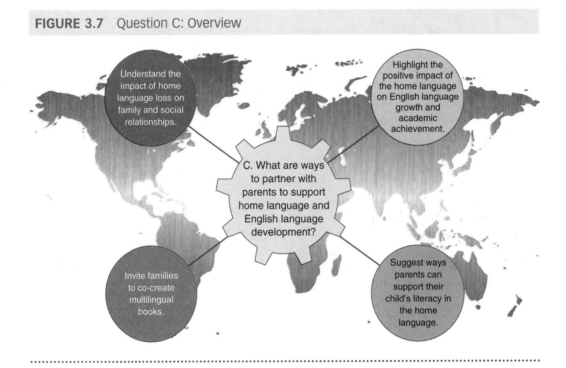

Understand the impact of home language loss on family and social relationships.

Highlight the positive impact of the home language on English language growth and academic achievement.

C. What are ways to partner with parents to support home language and English language development?

Invite families to co-create multilingual books.

Suggest ways parents can support their child's literacy in the home language.

POWERFUL PRACTICES FOR SUPPORTING ENGLISH LEARNERS

C. WHAT ARE SOME WAYS TO PARTNER WITH PARENTS TO SUPPORT BOTH THE HOME LANGUAGE AND ENGLISH LANGUAGE DEVELOPMENT?

- Powerful Practice 1: Highlight the positive impact of ongoing home language use and development on English language growth and academic achievement.

- Powerful Practice 2: Suggest ways parents can support their child's literacy development in the home language.

- Powerful Practice 3: Invite families to co-create multilingual books.

- Powerful Practice 4: Understand the effects of home language loss and its impact on family and social relationships.

Powerful Practice 1: Highlight the positive impact of ongoing home language use and development on English language growth and academic achievement.

What It Might Look Like

It is not uncommon for people to compare children to sponges, believing that they just "soak up" languages. Contrary to popular belief, children are not sponges (Paradis et al., 2011). Learning language in general is a complex process involving many variables. Children need to have meaningful opportunities to use language, for a range of functional purposes, and with a variety of communication partners. After all, people communicate in the real world for real reasons. Providing natural opportunities for authentic communication in the home language actively encourages home language use and development. Activities such as listening to music in the home language, attending community and religious events, seeing the home language in a variety of print media, video chatting with friends and families, and attending heritage or international language classes all provide students with opportunities to use the home language in rich and satisfying ways.

In addition to having opportunities for home language use, students require sufficient language stimulation with respect to quantity and quality, in order to continue to develop strong speaking and comprehension skills. Children need to hear and use complex forms of language (Wong Fillmore, 2000) and not just instructions regarding routines and behaviors. Encourage parents to use new vocabulary, concepts, and increasingly longer sentences in the home language. The use of longer sentences necessitates the use of more grammatically complex forms. Using and asking complex thinking and predicting questions is also helpful (e.g., I wonder what would happen if . . . ? How could we . . . ?). Retelling personal events and stories provides the opportunity for students to organize words into sentences and sentences into paragraphs to convey meaningful information. Using rich oral language in the home provides the foundation for all language skills, which in turn supports the acquisition of English, as well as academic skills.

Making It Your Own

Develop an awareness of real-life opportunities for the student to use the home language for functional reasons. You can find many subtle clues in your interactions with families. They may let you know about special events or outings, important people, celebrations, and places where the home language is the primary form of conversation. Use these opportunities to reinforce parents' best efforts to provide home language interactions.

Professionals have been busy creatively developing ways to impress parents with ideas that support the use of the home language. Multimedia options that have been translated and can be used with a wide audience can be particularly helpful. You may already have a handy list of resources that you use regularly. The following resources are offered as examples for your consideration and inspiration, with space for you to add your own resources and ideas:

Handouts

- A group of speech-language pathologists in Ontario created a handout for parents with suggestions on stimulating ways to read books to their young children. The resource has been translated into eleven different languages, and the handouts are available free of charge: *Reading Develops Language Skills: A Parent Handout in Eleven Languages* (Multicultural, Multilingual Interest Group of the Ontario Association of Speech-Language Pathologists and Audiologists, 2010, https.// cdn.ymaws.com/www.osla.on.ca/resource/resmgr/interest_groups/ osla-_reading_develops_langu.pdf).

- The New York State Education Department and The Office of Bilingual Education and World Languages has produced a guide for parents of English Learners. Available in twenty-six languages, the document dispels myths, provides various resources, and gives helpful tips for participating in their English Learners' education (http://www.nysed.gov/common/nysed/files/programs/bilingual-ed/guideforparentsofellsinnysenglish.pdf).

- Zelasko and Antunez (2000) co-authored a parent's guide entitled *If Your Child Learns in Two Languages: A Parent's Guide for Improving Educational Opportunities for Children Acquiring English as a Second Language* available for free downloading in English, Spanish, and five other languages (https://ncela.ed.gov/publications). It describes the benefits of learning two languages and paints a picture of the characteristics of effective schooling for students learning English as an additional language.

- _____

  _____

  _____

- _____

  _____

  _____

Flyers

- The Department of English as a Second Language/English Literacy Development and Speech-Language Pathology Services at the TDSB collaborated to create *Use Your Home Language: Building Skills with Young Children for School Success* (Toronto District School Board, 2016a), a colourful (FW: This refers to a Canadian publication, so use of "colourful" is preferred in this instance) flyer in multiple languages, explaining how parents can use the home language in stimulating conversational ways throughout the day (Speech-Language Pathology Google Site for Parents: Roll your cursor over the heading "More" for a drop down menu highlighting the flyers: http://bit.ly/slpconnection).

- Chumak-Horbatsch of the School of Early Childhood Education at Ryerson University in Toronto has produced a brochure called *Hold on to Your Home Language,* which is available in twenty-one different languages (https://www.ryerson.ca/mylanguage/brochures).

- _____

  _____

  _____

- _____

  _____

  _____

Videos

- Each of the multilingual flyers *Use Your Home Language: Building Skills with Young Children for School Success* (Toronto District School Board, 2016a) prepared by the TDSB have been set to music in two-minute video clips (Toronto District School Board, 2016b). These are very useful during parent interviews, conferences, workshops, and school registration (Speech-Language Pathology Google Site for Parents: Roll your cursor over the heading "More" for a drop down menu highlighting the video clips: http://bit.ly/slpconnection).

- The Toronto District School Board (2007) has prepared a fourteen-minute DVD in twelve languages, entitled *Your Home Language: Foundation for Success,* explaining the importance of the home language for academic success and how parents and caregivers can help maintain and develop their child's home language skills through simple family oracy and literacy-based activities.

- _____

  _____

- _____

  _____

- _____

  _____

Websites

- The School of Early Childhood Studies, Faculty of Community Services at Ryerson University in Toronto has a website with many different resources on home language maintenance. It is a website worth exploring (https://www.ryerson.ca/mylanguage/).

- The authoritative and comprehensive bilingual website for supporting English Learners, ¡Colorín colorado! (2019b) features an entire section devoted to *Raising Bilingual Kids.* English and Spanish articles focus on understanding the process of second language acquisition, providing encouragement, and suggestions for parents raising bilingual children (http://www.colorincolorado.org/raising-bilingual-kids).

- Multilingual Families (2013–2015) is an education project funded by the European Union to support parents in raising multilingual children. Their website contains parent and educator resources in a number of languages (http://www.multlingual-families.eu/home).

- _____
  _____
  _____

- _____
  _____
  _____

Other

- Listening to stories in different languages is often available through library activities, such as story time, or dial-in programs, such as Dial-A-Story, through the Toronto Public Library (2020). Dial-a-Story is a free program that allows families to call a phone number at any time to listen to stories in a multitude of languages (https://www.toronto publiclibrary.ca/services/dial-a-story.jsp).

- _____
  _____
  _____

- _____
  _____
  _____

Powerful Practice 2: Suggest ways parents can support their child's literacy development in the home language.

What It Might Look Like

Let's face it, many North American educators are not in the position to teach literacy in multiple languages. But they are well positioned to support their students becoming multiliterate. Educators can show their appreciation of literacy in other languages through their attitude and actions in the classroom, with profound results. Students who have literacy skills in the home language are less likely to lose the home language, have access to life-enriching literature not available in English, and experience the many benefits of being multilingual, multicultural, and multiliterate. It can begin with the simplest, most innocent of gestures on behalf of a teacher. When a teacher applauds a student's recognition of a word in the home language while reading a dual-language book in class or shares a family's joy of their child's reading achievements in a heritage/international language class, that educator is encouraging students to become multiliterate.

There are many ways to indirectly support students becoming multiliterate. You may have already been instrumental in encouraging students to achieve literacy in the home language. Here are a few more ideas to consider, with room to add your own initiatives:

- Encourage parents to be reading role models. Parents who actively model the pleasure and purpose of reading (in any language) teach their children that reading is an enjoyable, informative part of every day and not a school task to be completed before bedtime. Reading a variety of material (e.g., books, recipes, magazines) in the home language will promote a love of reading in a natural, nurturing way. Tom (2020) of *Scholastic Parents*, provides some easy tips in the handy article entitled *Be a Reading Role Model: If you want your child to be a good reader, be one yourself!* (https://www.scholastic.com/parents/books-and-reading/reading-resources/be-reading-role-model.html).

- Similarly, a tip sheet entitled *Encouraging Reading at Home* is available from the Speech-Language Pathology Department at the TDSB (https://sites.google .com/tdsb.on.ca/slpconnection/tip-sheets).

- Help families access dual- and home-language books (hard copies and electronically) and other reading material (e.g., magazines, newspapers, flyers, cook books, etc.).

- Promote multilanguage materials and activities in the classroom. Advocate for, display, and use dual-language books and reading material or invite guests who can read a story, recipe, or game instructions, in home languages.

- Talk about student participation in heritage/international language programs. Your interest and approval will be evident through simple conversations.

- Share information about heritage/international language programs, which are sometimes offered in public schools after school hours. Families may be seeking more formal reading instruction for their child.

- Celebrate the achievements and efforts of reading skills in other languages with genuine praise and joy.

- Educators often use newspapers, flyers, old cards, and magazines for crafts and lessons. Encourage families to donate printed material in other languages for use in the classroom.

- Literacy resources for families are available online:
  - The Reading Rockets website offers *Reading Tips for Parents (in Multiple Languages)* (2008) (https://www.readingrockets.org/article/reading-tips-parents-multiple-languages#english).

- The U.S. Department of Education (2005) offers online information for parents in English and Spanish to support their child's literacy development in the document entitled *Helping Your Child Become a Reader* (https://www2 .ed.gov/parents/academic/help/reader/index.html).

- International Literacy Association/National Council of Teachers of English (2020) provides a full slate of free resources to support family members in helping children with schoolwork and overall literacy development. This website offers a cornucopia of fun activities and projects, online tools to help children create book reports, cover pages and flip books and a slew of tips for parents to help their child with homework, choose a book to read, write a story, and stay safe online. All of these parent involvement materials are available on the site in both English and Spanish (www.readwritethink.org/ parent-afterschool-resources/).

Powerful Practice 3: Invite families to co-create multilingual books.

What It Might Look Like

Using available dual-language books at home and in the classroom is wonderful, but co-creating them with families elevates the use of dual-language books to a whole new level. An additional set of linguistic skills are needed to write and illustrate books. Producing dual-language books incorporates all linguistic areas (e.g., vocabulary, grammar, narrative grammar, sequencing) receptively and expressively, in both oral and written modes. In addition, students and families use the social skills of negotiation, communication, and collaboration as they work together on this special project. A sense of individual and family pride will prevail as the stories are enjoyed by family, friends, and schoolmates.

There are many inspirational bookmaking projects that could be used to create multilingual books on a variety of personal or academic themes. These books could be printed in hard copies, or made available online, and either format would be amazing additions to communal and personal libraries. Consider the work of Jeanette Voaden (2016), teacher with the Waterloo Region District School Board in Ontario, Canada. She uses Google Slides with students and their families to help them create meaningful and attractive multilingual books, and she happily shares the details so others can do the same (http://bit.ly/CreatingBooks).

Voaden's work has gone on to motivate others, including a group of educators at the TDSB who created the Books for Friends Gallery (https://sites .google.com/tdsb.on.ca/bffgallery/home), an online gallery of diversity inclusive books written and shared by students. In a companion site, The Books for Friends (BFF) Project, (https://sites.google.com/tdsb.on.ca/bff), they provide information so that others who are similarly inspired can create e-books. Stephanie Ledger and Kay Cairns (English as a second language and Grade 1/2 teachers respectively) at Winston Churchill Public School in Waterloo, Ontario, Canada, started a lunchtime dual-language book writing club with their students and parents. Together with participating parents, they guided students through a series of mini-lessons each day that encompasses brainstorming topics for dual-language books, creating a story plan, choosing vocabulary, writing mechanics, illustrating, and editing. The finished dual-language books in a variety of languages are professionally printed and bound and have since found a home on the shelves of the school library.

In an equally creative project to create dual-language books, Nadine Williams, a teacher-librarian at an elementary school in Toronto, was initially disappointed when she could not find commercially available Hungarian/English dual-language books. An influx of Hungarian-speaking students had recently arrived at the school, and she wanted to ensure that they would have access to books in their home language. The resourceful educator invited some of the bilingual Hungarian/English speaking parents to bring in Hungarian language books that they had brought from their home country and worked with them to add English text to create dual-language Hungarian/English books (e.g., Wilson & Chapman, 2003). This provided the students with the opportunity to read, hear, and share stories in their home language, as well as to see books in their home language proudly displayed among the school library's rich multilingual book collection.

Making It Your Own

Review some websites and programs for creating multilingual books (e.g., https://bookcreator.com/) and perhaps discover more! Many of these sites allow you to read existing books in addition to creating new ones (Figure 3.8). How can existing books be used in your classroom? Can you undertake a project to create a library of multilingual books for use in home, classroom, school, community, or global libraries? Could these books be part of a school fundraiser? What is needed to successfully complete such a project?

FIGURE 3.8 Creating Dual-Language Books

WEBSITE:	USING THE BOOKS:	CREATING BOOKS:
Creating Books. Jeanette Voaden (2016), Waterloo District School Board, Ontario, Canada: http://bit.ly/CreatingBooks		
Books for Friends Gallery, Toronto District School Board, Ontario, Canada: https://sites.google.com/tdsb.on.ca/bffgallery/home		
Books for Friends Project, Toronto District School Board, Ontario, Canada: https://sites.google.com/tdsb.on.ca/bff		
Unite for Literacy (2014) ww.uniteforliteracy.com		
Scribjab, Simon Fraser University, British Columbia, Canada www.scribjab.com		
Other resources:		

To create books, I need the following:

- Computer software:

- Administrative support:

- Funding:

- Project Schedule:

- Time:

- Translators:

- Partners:

- Other:

Powerful Practice 4: Understand the
effects of home language loss and its
impact on family and social relationships.

All families want their children to be healthy, happy, and successful. Parents make complex educational decisions to the best of their ability, sometimes influenced by their own academic experiences, the well-meaning (and sometimes uninformed) advice of others, and a good dose of common sense. Ideally, their decisions should also be influenced by research and evidence-based information. Some parents have hopes of their children becoming multilingual, multicultural, and multiliterate. Some parents may believe that they have to choose between their home language and English, the language of academic success. Each family has its own unique language personality and dynamics, which may change over time, influenced by a variety of planned and unplanned factors.

Responsive educators work to support parental choices while ensuring that families have the necessary data to make informed decisions. For example, a bilingual family may decide (intentionally or otherwise) to focus on the use of English in the home, and educator support should follow accordingly. Responsive educators are also aware that there are a variety of societal, educational, and personal factors that influence home language loss or maintenance, many of which are beyond their control or scope of practice. Nevertheless, educators themselves should try to avoid contributing to factors that promote home language attrition. Healthy and respectful attitudes regarding diversity and the incorporation of home languages and cultures into classrooms and schools goes a long way to preventing home language loss (Chumak-Horbatsch, 2019).

It never failed to surprise Mr. Silva, a Grade 5 teacher, to see parents speaking the home language to their children who responded only in English. He noted that the interactions were brief and usually specific to school entry or dismissal, such as remembering a lunch bag, gathering homework, and retrieving outdoor clothes. He wasn't sure why he was surprised—after all, this is the way he communicated with his own parents who spoke only Portuguese for as long as he could remember. As a child, they would instruct him to brush his teeth, get ready for bed, or finish his dinner. As an adult, the requests centered more around his parents' needs, grocery shopping, and scheduling medical appointments. There was still very little opportunity for real, heart-to-heart discussions. Mr. Silva did not speak much Portuguese, and his parents had never learned to speak English with confidence. He knew that many of his students had language worlds beyond the classroom that need not be sacrificed for the sake of English language acquisition and that much could be done to help students become multilingual, multicultural, and multiliterate (Chumak-Horbatsch, 2012) . Most importantly, he was saddened to think that some of his charges might end up like himself, unable to fully share their joys, successes, and struggles in a language shared with parents.

Making It Your Own

Getting to know families and the languages used in the home for various communication purposes can help you support their language-learning efforts. There are many different ways multiple languages can be organized in the home. Many families don't have an intentional plan, allowing communication to flow organically, with translanguaging leading the way. Other families use language more strategically, perhaps specifying language use by time, such as speaking the home language exclusively during meal times while being more relaxed regarding its use at other times in the day. Some might follow the one-parent, one-language formula, and others might designate language use by tasks, such as using the home language for social purposes and English for school and academic discussions. Whatever the plan, premeditated or otherwise, there needs to be a match between the language outcomes desired by parents and the actions that can lead to these outcomes. The one-parent, one-language plan will do little to promote bilingualism if the student does not have sufficient access to the languages of both parents, and the home language cannot be promoted sufficiently at mealtimes if the family seldom eats together.

When/if appropriate, how could you help families think about how their actions are aligned to promote their preferred language outcomes? Are they aware of the importance of having a language of shared proficiency between parents and children? How can you open up discussions? You might want to read or share the reflections of adults regarding their regret and struggles due to home language attrition, such as the dual-language poem (Gujarati and English) Search for "My Tongue" by Sujatta Bhatt (1988) included in Aamna Mohdin's moving article, "Even if You've Forgotten the Language You Spoke as a Child, It Still Stays With You" (2017) (https://qz.com/1155289/even-if-youve-forgotten-the-language-you-spoke-as-a-child-it-still-stays-with-you/). Zi-Ann Lum's (2017) echoes this conundrum in her poignant magazine article, "My Mother and I Don't Speak the Same Language, Literally" (https://www.chatelaine.com/living/my-mom-and-i-dont-speak-the-same-language/).

FIGURE 3.9 Question D: Overview

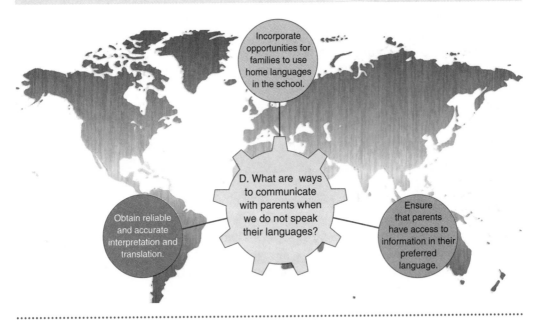

D. WHAT ARE SOME WAYS TO COMMUNICATE WITH PARENTS WHEN WE DO NOT SPEAK THEIR LANGUAGES?

- Powerful Practice 1: Incorporate opportunities for families to see, hear, and use their languages in the school and classroom.

- Powerful Practice 2: Ensure that parents have access to information in their preferred language.

- Powerful Practice 3: Obtain reliable and accurate interpretation and translation services.

Powerful Practice 1: Incorporate opportunities for families to see, hear, and use their languages in the school and classroom.

What It Might Look Like

Greeting families in their home language is a simple and effective way to connect with them. Some greetings might be indirect, such as multilingual announcements or music echoing down the hallways during transition times. Other greetings are more personal, such as those during entry and dismissal times or at the beginning of parent meetings. Even if your accent is terrible and you mispronounce a word or two, your efforts to make families feel more comfortable will be greatly appreciated and will help to build rapport. Greetings are not limited to one verbal exchange but are open to further social conventions, actions, creativity, and imagination. Once you are comfortable with a greeting, feel free to add another welcoming comment (e.g., "Please have a seat"; "Please come in") or a culturally appropriate gesture (e.g., bowing, nodding). Families will be eager to help you expand your repertoire of social greetings and gestures.

Greetings can also be extended to include social customs. For example, wishing families *Gong Hay Fat Choy* (congratulations and prosperity), a common Mandarin salutation during Chinese New Year, or *Shabbat Shalom*, a wish for good sabbath on a Friday for an observant Jewish family. During *Diwali*, the Festival of Lights, teachers at one Canadian school gathered to create their version of *rangoli*, a sand or coloured powder design on the floor of the home. Their educational interpretation of the greeting was created with coloured chalk in the foyer of the school and protected from foot traffic by mini construction cones. Parents were excited and deeply touched to know that the teachers used their break time to put thought and effort into recognizing this important holiday.

One creative school district decided on an efficient and formalized way to build capacity in the strategic use of home languages in the school. Recognizing that the school did not have enough interpreters of other languages to support families, leaders invited interested bilingual parents to participate in a certificate program of educational interpreter training. The program featured the benefits of "growing your own" cadre of local interpreters, as well as provided potential income for certified parents. This innovative initiative allowed for training of bilingual parents to provide qualified liaison and support to other families throughout the school year.

Making It Your Own

Remembering social greetings and customs from an array of language groups can be tricky. Knowing when and to whom to bow, whether or not you can shake hands with a member of the opposite sex, and the correct pronoun or preferred term of address to use with an elder can easily be forgotten if not used on a regular basis. It can be helpful to keep an inventory of tried and true sentences, gestures, and customs. You may already have a repertoire of greetings for daily or holiday use and be familiar with handy sources (e.g., Haghighat, 2005). Culture, however, is not static. Changes occur over time. Many resources outline greetings and customs typically used in the home country, some of which may be more formal than those adopted and used in North America. It is a good idea to double check your greeting intentions with a member of that language group and to learn from your own brave mistakes.

Once you have some greetings well established, how can you provide a deeper level of language experience? What else needs to be done to hear and see multiple languages throughout the school? How can you build capacity so everyone can enjoy a multilingual, multicultural, multiliterate environment?

Powerful Practice 2: Ensure that parents have access to information in their preferred language.

What It Might Look Like

Communicating effectively with all families is good educational practice, as well as a federal requirement in some districts (Collier, 2011; Staehr Fenner, 2014). To achieve equity in education, schools need to ensure that all parents have access to information regarding district, school, and class happenings (U.S. Department of Justice & U.S. Department of Education, 2015). Educators will need to use interpretation and/or translation services to best communicate with some parents.

Interpretation involves working with competent communicators to orally transmit information from one language to another (Metropolitan Toronto School Board, 1996). Interpretation is often used in group settings, such as an open house, curriculum night, school community council meetings, and special parent assemblies or conferences. Interpretation is also effective in one-on-one settings, such as school registration, various meetings, parent interviews, and in phone calls, especially the three-way phone call to connect the parent, interpreter, and yourself. Some schools have a dedicated telephone line that plays outgoing messages in multiple languages to inform parents of upcoming events and deadlines. Other districts have live access to remote interpreter services through telephone connections or itinerant personnel who can provide interpretation onsite. While interpreting in a one-on-one situation is useful, it can create inequities in the relationship between families and educators. Families can become dependent on educators to provide the interpreter and are subsequently unable to easily initiate contact when they have a concern or question. It is helpful to encourage parents to become self-sufficient in communication with the school, either by developing their own facility in English or finding their own language buddy, someone they trust who can provide interpretation when the parent wants to contact school personnel.

Schools also communicate in writing with families. The proof is in the varied types of documents crumpled at the bottom of little backpacks: newsletters, bulletins, invitations, report cards, notices, permission forms, data collection records, to name a few. Many schools choose to have important documents and website pages translated into the major languages spoken by their student population. Translation involves moving written information from one language to another. Professional translation can be costly, but because the outcome is a written product, translations can be produced in such a way as to be reusable. Suggestions for cost efficient and sustainable translation include the following:

- Translated materials should look as educationally professional and as similar as possible to original English documents. This means that translated documents are printed on the appropriate letterhead for the occasion, be it the school or district letterhead. The same grade and color of paper is used, as are salutations and signatures. Translated material should have the same status as the English material.

- Identify the key documents that would best serve the families in your school throughout the year. Have these documents translated first, adding on additional documents yearly.

- Identify several languages spoken by the majority of the student and family population. Have select documents translated into those languages first, adding on key documents in additional languages yearly.

- Connect with a nearby school to share the task and cost of translating documents. This should yield more documents translated into more languages, a benefit to both school communities.

- For ease of use, always indicate the name of the language somewhere on the document (e.g., footer, title). Be sure to include the English label on the English document. This can be helpful to a recipient still unfamiliar with English print and sends a very subtle but important message that the status of the English version is equal to that of translated versions. The language name should be clearly visible and located where it won't be easily cut off during rushed photocopying.

- Always send the English version of the document along with the translated version. Double-sided printing usually works well. Some recipients will appreciate being able to review their new language or may need to check their understanding of a particular message.

- Leave a blank line for content that might change over time, such as names, prices, locations, dates, or times. Use a smaller font under the line to indicate the information that is to be included in those spots. The translated template can then be reused over the years, with the specific data entered for each use. Don't worry too much about having to enter the data in English, if needed. Parents will appreciate having most of the information in the home language and can follow up regarding the specific details if required.

- When it is time to make substantial revisions to the original document, then it is time to have it translated again. Avoid taking short cuts or "making do" with translated copies (e.g., cut-and-paste, disintegrating handwritten revisions, overuse of whiteout). The translated versions should never be amended beyond recognition or look like an after-thought.

- Use visuals on documents when appropriate (e.g., picture of a pizza slice on a permission form for participation in pizza day). This provides a quick reference for parents who may struggle with literacy (English and/ or the home language) and prompt them to get more information (if needed) from their children, another parent, or the teacher.

- Organize and store documents securely. It is handy to have documents stored electronically, as long as your computer supports a wide range of fonts. Otherwise, your translation may look like a bunch of squares, dots, and squiggles. Hard copy backups should be of high quality printing so that they can be easily and reliably photocopied.

- The expectation following receipt of written communication is some action on the part of the parents. We expect them to complete and return a form, submit payment for a school trip, or indicate a preference for a meeting date. Their action confirms that the communication was successful. Don't be surprised if some parents ask clarification questions regarding a translated form before responding to the request. They may need to check the exact amount of payment needed or let you know about a conflicting schedule. Asking for clarification is another indicator of communication success. It means that families paid attention to the message and are doing their best to follow up accordingly.

- Use technology to your advantage. Create a dual-language blog or webpage that parents can consult to check on classroom and school information, download forms, review homework, check important deadlines, and see what their child is doing in class.

- While translation provides a huge service to many families, it is not always possible to translate all school documents. Establishing a repertoire of translated material is a work in progress. When translated versions are unavailable, districts may find it helpful to attach a translated tag to the English documents to indicate that the contents are particularly important.

Making It Your Own

Ideally, we want to work with professionally trained interpreters and translators. Some districts will use a local business that offers a roster of professional interpreters for hire (remotely or onsite), dedicate special education funds to cover interpretation expenses for high stakes special education meetings, or share professional interpreters and/or translators across districts. In the absence of professional interpreters, educators may use cultural and linguistic informants, someone who speaks the family's home language but who does not have professional certification (Westernoff, 2019). This would include valued bilingual employees (who provide interpretation services as needed and who may or may not receive a salary bonus), locally trained bilingual parents or volunteers, friends, or representatives from a social agency. Different districts and boards have their own rules and processes for securing interpretation personnel, so it is best to review the practices in your district. Once you are familiar with the guidelines and procedures, you can begin to develop a roster of people who speak the home languages of your students. It is handy to use the same trusted personnel as others in your building, in order to promote cooperation and skilled collaboration (Westernoff, 2019). Match the cultural and linguistic informant to the client, as well as the interpretation task for best outcomes. For example, in some cultures it might be best for the cultural linguistic informant to be the same gender as the client or from the same tribe or clan. Some cultural linguistic informants might prefer working in smaller settings, such as a parent meeting, and may be less comfortable interpreting in front of a large group of people. Others might be available for telephone interviews but unable to travel distances to provide interpretation services in person.

Some people who are competent providers of interpretation services may not be comfortable or able to provide translation services. You might need to develop another list of service providers who can move information from one language to another in written form. Brainstorm a list of important documents needed throughout the school year. Prioritize them by date and relevancy. Which documents will serve your students best? It might be more important to get a field trip permission form translated for immediate use rather than a notice about after-school programs that begins later in the year. Which languages are needed for this school year based on the current population? Where are the local schools that might be willing to partner in seeking relevant and sustainable translations?

Powerful Practice 3: Obtain reliable and accurate interpretation and translation services.

What It Might Look Like

It is not always easy to obtain quality interpretation and translation. Even the best intentions can fail miserably, as evidenced by international business advertising. For example, the car manufacturer Ford launched an ad campaign in Belgium with the slogan "Every car has a high-quality body," which translated into "Every car has a high-quality corpse." The brewing company Coors translated its slogan "Turn It Loose" into an expression commonly interpreted in Spanish as "Suffer from diarrhea" (Schooley, 2019). We really want to take necessary precautions to avoid such errors. Best outcomes can be achieved by combining the competencies of the interpreter/translator/cultural linguistic informant and the educator. It makes good sense to prepare for collaborative work at the planning stage, intervention stage, and debriefing stage (American Speech-Language and Hearing Association, 1997–2020a; Collier, 2011; Westernoff, 2019). Meeting ahead of time with the interpreter/translator/ cultural informant allows you to establish mutual expectations for the joint work. You can discuss how you want the interaction to be conducted, what you can do to make it successful, and clarify any unfamiliar terms. The actual interaction with the family occurs during the intervention stage, at which time the specific goals are met, or in the case of translation, the work is produced. In the debriefing stage, you and the service provider clarify messages and discuss what worked well in the intervention and any changes that could be made to improve further interactions.

Making It Your Own

Prepare for each part of the interpretation/translation event by identifying specific expectations, outcomes, and actions. What do you need? What does the interpreter/translator need? How will you and the interpreter/translator manage confidentiality? What are the expected timelines? What payment is expected, and what is the payment process? The following checklists, amended with your input, may be helpful.

FIGURE 3.10 Interpreter Collaboration Checklist

PLANNING STAGE ✓

- Matching the clients' language/dialect with that of the interpreter
- Consideration of cultural factors that could affect interaction (e.g., respective tribes, country of origin, gender of the clients and the interpreter)
- Type of interpretation (simultaneous, sequential, meeting, conference, telephone, or face-to-face, etc.)
- Roles and expectations
- Confidentiality
- Clarification of terms
- Review pertinent documents
- Payment
- Role-play or practice interpretation process, as needed
-
-

INTERVENTION STAGE

- Seating (e.g., educator facing the parents, speaking to the parents)
- Explanation of confidentiality, roles, and purpose of meeting
- Pacing of information
- Using short sentences and avoiding idioms in order to facilitate interpretation
- Providing parents with materials for writing notes
-
-

DEBRIEFING STAGE

- Review information and seek clarification as needed
- Review the process and discuss what worked and any amendments needed for future collaboration
-
-

Adapted from American Speech-Language and Hearing Association, 2020 (FW: I noticed that another ASHA reference was updated to 2020a, so this reference would need to be updated to distinguish it from other ASHA 2020 references); Westernoff, 2019)

FIGURE 3.11 Translator Collaboration Checklist

PLANNING STAGE	

- Purpose of translation
- Technological requirements (e.g., computer fonts, programs)
- Confidentiality
- Clarification of terms
- Review pertinent documents
- Payment
- Form of language (e.g., simplified, formal)
- Time lines

INTERVENTION STAGE

DEBRIEFING STAGE

- Review information and seek clarification as needed.
- Review the process and discuss what worked and any amendments needed for future collaboration.
- If possible, have a native speaker review the translation for feedback. Seek revisions as needed.

NEXT STEP

It is now your turn to integrate the information in Chapter 3, which discusses ways to partner with parents and families to support students from culturally and linguistically diverse backgrounds. You are invited to turn to page 255 of this guide. Begin to fill in the gear entitled "Families" with your thoughts, ideas, and impressions of ways to assist students at that level. Your reading and participation in the application exercises may have prompted you to think of other initiatives, which can also be included here. Now that you have personalized this gear, you are ready to begin Chapter 4, exploring aspects specific to the student.

FIGURE 4.1   Students: Overview

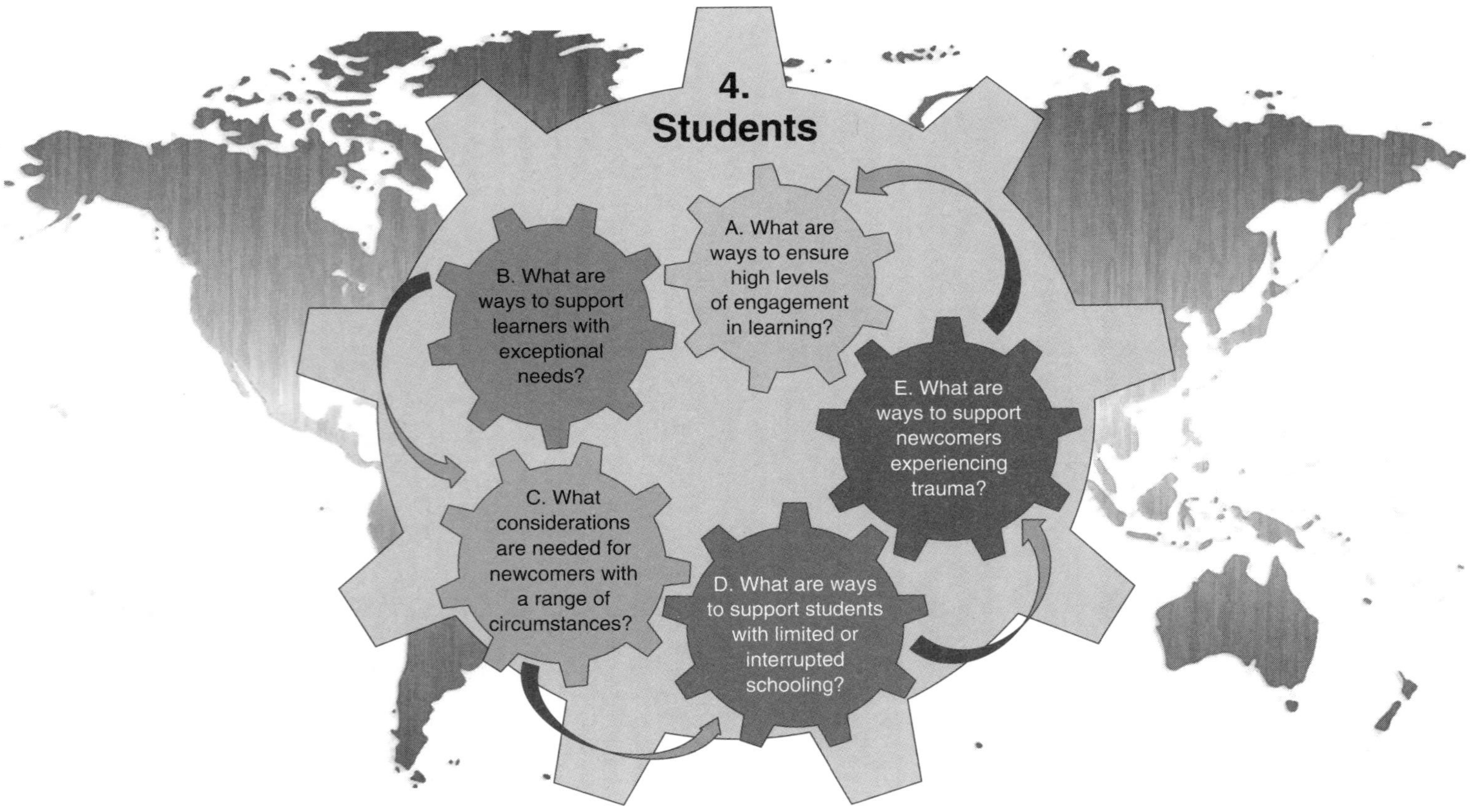

4.
Students

A. What are ways to ensure high levels of engagement in learning?

B. What are ways to support learners with exceptional needs?

C. What considerations are needed for newcomers with a range of circumstances?

D. What are ways to support students with limited or interrupted schooling?

E. What are ways to support newcomers experiencing trauma?

CHAPTER 4

Students

WHAT WE KNOW

Supporting individual English Learners, while being mindful of their strengths and needs, is at the heart of serving students, including those with vulnerabilities across a full range of unique personal circumstances. Many students respond to general strategies for ensuring that they experience high levels of engagement that build on their assets and bring personal background knowledge to the forefront as a springboard for learning. At the same time, other students arrive in our classrooms with physical, cognitive, or learning exceptionalities, which may or may not have been previously identified and/or addressed. As newcomers, they are likely to experience unfamiliar and varying needs as they adjust to the realities of their new environment, language, and education system. Still other newcomers experience vulnerability due to the fact that their previous education in another language or country does not align with that of their new age-level peers. Finally, untold other English Learners arrive in classrooms having endured unrevealed trauma, still reeling from its impact on their young psyches. Recognizing and responsively meeting all students' challenges with thoughtfulness, a sense of urgency, and advocacy is the collaborative charge of classroom educators and all other professionals in the school context.

Many competing demands vie for the attention of English Learners in our classrooms. Learning a new language and culture, adjusting to unfamiliar geography and climate, problem-solving family concerns, navigating a new social milieu, and many additional challenges consume students' personal resources needed for learning at school. Bearing this in mind, educators can select specific materials to support students. Seeing themselves reflected in classroom materials encourages student interest and engagement in the active learning process that promotes reading achievement and academic language development. Literacy engagement itself is a strong predictor of reading achievement and development of academic language (Cummins, Mirza, & Stille, 2011, 2012). Providing a safe and welcoming environment that embraces cultures and diverse backgrounds, promoting the use of prior knowledge and competencies, and implementing principles of good teaching all combine to maximize reading achievement and language development.

Every classroom will host its share of students with physical, cognitive, emotional, or learning differences that require special considerations. While some such differences might be immediately observable, others will be more subtle and only unfold over time. Some students will require the efforts of various medical and/or educational specialists to maximize their learning outcomes. The needs of others, such as gifted or talented English Learners, will only be revealed if current assessment and qualifying measures are adjusted in schools to consider the unique ways of exhibiting giftedness, without yet having achieved English language proficiency (U.S. Department of Education, 1998). The equitable inclusion of English Learners in Gifted and Talented programming calls for collaboration among English Learner/bilingual teachers, the gifted education specialist, and the general education teacher to ensure that the gifted potential of English Learners is readily recognized and served appropriately (Bianco & Harris, 2014). Such targeted and equitable inclusion in specialized programming is equally as important for students needing double support programs, such as an English Learner entitled to English language development services who is also a student with differing abilities entitled to special education services.

Like everyone else, some English Learners may present with conditions unrelated to learning a new language, such as language delay or disorder, attention deficit hyperactivity disorder, or learning disabilities. These students still continue to be English Learners. A myth persists that for such students, the home language interferes with English language development. There is no evidence that knowing or learning a home language will prevent, impede, or interfere with developing proficiency in another language (Paradis et al., 2011; U.S. Department of Health and Human Services & U.S. Department of Education, 2016b).

Children learning two languages simultaneously achieve early language milestones around the same time as monolingual children. First words are typically spoken around one year of age and two-word combinations emerge around two years of age (Paradis et al., 2011). The incidence of communication disorders in the multilingual population is estimated to be the same as that in the monolingual population, roughly around 10 percent. It is now accepted that all children have the capacity to learn more than one language (Paradis et al., 2011). Even students with identified disabilities can become multilingual to the extent of their overall difficulties (Genesee, 2016), including those with specific language impairment (Lowry, 2012a; Paradis et al., 2011), Down syndrome (Kay-Raining Bird et al., 2005), and autism spectrum disorder (Petersen, Marinova-Todd, & Mirenda, 2011). Significant research points to the notion that home language capabilities actually support additional language learning.

As described above, far from comprising a monolithic group, newcomers reflect a wide range of unique circumstances and experiences as reported in their enrolment papers and interviews. Some have instructional needs related to having received limited or interrupted schooling in their home countries.

Other students might arrive undocumented, requiring educators to be aware of contingencies and school responsibilities, while yet other students might be unaccompanied by a parent or guardian, which has specific implications for obtaining school permissions and the like. Some students experience yet another circumstance as international, fee-paying students seeking the benefit of an education abroad. Each of these divergent circumstances requires educators to respond sensitively and meaningfully in distinctly different ways.

Students who have had limited or interrupted schooling in their home countries benefit from specialized programs and services. Bajaj and Suresh (2018) describe multiple examples of the intentional practices that schools can engage in to foster mutual learning and community engagement. They assert that such a trauma-informed, curricularly responsive approach with reciprocal partnerships throughout the community is able to offer significant support for the socioemotional, academic, and material needs of immigrant and refugee youth. Rooting their highly successful programming in what is described as a "warm embrace" for refugees and immigrants and their families, an entire battery of responsive wrap-around services assist students and families to learn and thrive in their new and unfamiliar community. They note that, "When school becomes a place of support, and healing . . . students' trajectories can be significantly altered and improved" (Bajaj & Suresh, 2018, p. 96).

Becoming a trauma-informed educator requires specific knowledge and sensitivity and is an essential part of building relationships with today's students and families. For example, educators must internalize a "fundamental shift in providing support using a trauma-informed approach . . . to move from thinking 'What is wrong with you?' to considering 'What happened to you?'"(Sweeney, Filson, Kennedy, Collinson, & Gillard, 2018). In addition to the effects of war, flight, and persecution, today trauma additionally encompasses mental health issues induced by the fear of deportation of parents or family members living in communities with their school-aged children. Their deep fear of losing parents can impact academic achievement as well as behavior (Aganza, Gamboa, Medina, & Vuelvas, 2018). This thorny and untenable issue remains unresolved for educators due to its complicated nature and lack of clear guidance, often resulting in simply ignoring the irrefutable and significant short- and long-term impacts on immigrant children, including depression, anxiety, aggression, isolation, and other conditions that undermine well-being and productivity. In their suggested framework, the authors seek to empower others to support these most vulnerable young people who represent the hope of their families and members of their communities.

When working with a wide range of immigrant and refugee youth and families who have experienced severe physical trauma or emotional shock, the stress of learning their uniquely painful stories and challenges can deeply impact school professionals. Accordingly, educators with such students must develop the ability to practice self-care to preserve their own resilience and efficacy.

In this chapter, we examine the following questions.

A. What are some ways to ensure that English Learners maintain high levels of engagement in language learning?

B. What are some ways to support English Learners with exceptional needs?

C. What additional considerations are needed to help newcomers with a range of circumstances thrive and be successful?

D. What are some ways to support students with limited or interrupted formal schooling?

E. What are some ways to support newcomers who may be experiencing trauma?

FIGURE 4.2 Question A: Overview

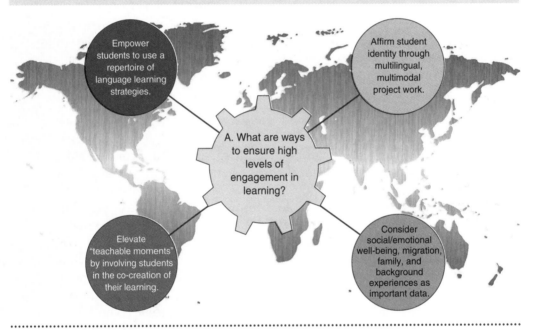

A. WHAT ARE SOME WAYS TO ENSURE THAT ENGLISH LEARNERS MAINTAIN HIGH LEVELS OF ENGAGEMENT IN LANGUAGE LEARNING?

- Powerful Practice 1: Affirm student identity through opportunities for multilingual, multimodal project work.

- Powerful Practice 2: Consider students' social/emotional well-being, migration stories, family situations, and other background experiences as important data.

- Powerful Practice 3: Elevate "teachable moments" derived from students' needs by involving them in the co-creation of their learning.

- Powerful Practice 4: Empower students to use a repertoire of language-learning strategies.

Powerful Practice 1: Affirm student identity through opportunities for multilingual, multimodal project work.

What It Might Look Like

Designing instruction for English Learners to include rich opportunities for them to express their linguistic, cultural, and social identities is a potent means of increasing student engagement at all age and grade levels. Cummins and Early (2015) contend that when learning makes connections to students' lives that result in the affirmation of their identities, literacy achievement at school is enhanced. The projects in which students creatively invest their identities, be they written texts, artwork, music, performances, or digital products, are known as identity texts (Cummins & Early, 2011). Identity text construction contributes to students' positive feelings about their identities, especially when they belong to socially marginalized communities, thereby leading to increased literacy engagement and facilitating enhanced cultural adjustment as newcomer students negotiate between multiple cultural and linguistic self-images. Such projects can also incorporate expression in both English and home languages, further adding to the boost of student identity and pride. Take a tour below of several schools and classrooms where teachers have facilitated powerful identity text work.

The Finding Home project, envisioned and brought to life by artist-educators Vanessa Barnett and Elena Soni, provided an opportunity for three hundred newly arrived refugee students from two Toronto high schools to work through their journeys of adjustment to Canada through artistic expression (Timson, 2016). The project culminated in sharing the students' work with the public at an exhibition mounted by the Aga Khan Museum, a major Toronto arts and culture institution. Students explored their relationships to their homes before arrival in Canada and to the homes they have established since coming to Canada. They created small, individual structures that contained their metaphorical visions of home, as well as written artist statements elucidating their work. Each unique artistic conception contained a combination of real and fashioned objects, drawings, backgrounds, and sometimes words or phrases in English and other languages. This project was a moving catalyst for students to confront the duality of their identities as New Canadians. Learn more about the project by viewing photos and videos at www.makingartmakingchange.com (Making Art Making Change, 2020).

TDSB elementary ESL teacher Dan Warden honoured his English Learners' first languages and rich cultural traditions, as well as their instincts as budding chefs with *The ESL Cookbook* project. Students from each of the five elementary schools that Dan supports surveyed their families to choose a favourite dish to feature in the cookbook, then researched the ingredients needed and the preparation instructions. Over a six-week period, each student cooked their recipe while the process was photographed. Using the computer program Book Creator (Tools for Schools Inc., 2011–2019), Dan's students each wrote up a two-page recipe spread in both English and their home languages, thanks to parental input and a bit of Google Translate. All the recipes were gathered together in a multilingual illustrated collection that was launched at a celebration meal showcasing the different prepared dishes. Yasmin Hasan, another Toronto ESL teacher also does a cooking unit with her English Learners. She added an additional multimodal layer by creating a video in which the students orally present their recipes, first in English and then in their home languages.

Yasmin Hasan also plans and organizes an annual English Learner group-identity book-writing project. Each year, her students engage in thinking, discussing, and writing about a particular topic. Their collected illustrated work, in both English and home languages, is published in a professional quality book and recognized with parents and community members in attendance at a group reading and celebration. Topics for Yasmin's book-writing projects have included fables from around the world in English and home languages; letters to family members in students' home countries telling of their lives in Canada; and recountings of their journeys to a new start in Canada.

TDSB ESL instructional leaders Shirley Hu, Sandra Mills-Fisher, and Ann Woomert coordinated a year-long project involving English Learners from a group of local elementary schools. Working together with the students' ESL teachers, they involved English Learners in co-creating a series of simplified readers based on their own experiences as newcomers in Canadian elementary schools. The students brainstormed aspects of their Canadian school life that were different from what they had experienced in their countries of origin. They collaboratively considered what information would be useful for newly arrived students in order to ease their transition to Canadian schools. Topics such as using an agenda book, going out for recess, packing a backpack, and touring the various facilities in the school were included. Students took photographs and co-created the text of each book with their teachers. The result is a series of highly relevant, locally published elementary newcomer readers that can be downloaded by any teacher in the district for use with newly arrived English Learners. In a similar vein, elementary ESL teacher Thursica Kovinthan Levi supported her English Learners to write informational procedural texts to help other newcomers adjust to cultural expectations in Canada. Students wrote about checking out books from the library, building a snowman, dressing for school in the winter, and a quintessentially Canadian activity: ordering a hot drink at the iconic chain restaurant Tim Horton's. Many of the student authors presented their contributions in dual-language format.

Making It Your Own

Many creative and thoughtful teachers have shared their ideas for facilitating multilingual, multimodal classroom work. Check out some of the following articles to get a glimpse of the range of imaginative project ideas that bring student voices and identities, diverse cultures, and languages into elementary and secondary classrooms. What projects might work for your teaching context, or how could they be adapted to serve your instructional setting? What new ideas for identity text projects are you inspired to bring to life with your students?

- *Improving Cohesion in Our Writing: Findings from an Identity Text Workshop with Resettled Refugee Teens* (Daniel & Eley, 2017). High school English Learners use semantic identity maps to compose texts and refine their writing skills.

- *Defining Identities through Multiliteracies: EL Teens Narrate Their Immigration Experiences as Graphic Stories* (Danzak, 2011). Florida middle school students retell their families' immigration stories in the form of comics.

- *The Multiliteracy Project.* A compilation of multimodal identity text work from Canadian classroom www.multiliteracies.ca.

- *Multiliteracies Pedagogy and Identities: Teacher and Student Voices from a Toronto Elementary School* (Giampapa, 2010). Grade 4 students from the greater Toronto area create dual-language texts and identity focused artwork, along with reflections on their use of home and second languages.

- *Amplifying Their Voices* (Roxas & Gabriel, 2016). Elementary and secondary school immigrant students in Colorado participate in a "photovoice" project where they tell their stories through a blend of photography and storytelling.

(Continued)

(Continued)

- *Inspired by Canadian Television: Ideas for Using Identity Texts and Digital Technology in the Classroom* (Sioumpas, 2016). Video projects for Grades 1 through 8 with a uniquely Canadian historical and social perspective.

- *"Imaginings": Reflections on Plurilingual Students' Creative Multimodal Works* (Stille & Prasad, 2015). A survey of multimodal and multilingual student identity texts at all grade levels showcased at an Ontario conference for ESL teachers.

- *"From the Koran and Family Guy": Expressions of Identity in English Learners' Digital Podcasts* (Wilson, Chavez, & Anders, 2012). Middle school students in Arizona use pictures, poetry, and prose to create individual identity stories in podcast format.

Powerful Practice 2: Consider students' social/emotional well-being, migration stories, family situations, and other background experiences as important data.

What It Might Look Like

Mrs. Grochala reviewed school enrolment papers and notes in an effort to get acquainted with her new student, Ying Li Hirsch. In particular, Mrs. Grochala was searching for clues that would help her to anticipate instructional implications and plan meaningful instruction for Ying Li. She knew that her student had lived in an orphanage in China until adopted at the age of three. Ying Li met Mr. and Mrs. Hirsch, an older, well-established couple, at the orphanage, as arranged by an international adoption agency. The lengthy adoption process had been completed, and Ying Li was adjusting to life with her new family in the United States. Now four years of age, she was enrolled at the local elementary school and placed in Mrs. Grochala's kindergarten program.

Mrs. Grochala wondered what early life might have been like for little Ying Li. She knew that the pre-adoption care of children could vary in the amount and quality of caregiver interaction, impacting significantly on physical, cognitive, social, linguistic, and overall developmental well-being. In addition, sometimes adoptees may be affected by adverse prenatal factors, such as alcoholism, drug abuse, and neglect (Paradis et al., 2011). Mrs. Grochala had no doubt that the love and support of her new family would help Ying Li flourish. Still, answers to important questions such as "When did Ying Li enter the orphanage and under what circumstances?" and "What was her care like in the orphanage, and how long was she there?" were unknown. Some institutions can be high-risk environments for children, impacting on interpersonal relationships and general development due to lack of stimulation and impoverished language experiences (Paradis et al., 2011).

Ying Li's adoptive family expressed questions about her language use and development. Unlike many English Learners who acquire two languages either simultaneously or sequentially, Ying Li's home language of Mandarin might have been abruptly replaced by English, an unfamiliar language. Some researchers describe this phenomenon as "a second first language" (in Paradis et al., 2011). She had other questions as well: Were Ying Li's monolingual English parents supporting her Mandarin development? How well was she now developing English language skills? Were there any indicators of language impairment based on pre-adoptive history? From her research, Mrs. Grochala learned that similar-aged adoptees, such as Ying Li, might be in need of speech-language pathology services if English language development is delayed beyond two years in the new country (Glennen, 2008). Mrs. Grochala also wondered how the family was adjusting to each other. She noticed that Ying Li was registered with both her Chinese name and her English name, Joyce. Which was the preferred name for use at school?

Mrs. Grochala gathered data from Ying Li's background to develop a student profile. She applied an English Learner lens of insight and advocacy to set out a plan to meet Ying Li's needs at school. Upon doing so, she realized that she needed more information about her young student and recognized that she might never get answers to some of the questions regarding Ying Li's pre-adoption history.

Making It Your Own

Review Figure 4.3, which invites readers to interpret Ying Li's social/emotional experiences, migration, linguistic background, and family context, to better understand and respond to her school needs. Do you have experience with internationally adopted children that could be used to enrich this activity? What other information would be helpful? What are the classroom implications of the data? Could the same type of approach be used or adapted to communicate the needs of English Learners with colleagues in your context?

FIGURE 4.3 Student Data and Implications

CATEGORY	STUDENT DATA	INTERPRETATION AND POSSIBLE CLASSROOM IMPLICATIONS
Name	Chinese Name: Ying Li English Name: Joyce Li Hirsch (Legal name on official records)	• Child's preferred name at school: Ying • Be sure to use student's preferred name with attention to correct pronunciation.
Age	4 years old	• Being the same age as classmates might not indicate the same level of social development.
Grade	Kindergarten	• Being placed in the same grade as similar-age peers often has more to do with the student's age than their content knowledge or language development.
Country of origin	China Pre-orphanage information:_____ Lived in an orphanage from _____ until adopted at 3 years of age.	• Overall development may be more at risk related to longer time spent in an orphanage.
First language experience and development	Mandarin Mandarin development is _____ Current level of exposure to Mandarin is _____ Loss of Mandarin skills receptively _____ and expressively _____	• Consult parents for their plan regarding maintenance and development of Mandarin. • Consider locating children's books with pictures that depict familiar cultural subjects and themes for school and home use.
English language experience and development	First introduced to English on a consistent basis upon being adopted at 3 years of age.	• Monitor English language development and possible need for speech-language pathology services closely for the first two years in case pre-adoption conditions significantly impacted linguistic development.
English language proficiency levels based on district test at enrollment	Level 1 in listening, speaking, reading, and writing.	• Prioritize social vocabulary development and peer interactions. • Incorporate routine playtime with English-speaking peers; consider assigning a "buddy for the day."
Family background	International adoption: English-speaking mother and father and two siblings, ages 7 and 9	• Supportive family, monolingual English. • Older siblings may likely facilitate speedy oral development in English. • Does the family have a bilingual language plan to include Mandarin? • In need of regular interaction with same-aged peers to ensure development of social language and vocabulary.

POWERFUL PRACTICES FOR SUPPORTING ENGLISH LEARNERS

CATEGORY	STUDENT DATA	INTERPRETATION AND POSSIBLE CLASSROOM IMPLICATIONS
Parental concerns	Parents are concerned about bonding with their newly adopted daughter. They express high academic expectations and an interest in tutoring.	• Resources for parents of internationally adopted children. • Organizations for connecting with other families with Chinese children.
Previous schooling	No previous formal schooling, since school begins at 6 years of age in China.	• Socializing with other children and learning classroom norms, similar to many non-English Learners in kindergarten, will be priorities.
Literacy background	Has not yet received formal instruction in literacy in Chinese. Exposure to literacy in Chinese _____ Is literacy in Chinese a parental priority?	• Support parental plan regarding literacy in Chinese (e.g., Read books together encouraging Ling to offer words in Mandarin. Does she know a song in Mandarin?). • Emphasize oral contextualized vocabulary development in English to promote comprehension to start. • Introduce appropriate books and story books for school and at home reading.
Parent connections	Teachers and parents have established a relationship with the special education team, the ESOL teacher, principal, and classroom teacher.	• Staff will collaborate to design appropriate instruction based on the student's literacy development needs while keeping parents informed. • Encourage parents to consult with the collaborative team—e.g., ESOL teacher, reading teacher, speech language pathologist—for general language development suggestions.

(Adapted from Fairbairn & Jones-Vo, 2016, pp. 76–88)

Powerful Practice 3: Elevate "teachable moments" derived from students' needs by involving them in the co-creation of their learning.

What It Might Look Like

Mrs. Colbert's high school students were facing an adverse and challenging environment outside of her ESL classroom. Unfortunately, harassment of English Learners by other students was on the rise. Some of the other students were hurling insults and exhorting the students to "go back where they came from." Sadly, this theme is one that calls for constant revisiting and response. By capitalizing on student concerns, Mrs. Colbert developed her most memorable lesson, later known as The Peace Project, following a soul-searching meeting with her English Learners, many of whom were diverse survivors of immigration, separation, and trauma.

Thirty-two diverse English Learners met in Mrs. Colbert's classroom. The students shared personal stories of how they were treated by fellow students and how unsafe they felt in the building. In some cases, this treatment brought up past emotions of trauma endured in the past. They wanted to stop the hurtful words and taunts and to feel safer and better understood. Under Mrs. Colbert's gentle guidance, the English Learners came to realize that their classmates did not really know or understand them or their backgrounds. She suggested that if the English Learners could tell their own stories to their classmates in a safe environment, there was a possibility of a breakthrough. In Mrs. Colbert's experience, when people know each other as human beings and develop personal relationships, bonds are likely to form. Her English Learners were motivated into action and agreed to share their personal stories as a way to build peaceful relationships with their peers.

With the principal's support, the English Learners asked teachers for an invitation into other classrooms to share their presentation of personal stories and experiences in a carefully planned format which the students had researched and prepared. They gathered photos of their previous homes, artifacts from their religions, practiced folk dances to be demonstrated, and devised how to break the ice at the beginning of their presentation. They wrote a script that infused culture and humor, leading to more serious content when English Learners shared moving descriptions of their personal and private experiences. During Black History Month alone, the principal arranged for English Learners to present their Peace Project program to 266 eighth-grade students over a two-day period.

During one of the impactful presentations, following the ice-breaking, dancing, and building of background, sitting in the semicircle alternating English Learners with non-English Learner hosts, one of the student presenters reached into his pocket and produced a pair of gray socks. He spoke haltingly, "These are the socks my father was wearing when they killed him. And then they made me bury him." Even Mrs. Colbert did not know of this tragedy and was amazed that her student had publicly shared it. Encouraged by their peer's example, other students followed, opening up with their previously unexpressed heart-wrenching experiences of violence and grief. Gasps were heard and tears began to flow, not only from English Learners, but from the other students and their teachers in the audience as well. Mrs. Colbert learned over and over through The Peace Project that when her students and their hosts were able to forge relationships with each other through this shared experience; they were softened and more empathetic toward one another.

At the conclusion of each session, the hosting teachers helped distribute feedback sheets that elicited reflections from the audience of non-English Learner classmates. Giving students time to sift and process their thoughts and to formulate meaningful conclusions in their feedback comprised an essential feature of The Peace Project. The feedback forms were returned to

Mrs. Colbert within forty-eight hours. Reading each honest reflection, humbled by the obvious deeper level of thinking that was prompted by those in attendance, truly meeting their English Learner peers on a personal level for the first time, Mrs. Colbert wept. Significant feedback from one eighth-grade audience included the following comments:

- I had a lot more respect for refugees in general. I also learned that many of the widespread rumors about refugees aren't true.

- After The Peace Project, I was amazed. I know some of their culture and some of their aching memories. I do have a different viewpoint.

- I think that if we keep having the ESL students come and talk that they will make an impact on our lives. Because of them, I'm going to try hard to not be rude or racist to anybody.

- I felt they were brave and courageous people for sharing their stories.

- I never knew refugees suffered so much.

- I will never say anything negative about a refugee again.

In retrospect, Mrs. Colbert realized that developing a project based on student needs, involvement, and voice, while incorporating academic requirements, were key elements to the success of The Peace Project. Only after the school year concluded was she able to dissect the lesson to truly understand why it was such an empowering and reciprocal experience for both her English Learners and their non-English Learner classmates. In her own reflection, Mrs. Colbert noted the following essential elements of the project, which would set criteria for future endeavors originating from students' needs:

A successful learning project for English Learners

1. Responds to students' authentic concerns and interests

2. Includes student voices, identities, and leadership

3. Requires communication across domains (listening, speaking, reading, writing)

4. Hones verbal presentation skills and organizational skills

5. Expects and supports participation by interested English Learners regardless of language levels

6. Situates English Learners in the midst of authentic experiences with peers

7. Recognizes that English Learners have valuable contributions to make

8. Develops academic skills (e.g., public speaking, conducting research, citing examples)

9. Requires written feedback answering specific reflective questions following each session within forty-eight hours from non-English Learner participants

10. Processes experiences and feedback with English Learners, identifies the impact in the school (e.g., increases English Learners' standing among peers, enhances self-esteem, improves relationships), and informs future actions

Making It Your Own

What are some of the troublesome concerns your students have shared about their lives in a new school, community, and country? What changes might they want to see? What changes would serve the school community well? How might you use the essential elements identified by Mrs. Colbert to create a reciprocal learning experience that addresses your students' needs, incorporates their voices, and also satisfies academic requirements?

Powerful Practice 4: Empower students to use a repertoire of language-learning strategies.

What It Might Look Like

English Learners must be equipped with the skills and tools to control and direct their own learning, so that they can continue to independently expand their language and content knowledge, both inside and outside of the ESL classroom. A wide range of language-learning strategies, many that teachers are already familiar with, are part of a student's full repertoire of learning strategies. When teachers design instruction on language-learning strategies, they provide English Learners with the capacity to accomplish their classroom-learning goals, increase positive and productive interactions with their peers, and build useful skills for learning that can last a lifetime. Researchers in the area of language-learning strategies concur that integrating explicit strategy instruction into language and content teaching is an important way to help students to build their English proficiency, manage their cognitive processes, and develop their autonomy in learning (Oxford et al., 2014).

In her seminal teacher's guide for learning-strategy instruction, Chamot (2009) categorized language-learning strategies into several broad areas: metacognitive, cognitive, and social/affective strategies. Chamot's model, known as CALLA (Cognitive Academic Language Learning Approach), is a five-phase instructional framework for language learners based on cognitive theory and research. A crucial component of CALLA is integration of language and content learning with explicit learning-strategy instruction. Research has shown that teaching of learning strategies to language learners has a positive impact on the development of oral and written English proficiency (Gunning & Oxford, 2014; Olson et al., 2012). Let's take a brief look at each of Chamot's sets of learning strategies and examine several examples of how strategy instruction for English Learners can be operationalized in the classroom.

Metacognitive strategies are actions and mental operations that learners use to influence their own overall learning process. Examples of metacognitive strategies in language learning would include setting learning goals for a lesson or task; planning, organizing, and managing learning; and engaging in self-assessment to evaluate progress in learning. Strategies to monitor comprehension, such as asking for clarification or repetition when the learner is experiencing difficulty understanding, also form part of the language learner's metacognitive strategy repertoire. Altering communication to get a message across by saying things in a different way (circumlocution) and using gestures and concrete objects to convey meaning are other examples of metacognitive strategies (See Figure 4.4 and Figure 4.6).

Diaz (2015) found that training elementary English Learners in metacognitive strategies for word learning contributed positively to their vocabulary improvement. Students in Grades 3 through 5 participated in a series of dynamic lessons in which the teacher modelled metacognitive strategies, such as articulating goals for learning and setting objectives for the number of words they might be able to assimilate into their vocabulary from a lesson. They also practiced word-learning strategies, like making associations between a new vocabulary item and a word already known and using imagery to fix the meaning of a new word in memory. Subsequent to the training, the students kept learning journals in which they recorded their use of various strategies and how they facilitated learning new words, affording them a bird's eye view to reflect on their own language-learning process.

In a study with ESL students in a Grade 6 classroom in the province of Quebec, students received instruction on strategy use to improve their English oral proficiency (Gunning & Oxford, 2014). These students also kept a log of the learning strategies they employed during various group oral tasks. Students improved their understanding of a range of communication strategies, such as effectively stalling for time while they processed their answer, expressing what they wanted to say in a different way when they didn't know specific words, and making inferences from the context of the conversation. The strategy training and log maintenance had a positive impact on the development of students' oral English competence, and the students were also able to demonstrate transfer of the strategies to new learning tasks.

FIGURE 4.4   What Strategies Did You Use in Your Talk Today?

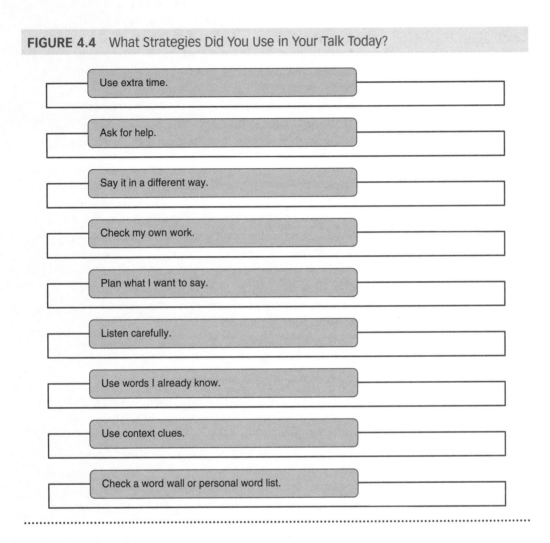

Cognitive strategies include actions involving critical thinking about how to accomplish various learning tasks in a particular skill area. Use of context clues, knowledge of English parts of speech, word roots and affixes, and cognates are all examples of cognitive strategies students can employ to help learn new vocabulary. Strategies such as predicting and asking questions before reading a text and using note-taking scaffolds during reading exemplify cognitive strategies for reading tasks.

Word-learning strategies are a highly productive subset of cognitive tools for students to use to expand vocabulary knowledge. Graves, Schneider, and Ringstaff (2017) have developed a clearly delineated program for vocabulary strategy learning that they call the "WLS Curriculum." Within the timeframe of a semester for middle school students, the program covers strategies focusing on the following: using prefixes and suffixes to understand new words; employing context clues to guess intelligently about an unknown word; using knowledge about parts of speech to grow vocabulary; and consulting dictionaries, peers, and teachers when other strategies don't bear fruit. The instructional technique moves from strategy training, where the teacher uses a think-aloud process with a shared text to model how to understand new words, to a gradual release of responsibility for students to use the strategy with teacher support, in pairs and finally in individual work. Consult the Graves, Schneider, and Ringstaff article for a step-by-step process on how to teach each strategy, as well as examples of classroom posters on learning strategy use.

Olson et al. (2012, 2017) carried out a large study on a strategy instruction intervention with students in Grades 6 through 12 in a California school district. In a far-reaching approach to integrating learning-strategy instruction, the district's English teachers took a lengthy professional development course in providing instruction in language-learning strategies and were given a cognitive strategies toolkit. One technique that formed an integral part of the intervention to keep strategy use firmly in the forefront of students' minds was the district-wide use of strategy bookmarks printed with sentence starters illustrating various cognitive learning strategies. Students who participated in the intervention classes improved their academic reading and writing skills through exposure to this cognitive strategies approach.

Social/affective strategies are ones in which relationships between the learner and others take center stage. Social strategies—such as cooperating in a group, coaching peers, and using appropriate expressions for participating in group discussions—enable English Learners to more effectively take advantage of the opportunities for language use inherent in conversation and discussion with their peers and teachers. Affective strategies—such as engaging in positive self-talk and controlling anxiety in language-learning situations—support learners to feel more relaxed and confident and to view themselves as capable participants in a second-language context.

Boisvert and Rao (2014) employed a procedure usually used with special education learners to create situations for positive image and self-talk among high school English Learners with limited or interrupted formal schooling in Hawaii. They used the technique of video self-modeling (VSM) to raise learners' levels of self-confidence and bolster their positive self-talk about their English language skills. VSM allows learners to view themselves successfully performing a language task that they may not yet be able to do independently at their current level of proficiency. It's done by first having the teacher record a self-modelling video reading a chosen text aloud. The student listens to the model, practices along with the recorded model, and finally video-records the reading in unison with the recorded model. The teacher's recorded voice is then edited out to produce the final video, which features the student performing the task competently and independently. Students thus perform tasks at a higher level than their current proficiency by reading together with the teacher model. They then view the final video of themselves accomplishing a task they would not yet have been able to do on their own. The VSM procedure helps instill in students the belief that they can achieve success at language tasks that have so far been out of their reach, giving a boost to their self-concept as language learners and their resulting self-talk.

FIGURE 4.5 Positive Self-Talk Affirmations

INSTEAD OF . . .	THINK . . .
I don't know.	I don't know how to do this *yet!*
I can't do it.	I can try again.
I'm not good at it.	I'll do better <u>if</u> I keep trying.
I'm not sure.	I'm going to try again!
I don't want to.	I need some thinking time.
I'll never be able to do that.	If I try again, it will be easier.
I'm not good at anything.	I can do something **AMAZING!!**
NO!	I can do this!!
This is impossible.	I can do hard things.

Making It Your Own

Are you currently incorporating a language-learning strategy instruction with English Learners in your classroom? Take a look at Figure 4.6 as a starting point for some of the learning strategies you may want to consider integrating into your teaching. Add your own list of strategies to the chart. While too many strategies exist overall to integrate on a daily basis, knowing the value and benefits of language-learning strategies helps educators to select carefully, using their artistry in teaching to choose those that are best suited for their unique learners and specific tasks.

If you'd like to take a deep dive into the area of language-learning strategies, get hold of a copy of landmark strategies author Rebecca Oxford's latest book, *Teaching and Researching Language Learning Strategies: Self-Regulation in Context* (2017), which includes recently updated research and practical applications in the field of learning strategies in the language-learning classroom.

FIGURE 4.6 Language-Learning Strategies

I model/facilitate/teach these learning strategies with English Learners:

→ Setting learning goals for a lesson or task

→ Planning the steps of a learning task

→ Monitoring comprehension of oral language

→ Asking for clarification when something is not understood

→ Gaining extra time to process language by stalling or using conversation fillers

→ Keeping a log or journal of learning strategies

→ Using context clues to determine the meaning of unknown words

→ Using gestures or objects to clarify meaning to others

→ Using parts of speech and word roots to learn and expand vocabulary

→ Engaging in positive self-talk about their capabilities as learners

→ Coaching each other in learning a language skill

→

→

→

FIGURE 4.7 Question B: Overview

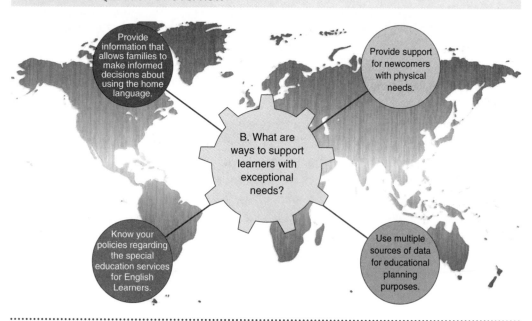

B. WHAT ARE SOME WAYS TO SUPPORT ENGLISH LEARNERS WITH EXCEPTIONAL NEEDS?

- Powerful Practice 1: Provide accommodations and support for newcomers with physical needs.

- Powerful Practice 2: Use multiple sources of data to best interpret student needs for educational planning purposes.

- Powerful Practice 3: Know your jurisdiction's policies regarding the provision of special education services to English Learners.

- Powerful Practice 4: Provide information that allows families of students with special education needs to make informed decisions regarding the use of the home language.

Powerful Practice 1: Provide accommodations and support for newcomers with physical needs.

What It Might Look Like

Approximately 15 percent of the world's population has some form of disability (World Health Organization, 2018). There are many different types of disabilities, ranging in severity from mild to severe and from temporary to permanent conditions. Some disabilities are more easily seen while others are less visible. Disabilities can be congenital (from birth) or acquired during one's lifetime due to illness, accident, or trauma. To complicate matters, some disabilities can precipitate secondary or tertiary conditions. For example, a young child with a significant hearing loss during the early language-learning years may experience a delay in speaking. Children with language delays are at risk for learning disabilities and challenges in acquiring reading and writing skills (Nelson, Nygren, Walker, & Panoscha, 2006; Paradis et al., 2011). Co-morbidity of conditions, when two separate conditions tend to occur together, can add further complications.

The notion of what constitutes a disability is socially constructed and varies from culture to culture. A condition that might be seen as disabling in one society may not even be recognized as problematic in another. Further, North American understanding of disabilities has been undergoing considerable change. The first significant change is the recognition that a medical condition in and of itself is not necessarily disabling but rather "disability arises from the interaction of health conditions with contextual factors—environmental and personal" (World Health Organization & The World Bank, 2011, p. 5). Functionality and participation are involved in determining a disability. The person who wears glasses to improve vision is not generally seen as having a disability because they can be highly functional and involved in society. A person with a condition that necessitates the use of a wheelchair might enjoy more mobility on the paved streets of North America than they might in bush areas of Africa. As such, the wheelchair user in Africa might be perceived as a greater disability. The second significant change is an expanding view of who the disability experts are. There is growing recognition of the individual as an expert on the impact of their condition, with a focus on strengths and abilities rather than on medical or intervention personnel as all-knowing (Holland & Nelson, 2014; Sánchez-López & Young, 2018).

As classrooms become more inclusive, it is likely that educators will have students with a range of familiar and unfamiliar physical conditions, whether they were born in North America or beyond. Health and physical conditions may have combinations of complex medical, rehabilitation, and educational implications. For example, in some countries, students with obvious physical disabilities may have been prohibited from attending school due to stigma, poverty, access barriers, or discriminatory practices. These students might arrive in classrooms without any prior formal education in addition to the original physical condition. Some students may not have had the diagnostic, medical, or rehabilitation services that might have improved their functionality and access to opportunities.

There is huge variability regarding access to professional rehabilitation services both within North America and in other countries. Rehabilitation services, designed to improve functionality, can be crucial for some to participate in education, employment, and social realms (World Health Organization & The World Bank, 2011). For example, a student with excessive drooling due to a neuromotor condition might not have been seen by professionals (e.g., dentist, ear-nose-and-throat specialist) or received saliva management services (e.g., behavioral strategies, medication, Botox injections). Excessive drooling in the classroom is a hygiene and health concern, with potential social and medical consequences.

Students with physical disabilities may need rehabilitation services in order to gain access to the curriculum. Some disabilities have seemingly accessible solutions, such as hearing aids or other amplification devices for those with hearing loss. However, factors such as funding, stigma, and compliance in caring for and wearing hearing aids may impede successful rehabilitation outcomes. Other conditions are quite complex and require a team of professionals. For example, a newly arrived student with cerebral palsy and a seizure disorder may require the involvement of a neurologist, occupational therapist, physiotherapist, dentist, speech-language pathologist, audiologist, ophthalmologist, and psychologist in order to clearly identify their needs. It can be stressful and confusing for families and students to be seen by so many different professionals, often in a variety of hospitals, clinics, and treatment centers, and sometimes undergoing invasive, embarrassing, uncomfortable, or painful procedures. These students may also miss many school days, as they attend assessment and intervention appointments. Understandably, children who are struggling with medical conditions might not be in optimal learning mode when they are at school (Hamayan et al., 2007), and families who must focus on their child's health concerns might be less available to focus on education (Staehr Fenner, 2014).

Educators can collaborate with students and their families to learn about what they feel is needed to participate more fully in school and community. Sometimes the slightest change can yield the greatest results. For example, the student with gross motor challenges might realize that they would benefit from a head start to get dressed in all the layers of clothing needed to participate in a cold winter recess. Providing an extra five minutes to prepare for the outdoors might help that student continue to enjoy and develop social interactions with peers while providing sufficient time for a much needed nutrition and movement break.

Educators might also need to connect and collaborate with professionals beyond the walls of their schools in order to further their understanding of their students' physical needs. Sharing information between agencies will require that the appropriate forms documenting parental consents to disclose information are completed and distributed and that the required information is obtained and reviewed for educational planning purposes or released accordingly. It does very little good if a consent to release information form is signed and sitting in a student's school file instead of having been forwarded to the appropriate service provider. It therefore makes good sense to be familiar with your jurisdiction's process and paperwork regarding the release of confidential information. Having a designated person who can manage and document the incoming and outgoing paperwork would also be helpful.

The information received from outside agencies should be used to inform educational planning and may result in accommodations that help students better participate in the classroom or school community. For example, a student with significant oral motor struggles that impede clarity of speech may be prescribed an augmentative communication system such as an iPad with communication software allowing voice output. That student may need classmates to wait patiently while preparing an outgoing message. Some teacher training may also be needed in order to have the device used to its full potential for communication and academic purposes.

Making It Your Own

Do you know the specialties of the different service providers in outside agencies who work with children? Here is a list of specialists whose work can impact student functioning in the class. Test your knowledge by identifying their respective areas of expertise and then identify by name some professionals associated with your school district who accept referrals in your area.

Audiologist _____

Optometrist _____

Ophthalmologist _____

Occupational Therapist _____

Physiotherapist _____

Speech-Language Pathologist _____

Neurologist _____

Developmental Pediatrician _____

Pediatrician _____

Otolaryngologist _____

Endocrinologist _____

Psychiatrist _____

Psychologist _____

Social Worker _____

Others _____

Powerful Practice 2: Use multiple sources of data to best interpret student needs for educational planning purposes.

Mr. Bouchard was reviewing the progress of his Grade 3 students. Most were coming along nicely, some with a variety of educational supports. One student, Jae-Ho, however, was not achieving as hoped. He had been attending the same North American school since first grade, arriving with one year of preschool experience in Korea. He spoke Korean as a first language, which was the primary language of the home. He had been receiving support for English Learners and seemed to be working diligently, but his literacy development was still much below grade level. Mr. Bouchard was wondering if Jae-Ho might be an exceptional learner as well as a learner of English as an additional language.

Mr. Bouchard recognized that diagnosing any exceptionality was beyond his scope of practice and that he would need to involve the school team to further understand and respond to Jae-Ho's educational needs. He looked forward to collaborating interprofessionally with colleagues in English as a second language and special education, knowing that a comprehensive approach merging the expertise of all educators would serve Jae-Ho well (Sánchez-López & Young, 2018). For his part, he wanted to gather pertinent information that would be useful in team discussions. To triangulate the data, he began to collect information from a variety of sources (e.g., parents, other teachers) and in a variety of formats (e.g., interviews, relevant documents, test performance, writing portfolio, class observations, school projects, assessment results) so that he could share details about Jae-Ho's background and academic progress. He organized his information into three main categories: background information, observations, and intervention and progress.

Background Information: Mr. Bouchard knew that some red flags regarding learning challenges might be found in Jae-Ho's early development, so he set out to gather the necessary background information. Details about the student's early language and overall development, behavioral considerations, family history, and information on how Jae-Ho manages in Korean (oral and written) would be key. Mr. Bouchard decided to obtain the necessary details by conducting a parent interview using *The Alberta Language Development Questionnaire* (Child English as a Second Language Resource Centre, 2020), a free, evidence-based survey. As a non-Korean speaker, this questionnaire would allow Mr. Bouchard to probe key areas with the family and then score parental responses in order to determine if there was any evidence of delay or difficulties in the home language. This could be one important piece of information to consider at a team meeting. He also requested that parents share copies of report cards from Korea and Jae-Ho's current Korean Heritage Class, which he had translated to English for ease of review. Finally, he asked parents to contribute any assessments from specialists outside of the school board (e.g., medical, hearing, developmental pediatrician) to share with the team.

Observations: Mr. Bouchard wanted to be better able to describe Jae-Ho's English language functioning in the class, so he began observing his communication and interactions more carefully. He noticed that Jae-Ho had great difficulty marking plurality (e.g., dogs, cats). He often omitted 's' when talking about many of the same items (e.g., "There were many dog at the park"). Mr. Bouchard wondered if this might be an interference error, so he consulted a guidebook (Swan & Smith, 2001) and found out that indeed, the error was common for Korean speakers learning English as an additional language. He made sure to reference this detail as such. He also noticed Jae-Ho had difficulty following instructions that had more than two steps. Longer, more complex directions had to be chunked and sequentially highlighted so that Jae-Ho could achieve success in completion. As the demands of the Grade 3 program were increasing, he worried about how many complicated instructions were unconsciously delivered and probably unsupported for his hard-working, struggling student. Mr. Bouchard vowed to pay closer attention to his verbal instructions and to request more insight about this observation from the teacher of English as a second language.

Intervention and Progress: Mr. Bouchard knew that it would be important to review the educational interventions that had been provided, as well as Jae-Ho's progress. His school used a response to intervention model (RTI), focusing on problem-solving and progress monitoring to identify and respond to learning needs (Collier, 2011; Echevarria, Richards-Tutor, & Vogt, 2015; Staehr Fenner, 2014). Jae-Ho had been receiving Tier I interventions, which focused on culturally and linguistically informed pedagogy delivered to the entire class. Over the years, Mr. Bouchard had been increasingly adopting a translanguaging perspective in his class and was using his growing library of dual-language books creatively. He had also received classroom consultation and mentoring from the school speech-language pathologist regarding focused vocabulary development and was using new strategies to improve word comprehension and use for all students in his lessons. This form of professional development was not available in all districts, and he was pleased that he had the opportunity for such meaningful collaboration. Jae-Ho was also receiving targeted support for learners of English as an additional language, a Tier II intervention. Fortunately, the teacher of English as a second language was part of the school team and would be available to share observations and results in a small group setting. Mr. Bouchard gathered some writing samples and reading test scores to bring to the meeting. He saw that Jae-Ho's reading was far below grade level and wondered if he might be in need of Tier III interventions, the most intensive level of support (Sánchez-López & Young, 2018). He also wondered if it was unrealistic to expect Jae-Ho to be reading at grade level. Mr. Bouchard appreciated that he could turn to the team for targeted programming suggestions, knowing that a referral for assessment could provide much more information than a diagnosis and ticket straight to a special education placement.

Making It Your Own

Each jurisdiction uses professional support staff in different ways, often governed by rules and guidelines. Are you familiar with the process and procedures of your area? Have there been recent changes in protocol? How are English Learners supported by your special education specialists? How are special education needs supported by your English as a second language specialist? Review the article *Using RTI Effectively With English Language Learners* by Zacarian (2011) (https://www.colorincolorado.org/article/rti-and-english-language-learners). Based on your understanding, identify the interventions at your school according to tiers.

Tier I: _____

_____

_____

Tier II: _____

_____

_____

Tier III: _____

_____

_____

Powerful Practice 3: Know your jurisdiction's policies regarding the provision of special education services to English Learners.

What It Might Look Like

Often, the literature on English Learners and special education seems to place significant emphasis on the misrepresentation of students in special education programs rather than on efforts to provide culturally, linguistically, and educationally appropriate identification of special needs. Attention to the overrepresentation of English Learners in special education (e.g., Collier, 2011; Hamayan et al., 2007) and underrepresentation of students with a gifted profile (Collier, 2011) has resulted in some well-meaning educators trying to shield students from any special education services whatsoever. Some have proclaimed that psycho-educational and speech-language pathology assessments could not be completed for up to seven years, despite the lack of substantive research, rationale, policy, or legislation. This myth persists in various locations, even though there have been efforts to educate to the contrary. Sometimes, English Learners suspected of having learning issues have been overlooked for assessment and intervention, as all their challenges are attributed to learning English as an additional language. As such, students who actually require assistance may be denied the benefits of early intervention, a beneficial protocol afforded to native English speakers.

It is generally accepted that English language proficiency is not a prerequisite to giftedness. However, the often sparse identification of English Learners who are gifted and talented has also come under scrutiny. Staehr Fenner (2014) notes that the talents of English Learners are not necessarily manifested in ways that are easily observable to educators. When talents of English Learners indicate signs of giftedness, complications related to measuring and documenting them may preclude English Learner qualification. English Learners benefit from an expanded repertoire of additional considerations to standardized testing for qualification in gifted and talented programming. Project GOTCHA (Galaxies of Thinking and Creative Heights of Achievement) outlines characteristics of gifted and talented English Learners (Iowa Department of Education, 2008; Staehr Fenner, 2014) and suggestions for changes in practices that promote equitable participation (e.g., Iowa Department of Education, 2008; Serrano & Scardina, Sousa, 2011). Sánchez-López (2017) explains that in schools with systems that are culturally and linguistically responsive, the representation of English Learners with educational exceptionalities is on par with that of native English speakers.

Educators and parents certainly want English Learners from diverse backgrounds who also present with exceptional learning needs to receive culturally and linguistically informed educational assessment and intervention in a timely manner, so they can achieve the best possible outcomes. There are systemic special education processes that have been undergoing transformations to be more culturally and linguistically responsive, such as access to services, qualifications of service providers, roles of service providers, and assessment.

Many educators are expecting special education assessments to answer the question, "Does the student qualify for ESL or special education services?" Implied here is that a student falls into either one group or the other, and therefore, interventions will either be allocated from special education or ESL funding. This question can be misleading. An English Learner with special education needs does not stop being a learner of English as an additional language (Sánchez-López & Young, 2018), and this student is entitled to special education services (e.g., U.S. Department of Education). It is now widely recognized that such students are eligible for services from both streams of education (e.g., Ontario Ministry of Education, 2008; Rosenthal, 2016; U.S. Department of Justice and U.S. Department of Education, 2015).

The qualifications of professionals who can complete assessments used to identify special learning needs has also been an issue of concern. Associations whose mandate is to protect the public by regulating professional practices have developed guidelines for working with clients from culturally and linguistically diverse backgrounds (e.g., American Psychological Association, 2020; American Speech-Language and Hearing Association, 1997–2020b; College of Audiologists and Speech-Language Pathologists of Ontario, 2016; Crago & Westernoff, 1997). In some districts, it is required or strongly recommended that assessments and interventions be completed by bilingual professionals, who often require certification. In other areas, such personnel do not exist for all the languages spoken by all students. To achieve equity in assessment and intervention, the combined expertise of a professional and native speaker of the home language are therefore required. Professionals are embracing their responsibility to provide culturally and linguistically appropriate services, even when the service provider does not share the same culture or language background as the student.

The roles and responsibilities of professional support staff vary greatly between districts and school boards. Some areas require professional assessments in order to "qualify" for services. Others have fallen into an assessment-to-placement pattern. Those systems with the most flexibility regarding the roles of support staff might be in a better position to provide culturally, linguistically, and educationally responsive services in a timely manner. In Ontario, for example, the need for involvement from professional support staff is determined by an interprofessional team that includes the parents, teacher, ESL teacher, administration, special educators, psychologist, speech-language pathologist, and social worker. The team reviews the student's needs and makes recommendations regarding programming and/or involvement from one or more professional support staff. Professional support staff would then be able to provide services at any tier of intervention, as needed. For example, a psychologist might collaborate with a teacher to conduct bilingual class lessons on mindfulness (Tier I), or a social worker and speech-language pathologist might use a dual-language book on how to be a good friend as the starting point to teach social communication skills to a small group of students (Tier II). Of course, there might still be students who could best benefit from special education support and/or placement (Tier III).

There are many different types of special education needs, varying in severity, occurring in isolation or as part of a greater diagnosis, changing across developmental stages, with both common and idiosyncratic features, and requiring various degrees of academic accommodations (Sánchez-López & Young, 2018). Criteria for identification of special educational needs varies from district to district. Professionals in special education have been seeking ways to improve diagnostic and intervention services for students and families from culturally and linguistically diverse backgrounds. They too have been adopting and incorporating culturally and linguistically informed practices. Rather than relying exclusively on test scores, practices have expanded to include formal and informal measures, the triangulation of data from multiple assessment sources (Collier, 2011; Staehr Fenner, 2014), and implementation of culturally and linguistically informed responses to intervention protocols (Sánchez-López & Young, 2018). Where feasible, assessments in the home language can also be completed (Staehr Fenner, 2014), for example, as is done in over 40 different languages for students in Toronto.

Making It Your Own

View the YouTube video *Bilingualism and SLI (DLD)* at https://www.youtube.com/watch?v=g7Sj_uRV7S4 (Raising Awareness of Language Learning Impairments, 2013), in which speech-language pathologists discuss bilingualism in students who have specific language impairment. Identify those key points that you already know and those that are new to you. Does any of the discussion remind you of a student in your classroom? What might be your next steps for that student?

Powerful Practice 4: Provide information that allows families of students with special education needs to make informed decisions regarding the use of the home language.

Personal and professional knowledge about bilingual children and disabilities varies greatly. Some professionals and families still subscribe to the "limited capacity hypothesis," that children with disabilities have an extra burden when raised bilingually, a belief unsupported by research (Paradis et al., 2011). We know now that bilingualism is attainable for children with disabilities (Paradis et al., 2011; Sánchez-López & Young, 2018) and that students won't automatically attain a high level of proficiency in English if deprived of their home language. Professionals may need to share this information with parents, so they can make informed decisions regarding family language planning. Nevertheless, some parents may feel that it is still in their child's best interest to switch to exclusive use of English, and in this case, professionals have a responsibility to support parents' informed decisions, even when in disagreement. Alternatively, some parents may be aware that their child with a disability can learn two languages but might be working with a professional who is not yet informed on the attainability of bilingualism for exceptional children. Parents must be brave and persistent advocates when working with a professional who continues to make recommendations that perpetuate the limited capacity hypothesis.

Informed professionals understand that interventions can (and usually should) be provided in dual languages (Kohnert, Yim, Nett, Kan, & Duran, 2005; Sánchez-López & Young, 2018), even when the service provider does not speak the language. The good news is that research supports the efficacy of parents as intervenors who play an important role in their child's language development (Ijalba, 2015; Lowry, 2012b). In the field of speech-language pathology, for example, parents and caregivers are often coached to complete language interventions in naturalistic settings, with successful results. After all, families spend more time with their children, communicating in multiple settings, than could a clinician in an office. This provides more opportunity for interventions throughout the day, as well as carryover of skills into different communication environments and with different communication partners. Some very successful intervention programs for children with language impairment and autism spectrum disorder are based entirely on the premise of parents as agents of change. The Hanen Centre in Toronto, Ontario, Canada, provides world-wide training to speech-language pathologists who are then certified to offer parent training programs to improve the oral language and social communication skills of young children. Their website offers excellent information, free tips, and suggestions, and some of their family-friendly resources for purchase are available from The Hanen Centre (2016) in multiple languages at www.hanen.org.

In addition to coaching parents to use the home language in communication interventions, home languages and cultures can be incorporated into intervention materials. Many schools and school districts are incorporating indigenous stories, culture, and art into beautiful sensory paths for students and staff to enjoy. Sensory paths are colorful activity guides along school hallways, corridors, and courtyards, inviting participants to hop, skip, balance, crawl, push-up, and more. Sensory paths provide increased physical activity and are found to be helpful for students who need a little physical movement to help them focus and concentrate (Donato, 2020). Puntledge Park Elementary School in Courtenay, British Columbia, provides an interesting video of the magic of a sensory path (Puntledge Park Sensory Path, 2019, https://youtu.be/EEWH08NZOJA).

Another example of bringing home languages into play in intervention material is the utilization of a visual schedule. The use of a visual schedule has gained in popularity, with impressive outcomes. Initially developed for students who have autism spectrum disorder, the visual calendar can also benefit other students, including English Learners. You might recognize first hand the benefits of having a calendar to outline your day, especially if you have ever felt lost after misplacing one. A visual schedule uses pictures of activities with accompanying words that are cut into cards and placed in a linear sequence to show the activities of the day. The sequence is reviewed at the beginning of the day and after each activity, at which time the completed activity card would be removed. A visual schedule allows all students to

FIGURE 4.8 Dual-Language Visual Schedule

醒来 wake up	洗脸 wash face	刷牙 brush teeth
吃早餐 eat breakfast	穿衣服 get dressed	走路去学校 walk to school
去上课 go to class	走路回家 walk home	吃零食 eat snack

Graphics by https://www.istockphoto.com/portfolio/leremy and https://www.istockphoto.com/portfolio/rhoon

understand the sequence of activities in a day as well as any changes in scheduling. This in turn can impact student behaviors, increase independence, improve comprehension, and reduce anxiety. Visual schedules can be used in the classroom (with the entire class or individual students) and at home. In Figure 4.8, pictures for a visual schedule to be used by parents in the home have been prepared electronically. The English text was written and translated into "simplified Chinese," a print form easily accessible to most readers of Chinese, using Google Translate. The Chinese translation was then reviewed and corrected by a native speaker for accuracy, before being shared with the family.

Making It Your Own

Staehr Fenner (2014) explains the need for educators to provide scaffolded advocacy for English Learners and their families. This means providing more support when needed and decreased support as the family is increasingly more comfortable to self-advocate. How can you support families' growing ability to advocate for themselves based on facts?

Parents may feel more confident in their decision to raise their child with a disability bilingually if they were familiar with and could share a handy, informative, comprehensible, and user-friendly article summarizing supporting research. Lowry (2012a) from the Hanen Centre in Toronto provides a synthesis of the research and rationale for continuing to use the home language in the article *Can children with language impairments learn two languages?* (http://www.hanen.org/Helpful-Info/Articles/Can-children-with-language-impairments-learn-two-l.aspx). This article can be used for discussion with parents and then, in turn, by parents with service providers.

Parents who are well informed are better prepared to make decisions. There are a variety of topics to support parents in their advocacy efforts, such as educational rights and responsibilities, structure and function of the school and/or district or board, extracurricular activities, grading and report card policies, parental involvement in advisory committees, and so forth (Staehr Fenner, 2014). What questions might your families need answered? Find out the topics that would best serve the parents at your school. How can you help them access the information they need to advocate for themselves and their families?

FIGURE 4.9 Question C: Overview

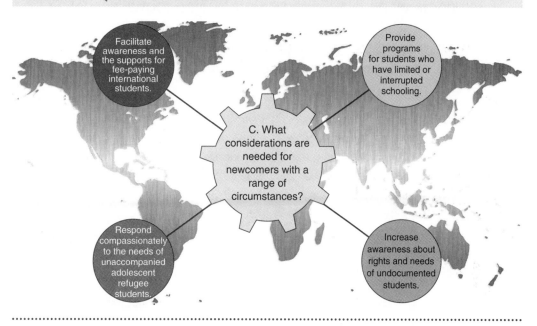

C. WHAT ADDITIONAL CONSIDERATIONS ARE NEEDED TO HELP NEWCOMERS WITH A RANGE OF CIRCUMSTANCES THRIVE AND BE SUCCESSFUL?

- Powerful Practice 1: Provide additional programs for students who have limited or interrupted formal schooling.

- Powerful Practice 2: Increase awareness about the rights and needs of undocumented students in your context.

- Powerful Practice 3: Respond compassionately to the needs of unaccompanied adolescent refugee students.

- Powerful Practice 4: Facilitate awareness and the creation of supports for fee-paying international students.

Powerful Practice 1: Provide additional programs for students who have limited or interrupted formal schooling.

Global unrest leading to dislocation and migration throughout the world continues to grow. Current worldwide political events mean that an increasing number of young people are arriving at our schools without enjoying the basic childhood human right to attend school regularly. Students with limited or interrupted formal schooling (often referred to as SLIFE) or limited prior schooling (LPS) come to North America from all over the world. They may have continuous or intermittent gaps of several years in their formal schooling, or they may have never had the opportunity to attend school at all. These young people's missed years of schooling may result from a wide range of causes and contributing factors: situations of war, conflict and displacement, political oppression and institutionalized persecution, stays in refugee camps lasting for many years, natural disasters and famine, lack of economic resources, and continuous migrant living as a means of support or survival.

The needs of learners with limited prior schooling extend well beyond academics. These young people and their families may be waiting on tenterhooks for the resolution of asylum claims; they may be experiencing reunification with family members after a lengthy period of separation and hardship; they may have lost close relatives as a result of war and flight; they may be existing under tight financial restrictions in their new country; and they may be going through a period of grief and mourning for their former lives as they adjust to a new country where they never expected their future would take them.

Regardless of the background circumstances of English Learners with limited or interrupted prior schooling, the all-embracing asset-based vision for these students must be that they are capable of achieving success at school when provided with the appropriate supports and opportunities. Young people who have had gaps in their formal schooling will most certainly have acquired a range of knowledge and skills that go well beyond academic learning. They will have strengths in areas as diverse as improvisation, problem-solving, and decision-making; experience and knowledge of areas such as agriculture, handiwork, and repair; an abundant reserve of survival skills, coping mechanisms, and resiliency; and often oral proficiency in several languages. All of these skills and experiences are assets for teachers to recognize, value, and build upon in the classroom. When we acknowledge and enhance their background strengths and skills, we pave the way for students who have not been in school regularly to see themselves as integral members of the school community who can begin to forge a path forward via school learning to reach their goals.

The TDSB proudly offers one of the largest specialized programs in North America to support students with limited or interrupted formal schooling. Known as LEAP (Literacy Enrichment Academic Program), this intensive upgrading initiative is offered to newcomers with limited or interrupted formal schooling, beginning in the fourth grade through to high school. (For snapshots of a few of the Syrian newcomer high school students in LEAP, take a look at the article by Ali Amad [2017] "The War Kids," from *Toronto Life Magazine* [https://torontolife.com/city/the-war-kids/].) This exemplary program provides a road map for other schools and districts needing guidance on how to best serve similar students in their schools. Where there is a critical mass of learners in one school, a program is located on site; in other cases, a magnet program is established at a central site that draws learners from many schools in the surrounding geographical area. LEAP class teachers are selected specifically for the program, have access to curriculum specially designed and written for the needs of students who have missed years of formal schooling, and regularly attend professional learning sessions focused on the needs of learners with gaps in their prior schooling. LEAP includes specific classes in English as a second language, English literacy development, and mathematics fundamentals, as well as sheltered academic courses, such as social studies and science. Integration with non-LEAP peers in some mainstream classes right from the beginning of the program is also a feature of LEAP. Social and emotional support for students as they adjust to the school environment, as well as guidance counselling with a view to helping students plan for their future goals, are all components of the program. At the time of writing, the TDSB was offering LEAP classes in twenty elementary and middle schools and seventeen high schools across the city of Toronto, in some locations with multiple classrooms. A high investment of teaching staff is dedicated to LEAP, with classes containing no more than thirteen to fourteen students. Students may remain in the program for up to three full years as they build their English proficiency, literacy skills, and academic knowledge, before transitioning to a mainstream academic program appropriate to their individual goals. The goal for students is to make gains of two grade levels in each academic year of study in the program. (For a full journalistic account of the TDSB's LEAP initiative in Canada's national newspaper, see Jill Mahoney's article [2007] "Leaping over educational adversity," in *The Globe and Mail*, [https://www.theglobeandmail.com/news/national/leaping-over-educational-adversity/article699294/].)

Yonas, a twelve-year-old boy from Eritrea, arrived in Toronto with his mother and six-year-old sister. The family had been granted refugee status to come to Canada after a three-year stay at a refugee camp in Ethiopia, where there was no opportunity to attend formal school. Yonas was welcomed at his local elementary school. He was placed in a half-day ESL reception program for newcomer students and integrated into an age-appropriate mainstream Grade 6 classroom for the remainder of the day. Over the succeeding weeks, Yonas's ESL teacher, Ms. O'Brien, worked with him on a number of initial placement tests, determining that he was at the very beginning stages of learning English as an additional language. She asked him to write a first language text in Tigrinya, his home language, in response to a prompt that has been translated into many home languages, including his own. Ms. O'Brien ascertained that Yonas's mastery of written Tigrinya was minimal. He had difficulty reading the simple writing prompt as well as in producing more than a few words in response. Yonas's initial math assessments showed that he was not working at a level in mathematics on par with his Grade 6 age peers. His academic mathematics proficiency was currently at the Grade 2 level. Ms. O'Brien's experience alerted her to the possibility that Yonas may have missed years of formal schooling before coming to Canada, and she requested a first language assessment for him in Tigrinya. A trained bilingual education worker came to the school to work informally with Yonas for several hours on literacy and numeracy tasks in Tigrinya. The first language assessment report indicated that Yonas's literacy skills in his home language, as well as his math skills, were years behind his age peers. As part of the first language assessment, the education worker also had a telephone conversation with Yonas's mother, in which she explained that Yonas did not attend school for several years when they lived in the refugee camp in Ethiopia.

Ms. O'Brien met with Yonas's mother and learned that in addition to having missed the opportunity to attend school during his stay at the refugee camp, Yonas also did not go to school regularly in their tumultuous year in Eritrea before the family fled from the country to Ethiopia. Ms. O'Brien compiled a portfolio for Yonas, including all his various assessment results, as well as examples of ongoing work from his ESL and mainstream classes, and submitted an application to the centrally appointed LEAP assessment and resource teacher Ms. Taylor for Yonas to be considered as a candidate for LEAP. The central LEAP assessment teacher reviewed Yonas's file and agreed that he would be an excellent candidate for the program since his limited academic knowledge and literacy skills were due to restricted educational opportunity before coming to Canada. Ms. Taylor consulted her district-wide school enrolment lists and found a spot available in a middle school LEAP classroom several miles from Yonas's local school. Ms. O'Brien, along with Yonas's mainstream classroom teacher and school principal, met with Yonas and his mother, who brought along a friend who translated from English to Tigrinya. They discussed how the smaller, specialized LEAP class could help Yonas close the academic gap with his age peers and explained that he would be eligible for bussing from his home school to the magnet LEAP school. Yonas and his mother signed a student/parent contract pledging that he would do his best to attend regularly, put forward his best behaviour and effort, and behave respectfully towards his peers and teachers in the LEAP classroom and host school. The following week, Yonas boarded the school bus and began his new school experience in LEAP where he joined a class-room community of ten other students of Grade 6 and 7 age, coming origi-nally from Syria, Mexico, Hungary, Afghanistan, and Sudan.

Making It Your Own

Have you worked with students who have arrived with minimal or interrupted schooling in your context? What have the prior experiences of these students been like? Does your jurisdiction have a specialized program to support such students in bridging the gap with their age-peers? How do students with limited prior schooling access support in your school or district?

What components of an overall initiative to serve students with limited or interrupted formal schooling are available in your jurisdiction? What com-ponents could be added? What changes would you make to tailor the pro-gram to the particular needs of your community? Use Figure 4.10 to further reflect on service delivery achievements and needs for these students.

FIGURE 4.10   Needs of SLIFE

SUPPORTS FOR STUDENTS WITH LIMITED OR INTERRUPTED FORMAL EDUCATION (SLIFE)	CURRENTLY AVAILABLE/ON THE "WISH LIST"	POSSIBLE ADAPTATIONS
Teachers trained to anticipate personal and academic needs of SLIFE		
Initial English and mathematics assessment materials geared for SLIFE		
Assessments for SLIFE available in home languages		
Specialized programs for SLIFE in • Grades 4–5 • Middle school • High school Program includes • ESL • Dual-language instruction • Mathematics • Content classes		
Contract or pledge for students and parents		

(Continued)

FIGURE 4.10 (Continued)

SUPPORTS FOR STUDENTS WITH LIMITED OR INTERRUPTED FORMAL EDUCATION (SLIFE)	CURRENTLY AVAILABLE/ON THE "WISH LIST"	POSSIBLE ADAPTATIONS
Central educator/coordinator dedicated to SLIFE		
Learning resources for unique needs of SLIFE		
Regular monitoring of SLIFE academic progress		
Professional learning for teachers of SLIFE		
Links with community partners to support SLIFE		

Powerful Practice 2: Increase awareness about the rights and needs of undocumented students in your context.

"I come to you as one of our country's eleven million undocumented immigrants, many of us Americans at heart, but without the right papers to show for it. . . . Too often we are treated as abstractions, subjects of debate rather than individuals with families, hopes, fears, and dreams."

(Jose Antonio Vargas, 2018, p. 179–180)

What It Might Look Like

Since the 1982 U.S. Supreme Court decision *Plyler v. Doe* (American Immigration Council, 2016), public school teachers are assured the responsibility of teaching all of the students in their classrooms, regardless of a student's immigration status. This landmark ruling grants a free public education to all students. As a result, teachers have been often uninformed or unaware of a student's lack of documentation. More recently, U.S. government policies have aggressively aimed to reduce the number of undocumented immigrants in the United States.

In Ontario, Canada, children also have the legal right to attend school, even though they or their parents may be undocumented. An unfortunate incident occurred in Ontario in 2006 when two undocumented siblings were removed from their school and used as bait to entice their parents to come forward in order to deport the entire family. Spurred by the desire to create a sanctuary space for undocumented students in light of this incident, the TDSB passed a policy called "Students Without Legal Immigration Status" (Toronto District School Board, 2007), colloquially referred to as "Don't Ask, Don't Tell," which allows all students access to a free public education. However, some critics maintain that the policy still creates exclusionary obstacles for undocumented students and their families (Villegas, 2018). Certainly, educators in both the United States and Canada (and perhaps other countries as well) need to be informed about the rights of students in their care in the case of a legal emergency.

This became abundantly clear in the following true scenario (the names of places and individuals have been changed). Two school buses of elementary children along with their teachers and chaperones departed the small rural town of Bear Creek, United States, taking a three-hour bus trip for the annual fourth-grade field trip to the state capitol. Teachers and their charges traditionally looked forward to this end-of-year celebration. They planned to arrive home that night, following their tour of the capitol building and grounds, meeting legislators, and enjoying a picnic lunch.

It was late afternoon, and the bus driver was preparing to drive back to Bear Creek. Mrs. Bui, a teacher and chaperone, checked her phone and noticed that she had received a text. The principal, Mr. Phomvisay, had sent a long, confusing message that alarmed her. Mr. Phomvisay reported that U.S. Immigration and Customs Enforcement (ICE) had conducted a raid at the local meat processing plant in Bear Creek. He said that ICE had arrested four hundred workers who were now being sorted into groups. Many mothers and fathers of the young children on the school bus were being processed for deportation. Dozens of children would find no one at home and no one to pick them up when the bus returned to Bear Creek. The raid constituted one of the largest ever carried out by the federal government. Horrified, Mrs. Bui gathered other teachers and chaperones to share the devastating news. What should they do now? What should they communicate to the children? Who would take care of the children after they arrived back in Bear Creek? Did the school have to cooperate with ICE? In what ways could they best keep the children safe?

Making It Your Own

Unforeseen events pose many questions and issues that educators have not often had to consider in the past. What are the legal rights and responsibilities of your students? Has your school shared the appropriate procedures in your district? What are your legal rights and responsibilities as their temporary guardian? How would you interact with immigration officials if they came directly into your classroom or onto your bus? What do you need to know and do in a legal emergency in order to keep yourself and your students safe? What do you need to know and do for the overall well-being of your students who might be citizens but whose parents might be undocumented?

Familiarize yourself with legal or local policies that your school district or school board has adopted. Create a well-prepared action plan for your school, and ensure that all staff is informed. Explore the resources that follow for ideas that can support educators in responding to safety issues for students in appropriate ways.

- National Association of Secondary School Principals. (2020): *Undocumented Students*. https://www.nassp.org/policy-advocacy-center/nassp-position-statements/undocumented-students/

- American Federation of Teachers. *Immigration*. https://www.aft.org/our-community/immigration

- ¡Colorín colorado! (2018) *Immigrant Students' Legal Rights: An Overview*. https://www.colorincolorado.org/immigration/guide/rights

- U.S. Department of Education. (2015): *Resource Guide: Supporting Undocumented Youth: A Guide for Success in Secondary and Postsecondary Settings*. https://www2.ed.gov/about/overview/focus/supporting-undocumented-youth.pdf

- Community Legal Education Ontario. (2020): *Helping parents without immigration status get their children into school*. https://www.cleo.on.ca/en/publications/rightschool

- Mary Wiens. (2018): *York first Canadian university to give "Dreamers" a chance at a degree*. https://www.cbc.ca/news/canada/toronto/canadian-dreamers-york-university-1.4488252

Powerful Practice 3: Respond compassionately to the needs of unaccompanied adolescent refugee students.

What It Might Look Like

Surrounded by the chaos and danger of a life-threatening situation, some young people fleeing from war, violence, and political instability become separated from their parents and families. Sometimes the separation happens suddenly in the midst of attack or flight. At other times, a deliberate decision is made in concert with family that a youth will set out on a journey to a safe country independent of family members. Families never undertake these steps lightly, and they are always taken in the hope that the family will be safely reunited one day in the future.

When youth in such situations arrive in Canada and the United States, they are often referred to as unaccompanied refugee minors (URM). The United Nations High Commission for Refugees defines URMs as "youth who are separated from both parents and are not being cared for by an adult who, by law or custom, is responsible to do so" (Franco, 2018, p. 552). Since 2014, it is estimated that more than one hundred thousand such unaccompanied refugee children and youth have entered the United States (Booi et al., 2016). In Canada, although the total is much smaller, unaccompanied minors claiming refugee status have been arriving in increasing numbers in the past several years (Walji, 2018).

Unaccompanied refugee minors might be living with older refugee youth who have come of age; they might be staying in refugee hostels or shelters; they might be living with foster families; or if they are nearing the age of majority, they might be living on their own in accommodations in the community. These vulnerable youth confront homesickness and disorientation, concern about the situations of their family members, fear of deportation, and worry over how they will financially maintain themselves. The distress experienced by unaccompanied refugee youth can be viewed as a tripartite accumulation of difficulty (Franco, 2018). Exposure to traumatic events, such as civil unrest, gang violence or military bombardment before their flight; the danger and strain of their journey to a safe country; and finally the stresses of a new life alone in an unfamiliar culture compose the three vertices of this triangle of difficulty. All these experiences in addition to the separation from or loss of their parents and other close family members put unaccompanied refugee minors at a much greater risk for depression, post traumatic stress disorder, and other mental health issues (Keles, Friborg, Idsoe, Sirin, & Oppedal, 2018; Tello, Castellon, Aguilar, & Sawyer, 2017). Jacobs (2018) points out that unaccompanied refugee youth are also particularly vulnerable to human trafficking operations during their dangerous and sometimes lengthy journeys to a safe country.

Sixteen-year-old Ameer fled Yemen after his family decided that he needed to leave for his own physical safety. He travelled to the United States and bought a bus ticket to Buffalo, New York, where he walked across the bridge to Canada and claimed refugee status at the Canadian border. Border officials directed him to a shelter for unaccompanied refugee youth in Toronto, where he lived for more than a year. Staff and volunteers at the shelter assisted Ameer in registering for school, finding part time work, and connecting with legal representation for his refugee claim. Ameer's guidance counsellor and some of his teachers were made aware of his challenging situation as soon as he registered at his secondary school. The school social worker met with Ameer regularly to provide support, including introducing him to a peer mentor at school, as well as a referral to an Arabic-speaking psychiatrist for counselling to alleviate the effects of the traumatic events he had witnessed in his home country and the stresses of adjusting to life on his own in Canada. The social worker also encouraged Ameer's participation on the school badminton team.

"Even though these children and adolescents walk thousands of miles and face hostile situations on their journey . . . they choose this path instead of the alternative, which for many, if they stay in their home country, is certain death."

(Tello et al., 2017, p. 371)

Making It Your Own

Watch the National Film Board of Canada documentary *Everybody's Children*, available for viewing at https://www.nfb.ca/film/everybodys_children/ (Delmos, 2008). Director Monika Delmos's film records a year in the life of two unaccompanied teenage refugees who have left their countries to make a new life in Canada. The film follows the youth as they face the normal pressures of teenage life while simultaneously undergoing the refugee claim process. Delmos underscores how the guidance and support of mentors and peers can make a significant difference in the lives of these young people.

View the interactive animated video presentation from the United Nations High Commissioner for Refugees, Canada (2020) *Children on the Run*, at https://www.unhcr.ca/children-on-the-run-experience/. This video experience allows children to interact with the story of Luis, an adolescent who is forced to flee from violence and poverty in Central America. How could you use this short film to help your students learn about and build empathy and understanding for the plight of unaccompanied refugee minors?

Do you know the backgrounds of your students? Kreuzer (2016) suggests ways to inform your thinking about getting started with newcomer students as well as those who might be unaccompanied. What difficulties can you anticipate that unaccompanied youth might experience when beginning to attend school? Does your school have a student handbook? How can educators ensure that the unique considerations of unaccompanied adolescent and minor students are included and considered in school guidance?

Powerful Practice 4: Facilitate awareness and the creation of supports for fee-paying adolescent international students.

In our globalized world, more students and their families are considering the advantages that study in an English-speaking country can convey to young people by increasing their linguistic and cultural competence and enhancing their future career options. Nowadays, for a growing number of international students, study abroad begins not in the university years but rather in high school, paving the way for increasing proficiency in English, obtaining a local graduation diploma, and gaining acceptance to a North American university. Especially in Canada, during the past decade there has been a surge in the number of international students coming to study at both high school and university levels (International Consultants for Education and Fairs, 2020; Semotiuk, 2018).

School districts across Canada and the United States offer programs of study for international high school students, both short-term study for English learning and cultural interchange, as well as long-term programs leading to high school graduation. Many mutual benefits accrue from welcoming international students to North American high schools. International students gain access to quality secondary school education, develop fluency in English, and experience living in a new culture and society. Local students gain valuable insights into other cultures and languages, expanding their perspective of the world and their intercultural competence without leaving home. And of course there are also definite economic benefits that emanate from thousands of international students who pay tuition, homestay fees, and other associated living expenses in the host country.

However, in contrast to immigrant adolescent students, who are most often living together with family members in their new country, the majority of international adolescent high school students are living abroad without their families for the first time in their lives as they settle in with a non-related homestay host family. If the student is under the age of eighteen, a custodianship with a local adult must be arranged and agreed to by parents for their child's safety and protection. In some instances, the custodian may be a homestay adult or a local friend or relative of the student, but in many other cases, the custodian is an international student agent who acts as custodian for a number of local teenaged international students. For the first time in their lives, many of these teenaged international students find themselves far from home and everything that is familiar. They may face challenges posed by feelings of homesickness, culture shock, language barriers, loneliness, and managing their finances on their own. Some adolescent international students are ambivalent about coming to study in another country and may feel they have been pressured to do so by their families. And according to some Canadian research, international students may feel more isolated than any other group of newcomer students (Wong, Homma, Johnson, & Saewye, 2010), living abroad and apart from their parents and social support systems for an extended period of time. Given the large financial investment their families are making in their education, international students may also experience feelings of guilt for not meeting parental and family expectations with regards to their grades or the speed of their progress (Kim & Okazaki, 2014).

While the majority of high school international students make a successful transition to life in Canada, some may experience isolation, depression, medical issues, or conflicts with their homestay host family (Xing, 2018). These students may be less inclined to seek assistance from counsellors or other helping professionals due to differing cultural perspectives on mental health issues (Popadiuk, 2010), as well as a lack of information on how to access help.

While school districts have always put an emphasis on providing high quality educational programs for adolescent international students, there has been much less focus on providing psycho-social supports to respond to the unique needs of this group of English Learners. School districts should focus on providing a welcoming and supportive environment for international students in order to promote their well-being, academic achievement, and intercultural learning. In addition to excellent programs for learning English and content, international high school students need advance preparation before leaving home, thorough and caring orientation once they arrive, local peer and teacher support, and rich opportunities to meet and share with their fellow students to help them integrate academically and socially. Research reveals the importance of creating strong social networks in the successful integration of international students (Kim & Okazaki, 2014; Popadiuk, 2010). Setting and maintaining standards for safe and caring homestays should also be part of a comprehensive strategy for international students. Wong, Homma, Johnson, and Saewye (2010) advocate for training for homestay families on maintaining a nurturing atmosphere that supports adolescent students separated from their parents. Regular check-ins with a counsellor or public health nurse and ongoing digital or phone conferences between the host family, the student, and his or her biological family are other initiatives that could be put in place to monitor the well-being of unaccompanied adolescent international students (Wong, Homma, Johnson, & Saewye, 2010).

An increasing number of international secondary students coming to Canada are choosing Ottawa, Canada's capital, as a base for their studies. In 2019, Tu Vuong, a secondary school ESL teacher in Ottawa, founded *Lead Your Way*, a unique ten-day orientation program for newly arrived international students in the weeks leading up to the start of their first Canadian school year. The program, open to international students in Grades 9 through 12, gives students a foundation in Canadian culture, an orientation to high school life in Canada, and a chance to begin to navigate their way around their new host city. English classes, field trips to sites around the city, and orientation activities are all part of this innovative two-week program that sets international students up for success by helping them to feel more empowered as they enter a new high school in a new country.

Many school districts also have a cadre of multilingual guidance counsellors who are dedicated to supporting the needs of the international students in their district. These counsellors have training and experience to understand the unique needs of international students and know that they will require support to adjust to life in a new country. They meet regularly with students, offering a listening ear and problem-solving strategies for a range of issues. Providing information about diploma requirements and career education pathways, as well as about admission and application to Canadian and American universities, is another aspect of the counsellor's role. Counsellors also organize social activities and cultural exchange workshops for international students in their district.

At the TDSB, a summer school orientation program has been started for incoming high school international students. High school diploma credits are offered in ESL and in ESL-sheltered content courses, such as family studies, career education, and drama. Each course has a specially designed curriculum for international students that integrates language and content learning with multiple opportunities for orientation to Canadian school life and culture.

Making It Your Own

Does your school or district offer programs for international fee-paying adolescents? Have you had personal experience teaching such students? Share your experiences with this group of students with your colleagues in an international student working group format. What are some of the social and psychological supports that could be put in place to support this vulnerable group of English language learners in your district?

FIGURE 4.11   Question D: Overview

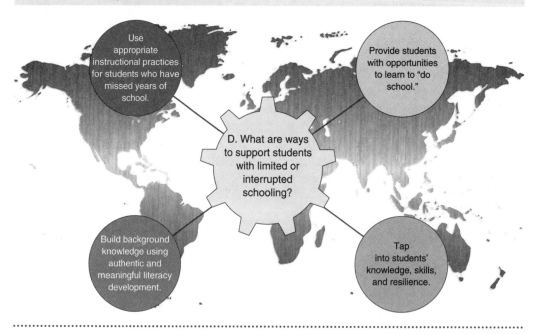

D. WHAT ARE SOME WAYS TO SUPPORT STUDENTS WITH LIMITED OR INTERRUPTED FORMAL SCHOOLING?

- Powerful Practice 1: Provide students with many opportunities to learn to "do school."

- Powerful Practice 2: Tap into the rich base of knowledge and skills and the core of resilience that students bring with them.

- Powerful Practice 3: Build students' background knowledge by surrounding them with authentic and meaningful literacy development.

- Powerful Practice 4: Use instructional practices that are appropriate for students who have missed years of school and may not have age-appropriate first language literacy skills.

Powerful Practice 1: Provide students with many opportunities to learn to "do school."

Ms. Alvarez is a highly experienced middle school teacher for *LEAP*, the TDSB's intensive special program for students who arrive with gaps in their prior schooling experience. After many years of teaching a class of LEAP students in Grades 6 through 8, she recognizes and appreciates that the students in her continuous enrolment class will arrive with diverse amounts of experience in formal schooling situations. Over the years, Ms. Alvarez has worked with some children who have never had the opportunity to attend school at all, as well as with other students who started their primary school careers in peacetime only to be torn away as their families fled to escape war, bombardments, or ethnic persecution. She's had students who never had the chance to learn to read in their home language and others who did learn to read but weren't able to keep up or advance their literacy skills over their long stay in a refugee camp. Some of Ms. Alvarez's students attended elementary school regularly in their countries of origin, but with classes containing upwards of 70 pupils, there were never enough books or writing materials for every student. Other students attended school in their home countries but had to be absent from classes for extended periods of time to help their parents during planting or harvest season, or perhaps they missed long periods of formal school learning due to natural disasters like earthquakes or hurricanes. A few of her students have been part of migrant worker families who spend part of the year in Canada and part in Mexico, according to the season. Ms. Alvarez knows that her students are eager to get back to childhood's most important work of school learning, but they often don't have the prior experience with the myriad of school contexts and situations that North American students almost unconsciously absorb during their continuous years in the classroom. Keeping this in mind, Ms. Alvarez is careful not to make assumptions about the background schooling experiences her students may have had and to build in plenty of repeat opportunities for them to become conversant with North American school life—or what we might call learning to "do school."

The rhythm of a typical middle school day makes a good starting point in supporting students with limited prior schooling to build familiarity and confidence with the classroom routines and procedures that their peers have already internalized through years of formal school attendance. Ms. Alvarez posts a large daily schedule prominently in her LEAP classroom, with all the times for each academic subject learning block, recess and lunch period, and rotational subjects like physical education, art, music, and school library visits. Her schedule is illustrated throughout with laminated picture cards depicting each subject and activity, and she also encourages students to write the words for various subjects and events in their home languages and add them to the schedule chart.

Earlier in her career teaching students with gaps in their prior formal schooling, Ms. Alvarez noticed that many students would ask to use the washroom at all kinds of inopportune moments, which would disrupt the rhythm of classroom learning. She has learned that it's worth spending some time to engage each new group of students in a group brainstorm of "good" versus "bad" times to ask to be excused to use the washroom, and this co-created class chart also hangs in her classroom to remind students of the protocols around washroom breaks.

FIGURE 4.12   Good Time to Use the Washroom

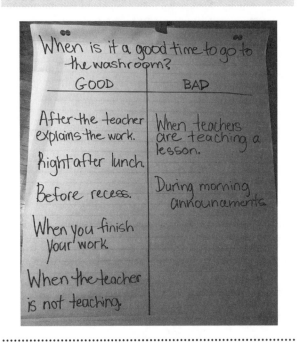

Ms. Alvarez takes extra time to ensure that her students can build the background knowledge needed to understand and participate in schoolwide initiatives and extracurricular events. For example, her whole school is involved in the annual "Jump Rope for Heart" event, a fundraising drive for the local Heart and Stroke Association. Ms. Alvarez didn't assume that all her students had prior experiences with jumping rope, so she crafted a brief experiential learning task about this physical fitness activity that allowed her students to discover more about jumping rope and to thus feel more prepared and confident about participating in the fundraiser with their school peers.

Ms. Alvarez has developed learning activities and visuals to provide her students with background knowledge relating to procedures and routines around the school. For example, she organizes a discussion about physical education classes, including the various sports students will do, what they should wear for gym class, as well as rules for appropriate and safe behaviour in the gym. She will often accompany her students to their first period of physical education to serve as an additional supportive presence for her newly arrived students as they become accustomed to gym routines. She spends time sensitively introducing her students to fire drill and lock down procedures and makes sure the students and their parents understand that the school must be notified when students are absent. Ms. Alvarez takes attendance every day and often asks her students to answer with a word in their home language that relates to one of the day's learning objectives in subjects like science, math, or geography.

Although already in middle school, some of Ms. Alvarez's students haven't ever had the opportunity to use computers or other digital devices before arriving at school in Canada. Some of them haven't had the chance to play with childhood games and toys such as jigsaw puzzles, Lego blocks, coloured pencils or markers, and modelling clay. Ms. Alvarez seeks out age-appropriate puzzles and games for her classroom and designs age-appropriate activities linked to her subject curriculum expectations to provide her students with many opportunities to make up for lost time with computers, puzzles, building blocks, and art materials. Her students enjoy learning with technology and manipulatives and, in this way, can build up a repertoire of shared experiences with their peers who have had the good fortune of uninterrupted schooling.

Customary school learning behaviors and tasks comprise another set of concepts that teachers should reinforce with students who have not had continuous opportunities for prior formal schooling. Maintaining an agenda book, recording and tracking homework assignments, keeping a notebook divided by subjects, and storing books and supplies for easy retrieval are some of the academic habits that children who have always been granted the right to continuous schooling have assimilated. Teachers working with students who have limited or interrupted formal schooling need to do a lot of modelling of these behaviors, and check in regularly with students to make sure they are getting the hang of organizing school learning tasks. Group project work is another learning task that may be new for students with limited prior formal schooling and often even for students with continuous schooling background from countries where group learning is not standard pedagogical practice. Assigning and rotating group roles, with lots of initial modelling, can be a way to help students become accustomed to learning in group settings.

In a touching example of "learning how to do school," Qudsia Ahmad, a secondary school LEAP teacher, noticed that most of her students had never before participated in a school graduation ceremony. She wants them to have the feelings of pride and accomplishment that come with achieving an academic milestone, and so she arranges for each teenager who is transitioning from the LEAP class to mainstream high school courses to be photographed in a cap and gown and receive a graduation certificate for completion of the LEAP program. Qudsia's classroom displays an ever-growing gallery of proud LEAP graduates beaming down from the walls.

Survey a typical school day and list all the different classes, events and activities that take place in your specific school and classroom. What strategies might you use to help students who may be unfamiliar with these routines (charts and visuals, modelling, class discussions, peer mentors, role play, etc.)? If you are currently working with students who have interrupted or limited formal schooling, what academic tasks and organization strategies do they find most challenging? What approaches might you employ to give your students familiarity and practice with these academic tasks?

Powerful Practice 2: Tap into the rich base of knowledge and skills and the core of resilience that students bring with them.

What It Might Look Like

Students with limited or interrupted formal schooling come to our schools with a depth of rich background experiences that have informed their lives as well as provided them with the resilience to overcome many challenges. Secondary school LEAP teacher Sally Bliss wanted to harness these strengths and diverse funds of knowledge that her adolescent students with limited or interrupted formal schooling brought with them from lived experiences around the world. Sally conceived of a multipronged unit of study that would allow students to leverage the knowledge and skills that they brought to her classroom. Her unit, The Growing Project, involved students in using their prior knowledge about growing food on family farms or gardening plots. The high school where Sally teaches contains a large room with a glassed-in atrium that is used as a greenhouse. Before beginning the project, her students first discussed which plants would grow best and have the most bountiful yield in the greenhouse conditions. Their school provided the funds to purchase pots, fertilizer, and seeds for marigolds, several tomato varieties, and a number of herbs. During classroom time, the students tended to their seedlings, interspersed with classroom literacy, mathematics, and science activities that reinforced and built on the academic learning inherent in the project. Students learned basic science concepts through keeping a plant observation journal in which they recorded the room temperature, sunlight level, soil conditions, and plant growth. Literacy activities included using sentence frames to compose a text about optimal growing conditions. In preparation for selling their products, students compared prices for similar plants at community groceries and plant nurseries. They organized two markets, complete with explanatory texts and signs for their produce tables: first at their school and later at the local farmers market. Setting up the tents and tables at the farmers market, students also included a small stage area and microphone so that some of their musically talented peers could entertain market shoppers with culturally diverse instrumentals. The Growing Project's market success netted each student $50 for their efforts, and the students made a heart-warming video clip of interviews on what each planned to do with the earnings. The pride expressed by many students in being able to contribute to their family's monthly expenses was palpable.

Artemis Kapakos, an art teacher in the TDSB who also has worked with LEAP students, wanted to initiate a project for her middle school SLIFE that would blend artistic expression with giving students a voice to express their individual identities and reserves of resilience. She developed the Living Portraits project for her students in which they explored their identities through a mixed-media collage art and text piece. Her learners experimented with language by using a series of English sentence stems such as: "I am . . .", "I like . . .", "I remember . . .", and "I believe . . ." to communicate the qualities, memories, experiences, and values that shape their self-image, feelings of resilience, and hopes for the future. This written component became a picture frame for the visual representation of each student's collage self-portrait. Through this project, Artemis's students developed a deeper sense of self-understanding and appreciation for the many strengths that they continue to bring to bear in successfully adapting to their new lives in Canada.

Making It Your Own

Amplifying the resilience, knowledge, and skills that students bring with them is a rewarding and essential practice in classrooms with English Learners. Such an approach helps build a solid academic foundation and language skills, while at the same time engaging students socially and emotionally. This amplification effect can be achieved through authentic activities involving collaboration with community partners in meaningful and relatable ways, such as those described above.

Based on your knowledge of the students and potential community partners in your context, what ideas do you have to ground learning in a similar approach to support the growth of English Learners? What academic standards could be addressed in your lesson idea? What types or examples of language development could you explicitly embed? Can you identify the essential knowledge or experience that you are tapping into that students brought with them? Develop a plan that names the ways you will build on their knowledge and what scaffolds and supports you will use. Be sure to think about practical and meaningful ways to make this authentic learning come to life.

Powerful Practice 3: Build students' background knowledge by surrounding them with authentic and meaningful language and literacy development.

What It Might Look Like

Students with limited and interrupted prior schooling come to us with a breadth of previous experiences and knowledge that we want to draw upon in our classrooms. At the same time, we also want to provide these students with many rich opportunities to widen the background knowledge that will support them for success in their literacy and content learning. All teachers who work with English Learners—but especially those who work with SLIFE—will want to draw upon many strategies in their instructional toolbox for building students' background knowledge, including the following:

- "Elbow partner" discussion and think/pair/share opportunities

- KWL charting

- Topic brainstorming

- Concept webbing

- Anticipation guides for pre-reading or pre-viewing focus

- Visuals and realia to illustrate new concepts

- Teacher modelled think-alouds

- Field trips with associated pre- and post-content-based literacy activities

Effective teaching for building background knowledge with SLIFE also encompasses involvement of students in the co-creation of texts based on the authentic and meaningful experiences of the students themselves. An exceptional example of this strategy can be found in the Making Good Choices Financial Literacy Project (ESL/ELD Resource Group of Ontario, 2014b), a series of teacher/student co-created literacy materials for SLIFE produced in Ontario. These materials provide an opportunity to assess and build students' background knowledge without assuming that students may have familiarity with various financial literacy topics. For example, paying sales tax, fines, and interest-bearing savings accounts may be new concepts for some students. Students also have opportunities to connect their new learning from the materials with what they already know and to share this information with their peers. When they read stories about their peers purchasing food, shoes, or clothing, they can compare shopping costs and product availability in North America with other countries where they have lived. Students can also discuss and explore the relationships between power, privilege, and economics through their experiences from around the world as they examine personal financial questions.

The Making Good Choices Financial Literacy Project series currently includes twenty-one levelled readers that reflect adolescent students' real experiences with personally relevant financial issues and challenges, including topics such as comparing cell phone plans, opening a bank account, budgeting and saving, calculating sales tax, fundraising for school activities, and finding a part-time job. A few of the most basic texts that introduce students to coins and bills and basic shopping can also be used with younger learners starting at Grade 4.

All of the readers are available at no charge and can be read online or downloaded and printed in PDF format. Guided reading lessons and three-part mathematics lessons accompany each text. Access the complete set of readers and lesson plans through the ESL/ELD Resource Group of Ontario (ERGO) (2014b) at htttps://www.ergo-on.ca/making-good-choices.

Making It Your Own

Brainstorm a list of potential background knowledge-building field trips in your area for your students with limited or interrupted schooling backgrounds. How can you integrate these offsite learning opportunities with your language and subject curriculum objectives? How can you enrich field trips with companion literacy activities? How can you bring cultural relevance to your field trips?

Powerful Practice 4: Use instructional practices that are appropriate for students who have missed years of schooling and may not have age-appropriate first-language literacy skills.

It can prove challenging for teachers to source age-appropriate, culturally relevant reading materials for learners who have missed years of formal schooling. A twelve-year-old student who is currently reading in the home language at the Grade 2 level needs reading materials that will facilitate engagement and curiosity yet won't talk down to their age group. Students with limited formal schooling want to feel that their reading materials are appropriate for their peer group. In the search for engaging and appropriate resources, a powerful technique for creating reading materials is to use the language experience approach to build texts that are relevant and interesting to students.

The language experience approach is an elementary school literacy instructional strategy that supports budding readers in starting with their spoken language knowledge to compose a shared class text. The co-created composition ties back to the class's shared experiences, giving added context and relevance that facilitates the students' reading comprehension. An excellent overview on using this approach with SLIFE is provided in the video *Language Experience Approach* (Bridges to Academic Success Project, 2017) available at https://bridges-sifeproject.com/language-experience-approach/.

The first step in composing a language experience story is for the learners to share an experience together, whether in class or on a trip outside the classroom. Any classroom participatory activity can become fodder for building a language experience story: a school tour, a shared viewing of a video, preparing food or making a craft item, learning or doing a sport together, playing a game, a shared reading of a wordless picture book, carrying out a simple science experiment. Field trips ranging from a walk around the neighborhood; a trip to the local grocery store, pharmacy, or park; an active outing to the community skating rink or jogging track; or a visit to a museum, zoo, art gallery, or street art exhibit can all provide a common experiential basis for the group creation of a language experience story.

After the participatory component, the teacher guides the students in a discussion of the experience and then records their shared narration and observations about the experience, shaping it collaboratively with the students into a cohesive text. The language experience story then becomes the basis for a variety of literacy activities focusing on the text, which can include the following:

- Choral and responsive reading aloud, leading to small-group and individual reading

- Recording the story for students to listen to as they read

- Vocabulary learning

- Contextualized grammar focus

- Further reading of simplified texts on the same topic

- Scaffolded writing using sentence patterns and stems drawn from the story

Another instructional strategy that provides meaningful literacy learning as well as an emotional sounding board for students with limited prior schooling is the use of dialogue journals. A dialogue journal is an extended reciprocal private written conversation, online or in a notebook, which takes place between the student and teacher or between two classroom peers. Dialogue journaling allows students to share their thoughts and experiences in a safe space through identity-focused writing while building positive and trusting relationships with their correspondents, whether a teacher or a peer. Linares (2018) describes the act of dialogue journaling as being part of "a pedagogy of care." Indeed, the process of continuous dialogue journal writing with students over an entire semester allowed two of the authors of this book to understand and empathize more deeply with some of the challenging experiences that SLIFE had on their journeys to Canada and the United States. As students gained a feeling of closeness and trust with the teacher through dialogue journaling, some chose to reveal details of their experiences in refugee camps and during flight, as well as about the fate of various close family members. Through the reciprocal process of dialogue journaling with learners, teachers become more aware of their students' lives and their emotional and academic needs.

Specially designed curriculum units for students with limited and interrupted formal schooling comprise another powerful strategy to create the classroom-learning environment for SLIFE to develop the background knowledge they may be missing in academic subjects such as science, social studies, and mathematics. Within the framework of the TDSB's LEAP program, teams of talented and creative teachers have developed units for SLIFE that can be used beginning in the fifth grade and right on through with high school-aged learners. The Go Green curriculum focuses on science topics, such as environmental stewardship and ecological sustainability, while Peace Talk explores issues of peaceful co-existence and anti-bullying. The Wavin' Flag unit features the coming to Canada story of Canadian rapper K'naan, as told in his autobiographical children's picture book (K'naan, 2012). These specially created units also promote the integration of a wide range of culturally relevant reading and viewing materials, selected with both the literacy levels and interests of SLIFE in mind.

Creative teachers also design their own integrated units in order to engage their learners and pump up the quotient of academic content learning along with age-appropriate literacy instruction. Each year in Qudsia Ahmed's high school LEAP class, students construct a "model city" and then use their model as a basis for reading and writing activities, as well as for learning in mathematics, science, social studies, and other content areas. In the process of planning and building the city, students will also share aspects of their identity through recounting their experiences in communities where they lived before migration, as well as their experiences in their new country.

Qudsia constantly collects large amounts of art and craft supplies and also obtains materials from the visual arts material depot in the school district. Drawing on their own experiences, the students first brainstorm all the facilities and components that would make up a city or town. Some of these components may be specific to particular cultural backgrounds, so students will have the opportunity to share information about places that are special to their heritage. Students then plan the city and build each part of the city in small groups. Components can include a city hall, an airport, a hospital, a mosque/church/temple and other places of worship, housing, schools, a university, an art gallery, parks, a train station, and so forth.

A wide range of language activities can be based on the planning and construction of the model city. Each place in the city can also be used as a jumping off point for lessons in mathematics (e.g., calculating area and perimeter of various buildings); social studies (e.g., discussing urban social issues and municipal government); career studies (e.g., exploring different careers of people who work in a range of urban institutions); and science (e.g., examining the sustainability of various features of the city). There are myriad opportunities to take advantage of the model city format as a catalyst for learning in every subject area.

Making It Your Own

For inspiration on how some Canadian teachers are using the learning experience approach, visit a website put together by teachers at the Algoma District School Board in northern Ontario that showcases the use of this approach with SLIFE in their district: www.dotalkwriteread.weebly.com. Examine some of the experiential learning that these teachers have used as catalysts for writing, as well as some of the texts co-written by the students.

FIGURE 4.13   Question E: Overview

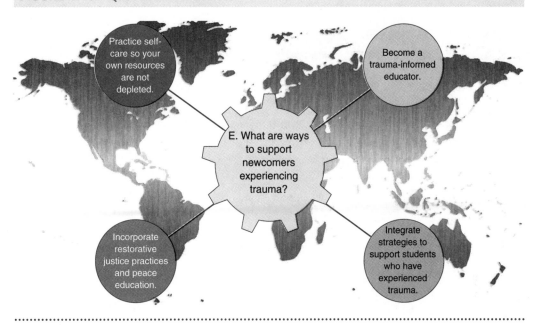

E. WHAT ARE SOME WAYS TO SUPPORT NEWCOMERS WHO MAY BE EXPERIENCING TRAUMA?

- Powerful Practice 1: Become a trauma-informed educator.

- Powerful Practice 2: Integrate approaches and strategies to support students who have experienced trauma.

- Powerful Practice 3: Incorporate restorative justice practices and peace education.

- Powerful Practice 4: Practice self-care so that your own resources are not depleted.

Powerful Practice 1: Become a trauma-informed educator.

Sixteen-year-old Ifeoma began high school in Canada on a warm early September day. She had recently arrived from a country in East Africa and was living with her aunt's family in the local community. By the time October rolled around, several of Ifeoma's teachers noticed that she was increasingly absent from class, and when she was there, she seemed to lack the ability to focus and was having difficulty remembering new concepts. Ifeoma's ESL teacher, Mr. Aziz, noticed she wasn't doing homework or coming to class prepared for assignments and tests. Ifeoma often appeared lethargic, and although athletically talented, she was increasingly reluctant to participate in her physical education class. She started skipping the gym class several times a week. Reciprocal dialogue journal interactions were a regular part of Mr. Aziz's classroom routine. He had found over the years that student/teacher dialogue journals provided a low-risk avenue for students to share stories about their lives and build a trusting relationship with him. One day, Ifeoma confided in her journal entry to Mr. Aziz that she had been kidnapped and beaten in her home country by a man to whom she had been promised in marriage by her father when she turned sixteen. She revealed that she had escaped from this man and had run away. Her mother quickly managed to raise the money to send her to Canada to claim refugee status and start a new life. After reading this disclosure and reflecting on Ifeoma's obvious signs of adjustment difficulty, Mr. Aziz became concerned about her well-being. He approached Ifeoma and asked if she would like to talk to him about how she was feeling about being new to Canada. Ifeoma talked privately with Mr. Aziz, during which she burst into tears and revealed her frequent nightmares and her fears that someone would emerge and forcibly take her back to her country to her dreaded fate as this hated man's wife. Mr. Aziz offered an empathetic, reassuring, and nonjudgmental ear in listening to Ifeoma's trauma story. Immediately afterwards, he went to his school's department head of guidance, and a team meeting was quickly organized with participation from all Ifeoma's teachers, as well as one of the school administrators. The team discussed how they could support Ifeoma, and subsequently invited Ifeoma and her aunt to consult together as a group on how they could help Ifeoma heal from her difficult experiences. Although for cultural reasons, Ifeoma's family were not sure that professional counselling was right for her, the school team impressed upon Ifeoma and her aunt that talking to a professional counsellor could prove to be an important mental health support for this young woman. Ifeoma began to meet regularly with a school counsellor trained in trauma support. Later on in the fall, the gym teacher gently convinced Ifeoma to join the girl's volleyball team, and Mr. Aziz encouraged Ifeoma to get involved with the school's newcomer peer-mentoring group, where she could meet other newcomers and contribute to the richness of the group through sharing aspects of her home culture and language.

Ifeoma's story represents but one from the growing number of such stories that educators are hearing as more children and youth arrive in schools after having undergone trauma difficult for us to imagine. Stewart and Martin (2018) use the following American Psychological Association definition: "a traumatic event is one that threatens injury, death, or the physical integrity of self or others and also causes horror, terror, or helplessness at the time it occurs" (2018, p. 24). Students coming from conflict zones, from regions ruled by drug lords or violent gangs, or from areas where individual human rights are not upheld may have experienced one, many, or even a prolonged period of traumatic events before they are granted asylum in a safe country. The traumatic events may have occurred in the pre-migration period and/or during the student's migration journey. Post-migration life also may be rife with stress, as students and their families deal with culture shock and isolation, separation from loved ones, grief over lives lost, financial concerns, and uncertainty about the future (Stewart & Martin, 2018).

FIGURE 4.14 Dictated Trauma Story

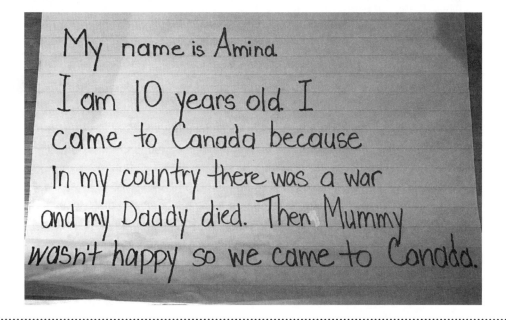

My name is Amina
I am 10 years old. I came to Canada because In my country there was a war and my Daddy died. Then Mummy wasn't happy so we came to Canada.

Although many young people who have experienced trauma will draw on their innate reserves of resilience and will not engage in behavior patterns revealing social-emotional distress, some children and youth may respond to their experience of trauma by:

- Exhibiting physical symptoms, such as headaches, poor bladder control, sleep disturbances, nausea, lethargy, lessening of appetite;

- Demonstrating signs of social-emotional maladjustment, such as depression, withdrawal, moodiness, anger, aggressive behavior, tantrums, and participation in high-risk behaviors;

- Experiencing difficulties with cognitive tasks due to memory problems, loss of concentration, task frustration, difficulty making decisions, lack of interest in school.

(Buchmüller, Lembcke, Ialuna, Busch, & Leyendecker, 2020; Medley, 2012; Stewart & Martin, 2018).

Lastly and importantly, educators supporting students who have experienced traumatic events must be mindful of "the danger of a single story." While some students from refugee backgrounds will most definitely have experienced trauma and will need support to heal from it, others will not have had these same experiences. Moreover, each student's response to the events of their migration story will be as unique as the strengths, talents, and aspirations that every student with a refugee background brings to the learning environment. Our goal as educators should be to move away from a stereotypical, deficit-based perspective of refugee learners that views them as the tragic victims of their circumstances, to a wider, asset-based stance that focuses on their resilience, determination, talents, and skills, which will be the key to fulfilling their hopes for the future. (Tweedie, Belanger, Rezazadeh, & Vogel, 2017).

Making It Your Own

Becoming a trauma-informed educator involves learning about the stories of war, political conflict, and oppression from students with refugee backgrounds, as well as learning about how educators can support students as they work through their trauma. The following resources are just the tip of the iceberg of those available for professional learning communities to spark reflection and discussion and to use as catalysts for action in their schools.

- Manitoba Education and Training. (2015). *Building Hope: Refugee Learner Narratives*, http://www.edu.gov.mb.ca/k12/docs/support/building_hope/index .html. Contains the stories of eleven youths from refugee backgrounds who made their way to the Canadian province of Manitoba to start a new life. An interactive version with links to background videos and readings on the various home countries is available on the website.

While by no means will all students from newcomer communities be refugees or experiencing the effects of trauma, a percentage of students from various communities will have undergone traumatic experiences on their journeys to Canada. All four of the following informative teacher resource guides, some with first-language inserts for parents, are available for free download.

- Ali, M., Franklin, K., Harvey, K., Hussein, G., Lees, S. J., Munro, J., & Yelich, B. (2012). *Teaching Somali immigrant children: Resources for student success.* Edmonton, Alberta: Canadian Multicultural Education Foundation & The Alberta Teachers' Association. https://www.cmef.ca/wp-content/themes/cmef/pdf/ CMEF-ATATeacherResourceSomaliStudents.pdf

- Coull, A. (Ed.). (2016). *Promoting success with Arab immigrant students: Teacher resources.* Edmonton, Alberta: Canadian Multicultural Education Foundation & The Alberta Teachers' Association. https://www.cmef.ca/wp-content/themes/ cmef/pdf/CMEF-ATATeacherResourceArabStudents.pdf

- Farrugia, L., Delcioppo, R., Wah, L. M., Thoo, L., Paw, H. N., & Ku, Ku, (2015). *Working with Karen immigrant students: Teacher resources.* Edmonton, Alberta: Canadian Multicultural Education Foundation & The Alberta Teachers' Association. https://www.cmef.ca/wp-content/themes/cmef/pdf/CMEF- ATATeacherResourceKarenStudents.pdf

- Kon, A., Lou, E., MacDonald, M. A., Riak, A., & Smarsh, L. (2012). *Working with South Sudanese immigrant students—Teacher resources.* Edmonton, Alberta: Canadian Multicultural Education Foundation & The Alberta Teachers' Association. https://www.cmef.ca/wp-content/themes/cmef/pdf/CMEF-ATATeac herResourceSudaneseStudents.pdf

- World Health Organization, War Trauma Foundation & World Vision International (2011). *Psychological first aid: Guide for field workers.* https://www.who.int/ mental_health/publications/guide_field_workers/en/. Available in over thirty languages, this document guides those who are not mental health professionals in learning the most supportive things to say and do for those who are very distressed.

- Ontario Ministry of Education (2016a). *Supporting students with refugee backgrounds: A framework for responsive practice.* Capacity Building Series, Special Edition #45. Toronto, ON. http://www.edu.gov.on.ca/eng/ literacynumeracy/inspire/research/cbs_refugees.html. This monograph offers

(Continued)

(Continued)

a framework for a whole-school approach to the successful integration of students with refugee background into the school community.

- Stewart, J. (2011). *Supporting Refugee Children: Strategies for Educators*. Toronto: University of Toronto Press. A landmark survey of the experiences and needs of refugee students that also provides classroom lessons and activities to support refugee children.

Powerful Practice 2: Integrate approaches and strategies to support students who have experienced trauma.

What It Might Look Like

Teaching approaches and strategies that are sensitive to the needs of English Learners affected by trauma have as their common goal the creation of a classroom climate of safety and trust, secure self-expression, cooperation, and empathy. Some specific instructional strategies that can be particularly supportive of this aim are storytelling, incorporating the arts for student expression and voice, and raising all learners' awareness about the realities of refugee flight, migration, and cultural adjustment.

Creating a safe and warm classroom community:

"With these kids, the relationship is the teaching" (Tweedie, Belanger, Rezazadeh & Vogel, 2017, p. 41).

Best practice in supporting newcomer students who have undergone trauma first and foremost aims for the creation of a safe and caring classroom community where students feel shielded from harm and free to express themselves (Stewart & Martin, 2018). Many individual classroom practices and actions taken together add up to students feeling safe and confident in the classroom. Greeting the new student with a smile, pairing the child up with a buddy or ambassador who perhaps can communicate in the same language, making a sincere effort to pronounce the student's name correctly, and displaying classroom signage and materials in a variety of languages, all set the stage for first impressions of a warm and welcoming classroom. A safe classroom community for newcomers encompasses predictable daily routines, the gradual introduction of new tasks, rich visual support to scaffold language, praise for incremental improvement, and opportunities for students to employ low-risk response techniques such as gestures, thumbs up/down signals, individual mini whiteboards for writing answers, and green/yellow/red signs on their desks for students to indicate when they need assistance with a learning task.

A crucial part of establishing a caring and supportive relationship with students who have undergone trauma is offering a listening ear whenever they need one. When teachers make themselves available to listen, students will tend to take advantage of that opportunity. Listening to students' thoughts and concerns can also take on a more physically distanced aspect in the form of dialogue journaling with students from refugee backgrounds to open up safe channels of communication (Ogilvie & Fuller, 2016). These educators also recount how after a level of trust had been established through the written journal conversations, a daily "tea-time" was also introduced into the class schedule to encourage relaxed communication, trust, and sharing amongst students and with the teacher.

At a high school for newcomer students in Brooklyn, New York, focus groups were conducted among students with refugee backgrounds to gather their input on what helped them most in adjusting to school in a new country. One student neatly summed up the importance of feeling supported and close to teachers when she said simply, "If you need help, they are always there for us." Another student commented about her science teacher, "If he see you feel sad or if . . . you are alone then he gonna come talk to you; . . . tell me what happened, we're gonna help you . . ." (Mendenhall, Bartlett, & Ghaffar-Kucher, 2017, p. 8).

> *Storytelling:* When teachers provide strategies to assist with healing and well-being, children and youth are more likely to have the capacity to deal with "the war without and the war within," the twin sources of difficulty and stress from both their present adjustment trials as well as their past horrors (Kyuchukov & New, 2016, p. 635). One classroom strategy that can promote resilience in children and adolescents is storytelling. Storytelling is a language and literacy development technique that simultaneously affords children and youth the opportunity to address and process emotionally difficult issues (Geres, 2016).

Emert (2013) engagingly used the "Where I'm from" poem to elicit stories from the refugee boys in his summer school program, also referred to by some as the "I am from . . ." poem. North of the forty-ninth parallel, teachers also often use a flipped version, the "If you're not from . . ." poem. Drawn from the popular classic Canadian children's book *If You're Not from the Prairie* by David Bouchard (1995), the stylistic device reverses the viewpoint to present the writer's wistful view of home in a different way.

TDSB teachers Shirley Hu, Shamira Mohamed, and colleagues and their Grades 4 and 5 English Learners, some from refugee backgrounds, co-created a book called *Flying Home: A Migration Story*. In science class, the students were learning about the migration patterns of Canada geese and reflected on the birds' journey to survive between two homes. As the students learned more about the seasonal flight of the birds, they connected what they were learning to their own migration stories. Thus was born a dual-text story with the sentences above the children's illustrations describing the migration of the geese while the text below related the experiences of the students and their families in coming to Canada. The teachers observed that some of their students who had heretofore rarely spoken in class became more vocal because the important life experiences they shared had been validated (Cummins, Hu, Markus, & Montero, 2015).

Storytelling by learners from refugee backgrounds can also help to reverse stereotypes by emphasizing students' strengths, resilience, and determination. Daniel (2019) conducted a series of workshops with teenage learners from refugee backgrounds in which they composed identity texts about their career goals, hopes, and dreams for the future. Her students wrote passionately about experiences that had informed their career aspirations, such as one girl who spoke about wanting to become a nurse because of her frustration that she could not do more to help when accompanying her ill mother on visits to the doctor. With their writing focusing on their goals of improving their lives and those of others, these students pushed back against often-held views of refugees only as victims who need help. Thus, students who have experienced trauma have the potential to transform deficit-based and marginalizing views about the refugee community through their writing (Daniel, 2019).

> *Arts-based learning:* Participation in expressive arts can yield an important avenue for children and youth who have experienced trauma to find ways to build hope and healing (Rousseau, Drapeau, Lacroix, Bagilishya, & Heusch, 2005; Stewart & Martin, 2018; Yohani, 2008). Making art allows refugee students to focus on creativity in the moment and offers cathartic opportunities to get in touch with their feelings. In the words of one art educator, "art can help you to talk about things that are essential, without necessarily having to talk strictly about yourself" (Chayder, 2019, p. 70). In Copenhagen, Denmark, the Louisiana Museum of Modern Art designed a special program for young learners with refugee backgrounds aged eight to eighteen. *Travelling with Art* spans several weeks of museum visits interspersed with school-based art activities. Students engage in a variety of creative activities, many self-directed, such as sketching their emotional reactions to painting and sculpture at the museum and making collages to express their personal identities. A sense of cultural relevance infuses many of the creative activities, as for example, when a group of Afghani students chose to build and decorate their

own kites, a project they would have continued to do had they been back in Afghanistan (Chayder, 2019).

In February 2021, the UNHCR, the UN Refugee Agency, and Franklin Watts Ltd. will publish in North America *Forced to Flee: Refugee Children Drawing on Their Experiences* (UNHCR, 2019), a compilation of children's pictures and words that express the thoughts and feelings of young refugees who have been forced to flee their homes in Syria, South Sudan, and Central America. This collection of children's art demonstrates the powerful combination of childhood resilience coupled with artistic creation.

Participation in music programs has similarly been shown to promote enhanced engagement with learning as well a greater sense of well-being and community inclusion for students from refugee backgrounds (Crawford, 2017).

> *Learning together about refugee realities to develop understanding and empathy:* Building a classroom community that is sensitive and supportive of students from refugee backgrounds includes expanding all class members' knowledge about the refugee experience. Some elementary age students may be unfamiliar with the concept of flight from one's country or with the kinds of life circumstances a refugee background might entail.

The Catholic Agency For Overseas Development (CAFOD) (2015) has developed *On the Move: A refugee simulation activity,* which invites students to follow a refugee family on their journey to safety. A group of participants simulates the travels of a family escaping from the dangers of war, progressing through nine different waystations. Difficult choices need to be made by the family grouping at each station, paralleling some of the difficulties that refugees may encounter in real life. The simulation is followed by discussion and reflection. *On the Move: A refugee simulation activity* is available at https://cafod.org.uk/content/download/32671/383774/version/ 8/file/On%20the%20move%20refugee%20game.pdf.

Even young children in the early grades, with guidance from the teacher, can share their background knowledge and learn from each other about the refugee experience. Using the picture book *What Is a Refugee* (Gravel, 2019), students brainstormed their ideas about refugees and sorted vocabulary describing the feelings an immigrant or refugee might have onto a multilingual Venn diagram.

> *Accessing resources and making connections:* Bridging Refugee Youth and Children's Services (BRYCS) (2018) offers many online resources to guide educators working with students who have experienced trauma. Whether you are looking for information on promoting student health and wellness, strengthening families from refugee backgrounds, early childhood resources,

or refugee resettlement issues, this organization is an excellent place to start. They also produce a useful series of three parent handbooks focused on raising young children, older children, and teenagers in a new country, available in English, Spanish, Somali, Nepali, and Arabic (https://brycs.org/).

Echo (2019) is an organization dedicated to educating families, communities, and professionals about trauma in order to break the cycle of generational trauma among survivors. They offer annual conferences, trauma trainings, and a variety of useful resources. View their infographic on the *Dos and Don'ts of a Trauma-Informed Compassionate Classroom* at https://www.echoparenting. org/dev/wp-content/uploads/2018/07/Echo_TIC_Web-8x11.pdf.

The Trauma and Learning Policy Initiative, based in Cambridge, Massachusetts, works to ensure that children exposed to trauma through family violence and other adverse experiences will meet with success in school. Their publications include several advocacy guides for establishing trauma-sensitive schools. Their website also contains many useful videos for educators to learn more about the impact of trauma on learning and on creating trauma-sensitive schools (https://traumasensitiveschools.org/about-tlpi/).

Distance learning became a sudden, confining reality for millions of children during the time the authors were writing parts of this book. The Trauma and Learning Policy Initiative preceding has prepared a valuable Q&A with experts to discuss how a trauma-sensitive approach can ease the effects of school closures and distance learning, so that everyone can continue to feel connected to a caring school community. Concerns about how to keep in mind the needs of the whole child in a remote learning environment, how to strategize distance communication with non-English speaking families, and how to maintain a sense of well-being among both students and teachers are addressed in their thoughtful publication, *Trauma Sensitive Remote Learning: Keeping Connections Strong* (Trauma Learning and Policy Initiative, 2020), available at https://traumasensitiveschools.org/trauma-sensitive-remote-learning-keeping-connections-strong/.

The ESL/ELD Resource Group of Ontario (ERGO) (2014a) provides the Live Well series, a compilation of dual-language booklets in English and Arabic to support the language and psychosocial/emotional needs of newcomer refugee learners. The books promote positive mental health strategies in simple English to help students and their families manage symptoms of trauma. Different sets of booklets for elementary and secondary students are available. Download for free at https://www.ergo-on.ca/live-well.

There will be times when you recognize that a child who is experiencing the effects of trauma needs more professional and specialized support than a teacher is equipped to give. Be sensitive about when you have reached the limit of helping as an educator and when a trained counsellor, social worker, therapist, or psychologist should take over. Work with administrators, school support staff, and guidance counsellors to find the appropriate referral.

Many urban centres are home to organizations whose mission is to provide specialized counselling and therapy to trauma victims. Toronto is fortunate to be home to the Canadian Centre for Victims of Torture (CCVT) (2018). The CCVT offers counselling for children and youth provided by culturally informed mental health professionals. They also organize a full roster of programs and events to support children from refugee backgrounds, including homework clubs, one-on-one tutoring, music and art programs, and local field trips over the summer. Network with colleagues to see if a similar organization exists in your community.

Making It Your Own

If you are currently working with students who have experienced trauma, what are some of the strategies and approaches that have met with success in your classroom? Connect with colleagues who also support students in this situation and brainstorm both a list of strategies that have worked, as well as a directory of agencies or practitioners for referral when needed.

Powerful Practice 3: Incorporate restorative justice practices and peace education.

What It Might Look Like

Incorporating restorative justice practices and peace education into school and classroom culture represents a promising approach for helping our students manage and move beyond the psychological and cognitive effects of trauma, violence, and displacement. Stewart and Martin (2018) advise teachers of refugee students to learn about the concepts and language of peace education and restorative justice and infuse these approaches into their classrooms, creating a safer, more caring, and more equitable participatory environment for all students.

Restorative justice is a centuries-old perspective on wrongdoing and its consequences, based on traditional ways of knowing held by many indigenous peoples around the world. While Western-style retributive justice is based on punitive measures for the violation of rules, restorative justice addresses the harm committed and asks those who have done harm to assume responsibility, provide input on how to rectify the harm, and restore the relationship with the harmed individual (Ogilvie & Fuller, 2016). In reflecting on how their behaviors affect others through restorative practices, students gain empathy and improve their interpersonal communication skills, promoting an atmosphere of community healing, interconnectedness, and reciprocity. Restorative justice represents "a process done *with* students rather than *to* them" (Ogilvie & Fuller, 2016, p. 89).

Restorative justice practices promote an asset-based view of refugee learners. Many students from refugee backgrounds have indeed gone through unimaginable trauma and may act out or withdraw as a result of their horrific experiences. But these students are also multi-faceted individuals who have so much more to contribute to their school, community, and country. Changing classroom perspectives to consider refugee students through a restorative lens, we appreciate their characteristics of resilience, strength, and determination as they participate actively in the process of promoting healing to those who have been harmed. Instances of conflict or misbehavior can thus be viewed as opportunities for social and emotional learning leading to healing rather than occasions for punishment and retribution (Stewart & Martin, 2018).

In one of the first studies in the United States that examined the use of restorative practices at the elementary school level, Ingraham et al., (2016) found that a schoolwide implementation of restorative justice practices in a highly culturally and linguistically diverse inner city California school led to a drastic reduction in behavior referrals, a drop in parental concerns about their children's' prospects of graduating, and an increase in parent and community engagement at the school. The research team introduced a number of foundational restorative justice practices to the school community, including classroom talking circles, teaching children the language to talk about and express their feelings, peer mediation of conflicts, and enacting the repair of harm approach. They were careful to pair the restorative justice approach with a raft of culturally and linguistically responsive adaptations, such as multilingual consultation and translation, frequent parental discussion and cooperative learning events, and simplified English materials for those parents who were less proficient in reading English.

In Australia, research with six Melbourne-area elementary and high schools applying a whole school restorative justice practices framework showed that significant benefits can accrue to students, teachers, and the community alike through the implementation of a schoolwide restorative practices approach (Kehoe, Bourke-Taylor, & Broderick, 2017). Interviews with students and teachers revealed increases in five crucial areas of social and emotional learning:

Harmony

Empathy for others

Awareness and accountability

Respectful relationships

Thinking in a reflective way

The aptly dubbed HEART program from "down under" provides an international model in the benefits of restorative justice practices in the school setting.

Bringing peace education into our classrooms can serve as another powerful catalyst to promote healing for traumatized students and foster critical thinking about human rights and relationships for all our students. Medley (2012) suggests teachers integrate content-based instruction for English Learners that illustrates the trauma healing journey by examining conflicts separate from those their own particular students have lived through. For example, learning about the Truth and Reconciliation process with Canada's indigenous peoples or the peoples of South Africa offers students a path to process their own experiences reflected through the prism of others' tribulations. This contemplation can help students to move on from their trauma and gain a sense of hope for the future.

> If there is to be peace in the world, there must be peace in the nations.
>
> If there is to be peace in the nations, there must be peace in the cities.
>
> If there is to be peace in the cities, there must be peace between neighbours.
>
> If there is to be peace between neighbours, there must be peace in the home.
>
> If there is to be peace in the home, there must be peace in the heart.
>
> —Proverb opening the Peace Talk unit by
> Chinese philosopher Lao-Tse, sixth century BC.

The Peace Talk curriculum developed by teachers in the TDSB for English Learners with limited or interrupted formal learning explores issues and concepts surrounding peace and encourages students to think critically about themselves and others in the world around them to promote equity, respectful and healthy relationships, and active, responsible civic participation. Throughout the units, the teacher establishes an atmosphere of mutual trust, validation, and inclusion in the classroom as students explore the concept of peace, investigate peace advocacy organizations, learn about diverse global peacemakers, and think critically about applying peace concepts to new situations. Students engage in a variety of activities, such as reading stories and texts about peace, creating a peace rock garden, practicing yoga and mindfulness, sharing culturally diverse symbols of peace, and performing random acts of kindness.

It's never too early to begin a program of peace education either. iACT (2019), a California-based nonprofit organization whose mission is to assist and empower refugees and populations subjected to mass atrocities, has developed a program that allows refugee children around the world to connect with young children in U.S. schools. Their Global Citizens curriculum for children ages three to five establishes a connection between American preschool and kindergarten children and their peers living in refugee camps to explore identity and practice empathetic learning. Fostering cross-border relationships among the youngest members of global school communities, this innovative program gives all children the chance to take "the first steps on the path to global ambassadorship" (iACT, 2019). Early years classes can apply online to become a "sister school" to a refugee camp school through the Global Citizens project.

Making It Your Own

Stewart and Martin (2018) have authored a comprehensive and practical guide to support teachers working with newcomer and refugee students. This excellent resource is available for free download, thanks to the Canadian Education and Research Institute for Counselling (CERIC), available at https://ceric.ca/resource/bridging-two-worlds-supporting-newcomer-refugee-youth/. The guide contains thirty professional development lesson plans through which teachers can engage in group learning on a range of topics about newcomer and refugee students. Form a learning group with interested colleagues to collaboratively raise your awareness about why and how to address negative behaviours with restorative justice practices using Lesson 7 from the guide (Stewart & Martin, 2018, p. 63).

Powerful Practice 4: Practice self-care so that your own resources are not depleted.

What It Might Look Like

We have all heard the instruction given by flight attendants in their pre-takeoff safety monologue: always make sure to secure the oxygen mask around your face first before helping others to do the same. As teachers, we also need to take care of ourselves in order to best support and help our students, but this is a maxim that is often overlooked where we are concerned. We may pay lip service to the notion of self-care; our supervisors and principals may remind us to take time to care for ourselves; but often we don't follow through with actions, and our mental well-being can suffer as a result.

At times when working with students who have experienced trauma, we may hear graphically disturbing stories that can be hard to forget. Students may also tell us of very challenging circumstances in their current lives, as they deal with situations of financial insecurity, family separation, uncertainty about the future, and painful memories. It can be emotionally taxing not only to deal with these disclosures but also to confront the limits to our power to make a difference in some of these difficult situations. Working with students who need every ounce of our support can bring on feelings of stress, exhaustion, and burnout. Teachers need to be able to call on a repertoire of self-care strategies when they are feeling emotionally depleted. The following suggestions may provide a starting point in looking for ways to practice self-care.

Talk to others (colleagues, family, friends) who you trust and can confide in. Having even one confidant who you can seek out when you need a listening ear can make a big difference in your capacity to deal with difficult circumstances. Consulting with a colleague to pool and increase knowledge about how to deal with a professional issue has been shown to be an effective work-related stress alleviation technique for teachers (Embse, Ryan, Gibbs, & Mankin, 2019).

Map out a wellness plan with intention that includes looking after your physical and mental well-being through healthy eating, sufficient rest and sleep, physical activity, and spending time regularly doing something that you love and that brings you joy.

Make time to regularly get out into nature, as well as to engage in any type of exercise or physical activity that you enjoy, alone or with family or friends.

Attend to your spiritual needs by attending faith-based events and services, speaking with clergy or lay leaders, reading spiritually nourishing texts, or taking time for personal contemplation and reflection.

Practice mindfulness meditation. Many people find that engaging in the practice of mindfulness meditation can bring about an immediate state of relaxation as well as longer-term positive changes in mental and physical health. Mindfulness can help people to accept their experiences and gain a better perspective on their anxiety-provoking and self-defeating thoughts and behaviors, enhancing their capacity to deal with adverse and challenging situations. In their recent literature review of teacher stress interventions, Embse, Ryan, Gibbs, and Mankin (2019) found that mindfulness practice was among the most effective techniques to alleviate teacher burnout and stress. Roeser et al. (2013) also showed mindfulness was significantly beneficial in alleviating teacher stress. Group courses, online sessions, podcasts, and books are all available tools for becoming involved in the practice of mindfulness meditation. Many workplaces today, including schools and universities, offer regular mindfulness sessions for employees.

Demonstrate self-compassion. When working with students who have undergone trauma and are still dealing with its effects on their well-being, educators are focused on showing compassion and caring to these students who are so in need of our support. Much less often do we think about showing this same compassion to ourselves. In our fast-paced and hard-working, outcomes-oriented culture of education, we often brush aside feelings that we ourselves are deserving of caring and compassion. We push ourselves intensely and are hard on ourselves when things are not progressing according to expectations. But just as with the airplane oxygen mask, self-compassion allows you to develop the emotional skills and self-awareness to be able to show compassion toward others. (Nelson, Hall, Anderson, Birtles, & Hemming, 2018). Instead of allowing your thoughts to move along a self-punishing track, show yourself kindness and understanding when you find it difficult to continue to support students who need so much emotional investment. Adjust your self-talk to show the same understanding and acceptance that you would offer to a friend in similar circumstances.

Recognize when you may be at your limit and seek help. If it becomes difficult to continue to work with students who are dealing with past and present trauma, it's vital to remember that there are many resources to turn to for support and self-care. A family physician, psychiatrist, counsellor, social worker, or therapy support group can provide much-needed support to help you clarify and manage your feelings. Many school districts offer a series of sessions at no charge with a professional counsellor as part of their employee workplace assistance program. If your school district provides this benefit, seek out expert assistance through this avenue. Reviewing your workload and involvement in extracurricular activities, professional learning groups, and school committees may also be part of a strategy to scale back when you have temporarily reached your limit in supporting others. Stewart (2011) quotes an administrator at a school where some students suffered serious mental health issues as a result of their harrowing experiences before coming to Canada. The administrator talks about the toll that supporting refugee students may take on his staff. "That person I told you about earlier, the colleague who took the girl to the hospital because she was on suicide watch, the teacher went directly to her own doctor after that session with the student" (p. 181). This dedicated teacher recognized that she had to seek out assistance to take care of herself and continue to provide that all-important caring to others.

Making It Your Own

What actions do you need to take for yourself to minimize stress at work and prevent burnout? Make a list of actions that would be best suited to you, keep it visible, and commit to following through with at least one or two of the actions as soon as you can.

POWERFUL PRACTICES FOR SUPPORTING ENGLISH LEARNERS

Doing things that bring you joy should be part of every teacher's self-care plan. Psychologist Karen Horneffer-Ginter (2017) has put together a list of fifty activities to help you take a break from life's stressors in a colorful poster called *50 Ways to Take a Break*. Your favorite way to de-stress might be illustrated, or perhaps one of the entries will encourage you to find a new, restorative activity. Even better, you might have to break out the crayons or colored pencils to create your own personalized poster—stained glass, rappelling, baking, biking? What activities bring you joy? How can you replenish yourself? Could this be an activity to share with your colleagues or students to help everyone create their own list of preemptive self-care practices that could be used during times of stress?

NEXT STEP

Chapter 4 has explored Powerful Practices that respond to the unique needs of students from various contexts. Some of these contexts might be very familiar to you, while others might be less so. You may choose to add labels to the "Student" gear of the English Learner Interconnected Ecosystem Model on page 255 of this guide with ideas, beliefs, and first steps that will be most applicable to your context. Of course, feel free to add whatever else inspires you, before joining us in the conclusion of this guide.

Conclusion

We are now nearing the end of our interprofessional, transnational, and asset-based journey together. Along the way, we have shared research, powerful practices, stories of triumphs and challenges, and have encouraged you to think deeply through application, reflection, and exercises. We hope your guidebook looks a little dog-eared from flipping back and forth to review ideas that sparked your curiosity and from personalizing your English Learner Interconnected Ecosystem Model. In doing so, you will have designed your own way to expand your interactions and connectedness with the school/community, classroom, families, and English Learners in your area. We now invite you to examine your creation and add any other insights.

Maybe the gears of your model are decorated by entries in various colors of ink and punctuated with enthusiastic exclamation marks. Perhaps you needed to add more space or arrows to your model to best represent your thinking. The teacher, paraprofessional, administrator, support staff, volunteer, or other school personnel who apply English Learner-based research, strategies, instruction, and advocacy, are actively engaging with each of the gears. When implementing powerful practices, educators are reminded of their own unique and creative artistry produced through their collaborations connecting the school, community, classroom, families, and students.

Each reader of this guide may have created their own distinctive model, and each model may be shared and linked with others to gain strength and efficacy. Consider sharing your model with a colleague, perhaps one from another profession, to bridge ideas and resources. Perhaps you can learn from their model or inspire them to launch new initiatives. Can your models be merged into something stronger and actionable for your students and families? Through reaching out to others with a culturally and linguistically sensitive lens, all educators are reminded of our potential for greater interconnectedness and the power within to make a significant difference in the lives of English Learners, their families, schools, and communities. We hope that the English Learner Interconnected Ecosystem Model encourages new asset-based collaborations and partnerships across professional and national frontiers.

We leave you with one final question: What are your next steps for supporting English Learners by elevating their assets and identities?

_____

_____

_____

_____

_____

_____

_____

_____

_____

_____

_____

_____

_____

_____

FIGURE CONCLUSION 1 English Learner Interconnected Ecosystem Model

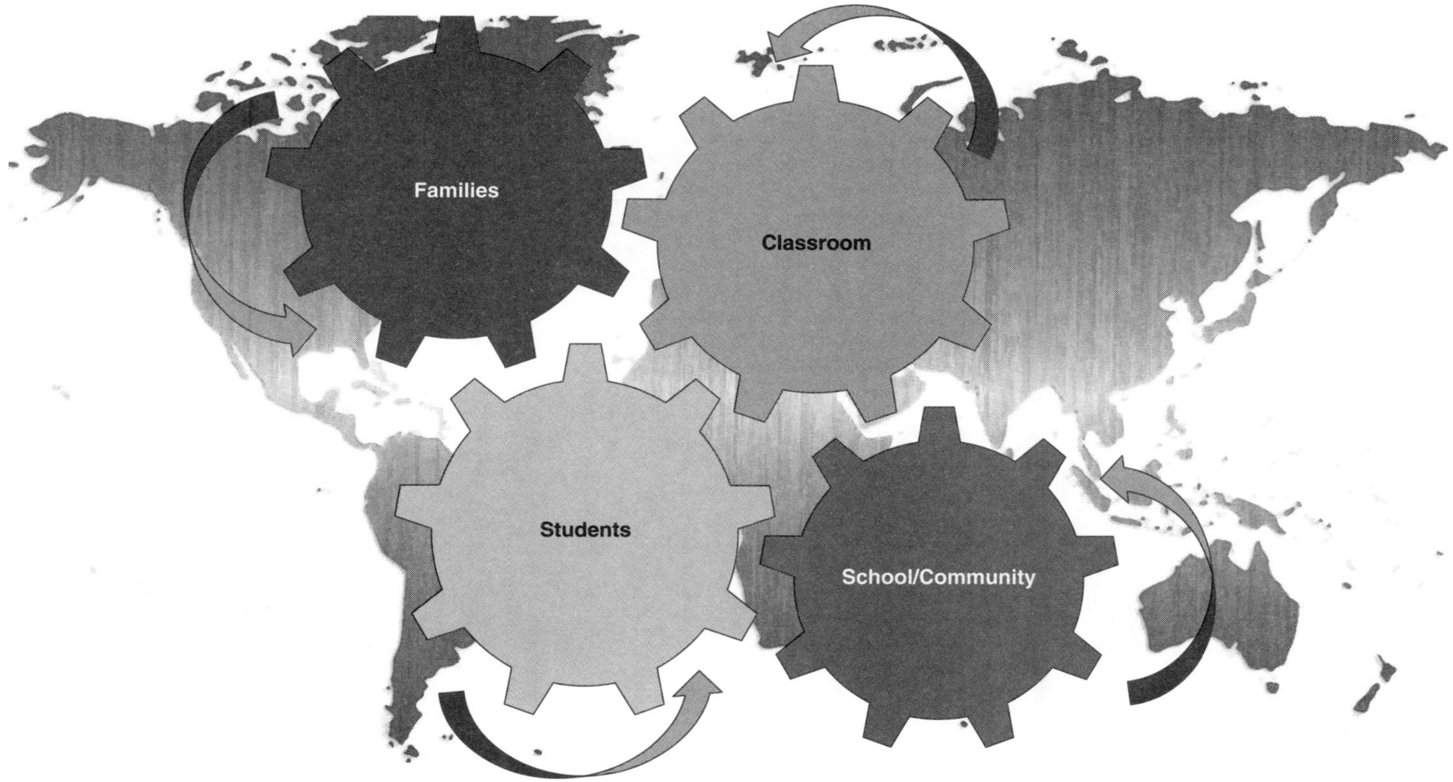

References

Adelson-Goldstein, Jayme, & Shapiro, Norma. (2016). *Oxford picture dictionary* (3rd ed.). Oxford, UK: Oxford University Press. (available in dual language editions and in a Canadian edition)

African Storybook. (2015–2019). https://african storybook.org/

Aganza, Joaquin, Gamboa, Angélica, Medina, Elizabeth, & Vuelvas, Stephanie. (2018). Breaking the silence: A framework for school psychologists working with students of undocumented immigrant families. *Contemporary School Psychology, 23*, 10–19, https://doi.org/10.1007/s40688-018-0210-1

Alberta Government. (1995–2020a). *Alberta K–12 ESL proficiency benchmarks.* http://www.learnalberta.ca/content/eslapb/search.html

Alberta Government. (1995–2020b). *Supporting English language learners: Tools, strategies and resources.* https://www.learnalberta.ca/content/eslapb/index.html

Ali, Mulki, Franklin, Kelsey, Harvey, Kerry, Hussein, Guled, Lees, Sarah Jane, Munro, Jill, & Yelich, Bette. (2012, August). *Teaching Somali immigrant children: Resources for student success.* Edmonton, Alberta: Canadian Multicultural Education Foundation & The Alberta Teachers' Association. https://www.cmef.ca/wp-content/themes/cmef/pdf/CMEF-ATATeacherResourceSomaliStudents.pdf

Amad, Ali. (2017, November 6). The war kids. *Toronto Life.*https://torontolife.com/city/the-war-kids/

American Immigration Council. (2016, October 24). *Fact sheet: Public education for immigrant students: Understanding* Plyler v. Doe. https://www.americanimmigration council.org/research/plyler-v-doe-public-education-immigrant-students

American Psychological Association. (2020). *Guidelines for providers of psychological services to ethnic, linguistic, and culturally diverse populations.* https://www.apa.org/pi/oema/resources/policy/provider-guidelines

American Speech-Language and Hearing Association. (1997–2020a). *Collaborating with interpreters.* https://www.asha.org/PRP SpecificTopic.aspx?folderid=8589935334 &section=Key_Issues

American Speech-Language and Hearing Association. (1997–2020b). *Working with culturally and linguistically diverse (CLD) students in schools.* https://www.asha.org/slp/CLDinSchools/

American Speech-Language and Hearing Association. (2020, August 4). COVID-19: Tracking of state laws and regulations for school-based telepractice and state school reopening plans. https://www.asha.org/uploadedFiles/State-Laws-and-Regulations-for-School-Based-Telepractice.pdf

Anderson-Lopez, Kristen, & Lopez, Robert. (2013a). Let it go. [Frozen Song—Let it Go Sang (sic) in 25 Languages. YouTube]. ReadySetLOL. www.youtube.com/watch?v=v7GB4l881Es

Anderson-Lopez, Kristen, & Lopez, Robert. (2013b). Let it go. [Recorded by Travys Kim on YouTube, February 19, 2019, in 25 languages, YouTube]. www.youtube.com/watch?v=X_dcTc3CPxU&list=RDX_dcTc3CPxU&start_radio=1&t=210

Arab American National Museum. (2020). *English-Arabic storytime: Online storytime* https://arabamericanmuseum.org/storytime/

Argitis, Theophilos, & Hertzberg, Erik. (2019, March 22). Canada sees 300,000 new immigrants—the largest influx in a century. *The National Post*. https://nationalpost.com/news/canada/canada-sees-300000-new-immigrants-the-largest-influx-in-a-century

Argueta, Jorge. (2015). *Salsa: Un poema para cocinar/A cooking poem*. Toronto, ON: Groundwood Books.

Asgedom, Mawi, & Even, Johanna. (2017). *Empowering English learners for classroom success: 6 keys to academic and social-emotional growth*. Elmhurst, IL: Mawi Learning, Inc.

Asia Society: Center for Global Education. (2020). Islamic belief made visual. https://asiasociety.org/education/islamic-belief-made-visual

Attendance Works. (2018). https://www.attendanceworks.org

Bajaj, Monisha, & Suresh, Sailaja. (2018). The "Warm Embrace" of a newcomer school for immigrant & refugee youth. *Theory Into Practice*, 57(2), 91–98.

Barasch, Lynne. (2007). *Hiromi's hands*. New York, NY: Lee and Low Books.

BBC News. (2015, December 11). *Canada: PM Justin Trudeau welcomes Syrian refugees*. YouTube. https://www.youtube.com/watch?v=e48U2pmc8Do

Bergman, Peter, & Chen, Eric W. (2019, July 8). Leveraging parents through low-cost technology: The impact of high-frequency information on student achievement. *Journal of Human Resources*. doi:10.3368/jhr.56.1.1118-9837r1

Bernard, Sara. (2010, December 1). Science shows making lessons relevant really matters: Personal relevance is as vital to the learning brain as it is to the person learning. *George Lucas Educational Foundation: Edutopia*. https://www.edutopia.org/neuroscience-brain-based-learning-relevance-improves-engagement

Bhatt, Sujata. (1988). *Search for my tongue in Brunizem*. Manchester, United Kingdom: Carcanet Press.

Bialik, Kristen, Scheller, Alissa, & Walker, Kristi. (2018, October 25). 6 facts about English language learners in U.S. public schools. *Fact Tank: News in numbers*. https://www.pewresearch.org/fact-tank/2018/10/25/6-facts-about-english-language-learners-in-u-s-public-schools/

Bialystok, Ellen, Craik, Fergus I. M., & Freedman, Morris. (2007). Bilingualism as a protection against the onset of symptoms of dementia. *Neuropsychologia*, 45, 459–464.

Bianco, Margarita, & Harris, Bryn. (2014, July). Strength-based RTI: Developing gifted potential in Spanish-speaking English language learners. *Gifted Child Today*, 37(3), 169–176.

Binogi Canada. (n.d.). https://www.binogi.ca/

Bloom: Let's Grow a Library—Book Library. (2020). https://bloomlibrary.org/browse

Boisvert, Précille, & Rao, Kavita. (2014). Video self-modeling for English Language Learners. *TESOL Journal* 6 (1), 36–58.

Booi, Zenande, Callahan, Caitlin, Fugere, Genevieve, Harris, Mikaela, Hughes, Alexandra, Kramarczuk, Alexander, Kurtz, Caroline, Reyes, Raimy, & Swaminathan, Sruti. (2016). *Ensuring every undocumented student succeeds*. Washington, DC: Georgetown Law Human Rights Institute.

Bouchard, David. (1995, April 1). *If you're not from the prairie*. New York, NY: Atheneum Books for Young Readers.

Brayko, Kate. (2018, April). *Trying on their shoes: Empathy as pedagogy for teachers of English language learners*. https://www.researchgate.net/publication/330842194_Trying_on_Their_Shoes_Empathy_as_Pedagogy_for_Teachers_of_English_Language_Learners

Breiseth, Lydia. (2020a). *Making the connection: Communicating with ELLs and their families during school closures*. ¡Colorín colorado! https://www.colorincolorado.org/article/coronavirus-ells-families

Breiseth, Lydia. (2020b). *School responses to COVID-19: ELL/immigrant considerations*. ¡Colorín colorado! https://www.colorincolorado.org/coronavirus-ell

Bridges to Academic Success Project. (2017, February 28). *Language experience approach*. https://bridges-sifeproject.com/language-experience-approach/

Bridging Refugee Youth and Children's Services (BRYCS). (2018, February 28). https://brycs.org/

Buchmüller, Thimo, Lembcke, Hanna, Ialuna, Francesca, Busch, Julian, & Leyendecker, Birgit. (2020). Mental health needs of refugee children. *Journal of Immigrant and Minority Health* 22(1), 22–33.

Californians Together. (2020). https://www.californianstogether.org/

Canadian Centre for Victims of Torture. (2018). http://ccvt.org/

Capstone. (2020). *Pebblego.* www.pebblego.com

Carle, Eric. (1969). *The very hungry caterpillar.* Cleveland, OH: World Publishing Company.

Catholic Agency For Overseas Development (CAFOD). (2015). *On the move: A refugee simulation activity.* https://cafod.org.uk/content/download/32671/383774/version/8/file/On%20the%20move%20refugee%20game.pdf

Cecco, Leyland, & Sakkab, Annie. (2017, March 31). Canadian entrepreneur invests millions in Syrian refugees: Jim Estill explains why he is teaming up with community leaders to help resettle and employ refugees in Guelph, Ontario. *The UNHCR: USA.* https://www.unhcr.org/news/stories/2017/3/58be80ed4/canadian-entrepreneur-invests-millions-syrian-refugees.html

Celic, Christina, & Seltzer, Kate. (2013). *Translanguaging: A CUNY-NYSIEB guide for educators.* New York: CUNY-NYSIEB, The Graduate Center, The City University of New York. https://www.cuny-nysieb.org/wp-content/uploads/2016/04/Translanguaging-Guide-March-2013.pdf

Centre Ontarien de Prévention des Agressions (COPA). (2018a). *Elementary school guide for newcomers to Ontario.* https://settlement.org/ontario/education/elementary-and-secondary-school/newcomers-guides-to-education/

Centre Ontarien de Prévention des Agressions (COPA). (2018b). *Secondary school guide for newcomers to Ontario.* Immigration, Refugees and Citizenship Canada. https://settlement.org/ontario/education/elementary-and-secondary-school/newcomers-guides-to-education/

Chamot, Anna Uhl. (2009). *The CALLA handbook: Implementing the cognitive academic language learning approach* (2nd ed.). Boston, MA: Pearson.

Chayder, Line Ali. (2019). Art as a bridge-builder: A program for young refugees. *Journal of Museum Education,* 44(1), 69–80.

Cheng, Andrea. (2000). *Grandfather counts.* New York: Lee & Low Books.

Child English as a Second Language Resource Centre. (2020). *The Alberta language development questionnaire.* The University of Alberta, Faculty of Arts. https://www.ualberta.ca/linguistics/cheslcentre/questionnaires.html#ALDeQ

Childress, Greg. (2020, May 6). School buses to carry Wi-Fi hotspots to rural, underserved students. *A Blog from NC Policy Watch: The Progressive Pulse.* http://pulse.ncpolicywatch.org/2020/05/06/school-buses-to-carry-wi-fi-hotspots-to-rural-underserved-students/

Choi, Yangsook. (2001). *The name jar.* Decorah, IA: Dragonfly Books.

Christensen, Linda. (2009). Uncovering the legacy of language and power. In *Teaching for joy and justice* (pp. 207–217). Milwaukee, WI: Rethinking Schools. https://lead.nwp.org/wp-content/uploads/2016/06/Language_Power_Sample_Chapter.pdf

Chumak-Horbatsch, Roma. (2012). *Linguistically appropriate practice: A guide for working with young immigrant children.* Toronto, ON: University of Toronto Press.

Chumak-Horbatsch, Roma. (2019). *Using linguistically appropriate practice: A guide for teaching in multilingual classrooms.* Bristol, UK: Multilingual Matters.

City of Toronto. (2020, April 28). *City of Toronto and partners help connect vulnerable populations with internet access during COVID-19 pandemic.* https://www.toronto.ca/news/city-of-toronto-and-partners-help-connect-vulnerable-populations-with-internet-access-during-covid-19-pandemic/

Clark, Christina, & Rumbold, Kate. (2006, November 1). Reading for pleasure: A research overview. *The National Literacy Trust 2017.* https://literacytrust.org.uk/research-services/research-reports/reading-pleasure-research-overview/

College of Audiologists and Speech-Language Pathologists of Ontario. (2016, September). *Guide for service delivery across diverse cultures.* Toronto, Ontario. http://www.caslpo.com/sites/default/uploads/files/GU_EN_%20Service_Delivery_Across_Diverse_Cultures.pdf

Collier, Catherine. (2011). *Seven steps to separating difference from disability.* Thousand Oaks, CA: Corwin.

Collins, Cory. (2020, March 19). Teaching through coronavirus: What educators need right now. *Teaching Tolerance.* https://www.tolerance.org/magazine/teaching-through-coronavirus-what-educators-need-right-now

¡Colorín colorado! (2018). *Immigrant students' legal rights: An overview.* https://www.colorincolorado.org/immigration/guide/rights

¡Colorín colorado! (2019a). https://www.colorincolorado.org/

¡Colorín colorado! (2019b). *Raising bilingual kids.* http://www.colorincolorado.org/raising-bilingual-kids

Community Legal Education Ontario. (2020). *Helping parents without immigration status get their children into school.* https://www.cleo.on.ca/en/publications/rightschool

Corwin. (2020). Webinar archive. https://us.corwin.com/en-us/nam/webinars-archives

Coull, Adrienne (Project Editor). (2016, April). *Promoting success with Arab immigrant students: Teacher resources.* Edmonton, Alberta: Canadian Multicultural Education Foundation & The Alberta Teachers' Association. https://www.cmef.ca/wp-content/themes/cmef/pdf/CMEF-ATATeacherResourceArabStudents.pdf

Crago, Martha B., & Westernoff, Fern. (1997, September). CASLPA position paper on speech-language pathology and audiology in the multicultural, multilingual context. *Journal of Speech-Language Pathology and Audiology, 21*(3), 223–224. https://www.sac-oac.ca/sites/default/files/resources/multicultural%20multilingual%20contexts%20for%20pdf.pdf

Crawford, Renée. (2017). Creating unity through celebrating diversity: A case study that explores the impact of music education on refugee background students. *International Journal of Music Education, 35*(3).

Cummins, Jim. (1996). *Negotiating identities: Education for empowerment in a diverse society.* Ontario, CA: California Association for Bilingual Education.

Cummins, Jim, & Early, Margaret. (Eds.) (2011). *Identity texts: The collaborative creation of power in multilingual schools.* Stoke-on-Trent, England: Trentham Books.

Cummins, Jim, & Early, Margaret. (2015). *Big ideas for expanding minds: Teaching English language learners across the curriculum.* Toronto, ON: Pearson Canada.

Cummins, Jim, Hu, Shirley, Markus, Paula, & Montero, M. Kristiina. (2015). Identity texts and academic achievement: Connecting the dots in multilingual school contexts. *TESOL Quarterly, 49*(3), 555–581.

Cummins, Jim, Mirza, Rania, & Stille, Saskia. (2011). Frames of reference: Identity texts in perspective. In Jim Cummins & Margaret Early (Eds.), *Identity texts: The collaborative creation of power in multilingual schools* (pp. 21–43). Stoke-on-Trent, England: Trentham Books.

Cummins, Jim, Mirza, Rania, & Stille, Saskia. (2012). English language learners in Canadian schools: Emerging directions for school-based policies. *TESL Canada Journal/Revue TESL du Canada, 29*(6). https://www.researchgate.net/profile/Jim_Cummins5/publication/304550714_English_Language_Learners_in_Canadian_Schools_Emerging_Directions_for_School-Based_Policies/links/5862049408ae329d61ff3fde/English-Language-Learners-in-Canadian-Schools-Emerging-Directions-for-School-Based-Policies.pdf

Curts, Eric. (2018, August 6). Google Tools for English language learners. *Control Alt Achieve,* https://www.controlaltachieve.com/2018/08/google-ell.html

Dagenais, Diane, Toohey, Kelleen, Bennett Fox, Alexa, & Singh, Angelpreet. (2017). Multilingual and multimodal composition at school: *Scribjab* in action. *Language and Education, 31*(3), 263–282.

Daniel, Shannon M. (2019). Writing our identities for successful endeavors: Resettled refugee youth look to the future. *Journal of Research in Childhood Education, 33*(1), 71–83.

Daniel, Shannon M., & Eley, Caitlin. (2017). Improving cohesion in our writing: Findings from an identity text workshop with resettled refugee teens. *Journal of Adolescent and Adult Literacy, 61*(4), 421–431.

Danzak, Robin L. (2011). Defining identities through multiliteracies: EL teens narrate their immigration experiences as graphic stories. *Journal of Adolescent and Adult Literacy, 55*(3), 187–196.

Delmos, Monika. (2008). Everybody's children. *National Film Board of Canada.* https://www.nfb.ca/film/everybodys_children/

Diaz, Itala. (2015). Training in metacognitive for students' vocabulary improvement by using learning journals. *PROFILE Issues in Teachers' Professional Development, 17*(1), 87–102.

Dolly Parton's Imagination Library. (2020). *Good night with Dolly,* https://imagination-library.com/

Donato, Al. (2020, February 26). *What is a sensory path? How hallway decals help kids focus, exercise and learn.* HuffPost. https://www.huffingtonpost.ca/entry/sensory-paths-canadian-schools_ca_5e568ee6c5b649ec43313c8f

Dove, Marie G., & Honigsfeld, Andrea. (2020). From isolation to collaboration. In Margarita Espino Calderón, Diane Staehr Fenner, Andrea Honigsfeld, Shawn Slakk, Debbie Zacarian, Maria G. Dove, Margo Gottlieb, Tonya Ward Singer, & Ivannia Soto, *Breaking down the wall: Essential shifts for English learner's success.* Thousand Oaks, CA: Corwin.

Dubinski, Kate. (2016, January 27). GENTLE Centre teaches refugees about how the education system works. *The London Free Press.* https://lfpress.com/2016/01/27/gentle-centre-teaches-refugees-about-how-the-education-system-works/wcm/6e6691e4-ca30-42a1-b3f4-4f5a0408efd4

Early Head Start National Resource Center. (2008). *Revisiting and updating the multicultural principles for Head Start Programs serving children ages birth to five.* https://eclkc.ohs.acf.hhs.gov/sites/default/files/pdf/principles-01-10-revisiting-multicultural-principles-hs-english_0.pdf

Echevarria, Jana, Richards-Tutor, Cara, & Vogt, MaryEllen. (2015). *Response to intervention (RTI) and English Learners: Using the SIOP model* (2nd ed.). New York, NY: Pearson.

Echo. (2019). www.echoparenting.org

edWeb. (2020). https://home.edweb.net/

Embse, Nathaniel, Ryan, Shannon V., Gibbs, Tera, & Mankin, Ariel. (2019). Teacher stress interventions: A systematic review. *Psychology in the Schools, 56*(8), 1328–1343.

Emert, Toby. (2013). "The Transpoemations Project": Digital storytelling, contemporary poetry, and refugee boys. *Intercultural Education 24*(4), 355–365.

English Language Proficiency Assessment for the 21st Century (ELPA21). (2018). *What Is ELPA21? The ELP assessment system.* https://www.elpa21.org/

Erickson Translations. (2020). *COVID-19 glossary in 18 languages.* https://www.eriksen.com/general/translation-importance-during-covid19/

ESL/ELD Resource Group of Ontario (ERGO). (2014a). Live well series. https://www.ergo-on.ca/Classroom-Resources.htm

ESL/ELD Resource Group of Ontario (ERGO). (2014b). *Making good choices financial literacy series.* https://www.ergo-on.ca/Classroom-Resources.htm

Esteban-Guitart, Moisès, & Moll, Luis C. (2014). Funds of identity: A new concept based on the funds of knowledge approach. *Culture & Psychology, 20*(1), 31–48.

Facebook. (2020a). *Global educator collective network.* https://www.facebook.com/groups/Temporaryschoolclosuresupport

Facebook. (2020b). *Teachers helping teachers.* https://www.facebook.com/groups/100879116923919/

Facebook. (2020c). *Trauma informed educators network.* https://www.facebook.com/groups/1950824761646206/

Fairbairn, Shelley, & Jones-Vo, Stephaney. (2010). *Differentiating instruction and assessment for English Learners: A guide for K–12 teachers.* Philadelphia, PA: Caslon Publishing.

Fairbairn, Shelley, & Jones-Vo, Stephaney. (2016). *Engaging English learners through access to standards: A team-based approach to schoolwide student achievement.* Thousand Oaks, CA: Corwin.

Fairbairn, Shelley, & Jones-Vo, Stephaney. (2019). *Differentiating instruction and assessment for English language learners: A guide for K–12 teachers* (2nd ed.). Philadelphia, PA: Caslon Publishing.

Far Eastern Books number posters (Arabic, English, Gujarati, Panjabi, and Urdu) (1975–2008). Far Eastern books online. fareasternbooks.com/search.php?search_query=numbers&x=0&y=0

Farrugia, Lynn, Delcioppo, Renato, Wah, Lah May, Thoo, Lei, Paw, Hse Nay, & Ku, Ku. (2015, January). *Working with Karen immigrant students: Teacher resources.* Edmonton, Alberta: Canadian Multicultural Education Foundation & The Alberta Teachers' Association. https://www.cmef.ca/wp-content/themes/cmef/pdf/CMEF-ATATeacherResourceKarenStudents.pdf

Fenton Smith, Kay, & Spaulding, Carol. (2011). *Zakery's bridge: Children's journeys from around the world to Iowa.* Des Moines, IA: Shrieking Tree.

Food and Agriculture Organization of the United Nations. (2020). http://www.fao.org/home/search/

Franco, Diana. (2018). Trauma without borders: The necessity for school-based interventions in treating unaccompanied refugee minors. *Child and Adolescent Social Work Journal, 35,* 551–565.

Fynes, Laurel. (2013, June 23). *We can count.* This Kindergarten Life. https://thiskindylife.blogspot.com/search?q=We+Can+Count

Fynes, Laurel. (2014, April 28). *How do you say Hello?* This Kindergarten Life. https://thiskindylife.blogspot.com/search?q=Hello+Goodbye

García, Ofelia. (2020). Translanguaging and Latinx bilingual readers. *The Reading Teacher, 73*(5), 557–562.

García, Ofelia, & Lin, Angel M. Y. (2016). Translanguaging in bilingual education. In O. García, A. Lin, & S. May (Eds.), *Bilingual education* (Vol. 5, pp 117–130).

Encyclopedia of Language and Education. Switzerland: Springer Publishing. doi: 10.1007/978-3-319-02324-3_9-1

García, Ofelia, & Seltzer, Kate. (2015). The translanguaging current in language education. https://ofeliagarciadotorg.files.wordpress.com/2011/02/garcia_seltzer47122073-1.pdf

Genesee, Fred. (2016). *At-risk learners and bilingualism: Is it a good idea?* ¡Colorín colorado! http://www.colorincolorado.org/article/risk-learners-and-bilingualisgood-idea

Geres, Koreen. (2016). Resilience through storytelling in the EAL classroom. *TESL Canada Journal 33*(10), 62–85.

Geva, Esther, Barsky, Allan E., & Westernoff, Fern. (2000). Developing a framework for interprofessional and diversity informed practice. In A. E. Barskey, E. Geva, & F. Westernoff (Eds.), *Interprofessional practice with diverse populations: Cases in point* (pp. 1–28). Westport, CT: Greenwood Pub.

Giampapa, Frances. (2010). Multiliteracies pedagogy and identities: Teacher and student voices from a Toronto elementary school. *Canadian Journal of Education, 33*(2), 407–431.

Glennen, Sharon. (2008, December 1). Speech and language "mythbusters" for internationally adopted children. *ASHAWire: The ASHA Leader.* https://leader.pubs.asha.org/doi/10.1044/leader.FTR1.13172008.10

Global Beer Fridge Extended Molson Canadian. (2015, November 17). YouTube https://www.youtube.com/watch?v=CfpatqyujM0

Goldenberg, Claude. (2008, Summer). Teaching English language learners: What the research does—and does not—say. *American Educator,* 8–44. https://www.aft.org/sites/default/files/periodicals/goldenberg.pdf

Goldsmith, Jill S., & Robinson Kurpius, Sharon E. (2018). Fostering the academic success of their children: Voices of Mexican immigrant parents. *The Journal of Educational Research, 111*(5), 564–573.

Government of Canada. (2017). *Getting involved in your child's education.* https://www.canada.ca/en/immigration-refugees-citizenship/services/new-immigrants/new-life-canada/enrol-school/participate-child-education.html

Government of Canada. (2020, January 13). *Canada's food guide.* https://food-guide. canada.ca/en/

Grande, Reyna. (2013a). *La distancia entre Nosotros.* New York: Atria Books.

Grande, Reyna. (2013b). *The distance between us.* New York: Washington Square Press.

Grande, Reyna. (2016). *The distance between us* (Young Reader's ed.). New York: Aladdin, Simon and Schuster Children's Publishing.

Grantmakers for Education. (2013, April). *Educating English language learners: Grantmaking strategies for closing America's other achievement gap.* https://edfunders.org/ sites/default/files/Educating%20English%20 Language%20Learners_April%202013.pdf

Gravel, Elise. (2019). *What is a Refugee?* Toronto: Penguin Random House Canada.

Graves, Michael F., Schneider, Steven, & Ringstaff, Cathy. (2017). Empowering students with word-learning strategies: Teach a child to fish. *The Reading Teacher, 71*(5), 533–543.

Grey, Mark A. (2006). New Americans, new Iowans: Welcoming immigrant and refugee newcomers. Cedar Falls, IA: University of Northern Iowa Center for Immigrant Leadership and Integration. https://bcs.uni. edu/icili/pdfs/icili_booklet.pdf

Gunning, Pamela, & Oxford, Rebecca L. (2014). Children's strategy use and the effects of strategy instruction on success in learning ESL in Canada. *System, 43,* 82–100.

Habib, Samra. (2019). *We Have Always Been Here: A Queer Muslim Memoir.* Toronto: Penguin Random House Canada.

Haghighat, Cathy. (2005). *Language profiles* (Vol. I, II, III). Toronto, ON: World Languages Publishing House, Canadian Cataloguing in Publication Data.

Hall, Gaynor. (2020, June 25). *Mayor Lightfoot announces $50M plan to bring high-speed internet to CPS students in need. WGN Web Desk.* Chicago News. https://wgntv.com/ news/chicago-news/watch-live-mayor-light foot-announces-plan-to-bring-high-speed- internet-to-cps-students-in-need/

Halton District School Board. (2017, October 5). *ESL innovation project.* YouTube. https:// www.youtube.com/watch?v=XY9Ytbk WWys&feature=youtu.be

Hamayan, Else V., Marler, Barbara, Sánchez-López, Cristina, & Damico, Jack S. (2007). *Special education considerations for English language learners: Delivering a continuum of services.* Philadelphia, PA: Caslon Publishing.

Han, Young-chan, & Love, Jennifer. (2015). Stages of immigrant parent involvement— survivors to leaders. *Kappan, 97,* 21–25.

Holland, Audrey L., & Nelson, Ryan L. (2014). *Counseling in communication disorders: A wellness perspective* (2nd ed.). San Diego, CA: Plural Publishing.

Horneffer-Ginter, Karen. (2017, December 6). 50 ways to take a break, and the essential first step of remembering. *HuffPost.* https://www. huffpost.com/entry/gps-guides_b_1632700

iACT. (2019). *Global Citizens: An iACT education program.* https://www.iact.ngo/impact/ global-citizens/

Ijalba, Elizabeth. (2015). Effectiveness of a parent-implemented language and literacy intervention in the home language. *Child Language Teaching and Therapy, 31*(2), 207–220.

Ingraham, Colette L., Hokoda, Audrey, Moelenbruck, Derek, Karafin, Monica, Manzo, Caroline, & Ramirez, Daniel. (2016). Consultation and collaboration to develop and implement restorative practices in a culturally and linguistically diverse elementary school. *Journal of Educational and Psychological Consultation, 26*(4), 354–384.

Instagram. (2020). tdsb_slp. https://www. instagram.com/tdsb_slp/

International Consultants for Education and Fairs. (ICEF). (2020, February 26). Canada had another strong year of growth in 2019. *ICEF Monitor.* https://monitor.icef. com/2020/02/canada-had-another-strong- year-of-growth-in-2019/

International Literacy Association/National Council of Teachers of English. (2020). *Parent & after school resources.* Read-writethink. http://www.readwritethink.org/ parent-afterschool-resources/

Iowa Department of Education. (2008). *Identifying gifted and talented English language learners* (Grades K–12). Des Moines, IA: Iowa Department of Education. https:// educateiowa.gov/sites/files/ed/documents/ IdentifyGiftedTalentedELL.pdf

Iowa Department of Human Services. (2020). RefugeeServices.https://dhs.iowa.gov/refugee-services

Iowa Public Television. (2007). *A promise called Iowa* [DVD Video]. Johnston, IA: Commission on the Status of Iowans of Asian and Pacific Islander Heritage.

Iowa Public Television. (1995–2020). *Robert D. Ray: An Iowa governor, a humanitarian leader*. Iowa Pathways.

Jacobs, Suzan F. M. (2018). Collective narrative practice with unaccompanied minors: "The Tree of Life" as a response to hardship. *Clinical Child Psychology and Psychiatry*, 23(2), 279–293.

Jenkins, Ella. (2020, July 17). More multicultural children's songs from Ella Jenkins. YouTube. www.youtube.com/playlist?list=OLAK5uy_mEuG2Qc5fT5eaICppg2W09z731RlA4mN0

John McCrae Public School. (2019, October 16). TDSB Twitter. twitter.com/John_McCraePS/status/1184449679662206976

Jones, Stephanie, Weissbourd, Rick, Bouffard, Suzanne, Kahn, Jennifer, & Ross Anderson, Trisha. (2020). *For educators: How to build empathy and strengthen your school community*. Making Caring Common Project at the Harvard Graduate School of Education. https://mcc.gse.harvard.edu/resources-for-educators/how-build-empathy-strengthen-school-community

Jordan, Phyllis. (2020, June). *Attendance playbook: Strategies for reducing chronic absenteeism in the Covid era*. Georgetown University: FutureEd and Attendance Works. https://www.future-ed.org/attendance-playbook/

Kahoot! (2020). https://kahoot.com/

Kantor, Jodi, & Einhorn, Catrin. (2016, June 30). Refugees encounter a foreign word: Welcome, how Canadian hockey moms, poker buddies and neighbors are adopting Syrians, a family at a time. *The New York Times*. https://www.nytimes.com/2016/07/01/world/americas/canada-syrian-refugees.html

Kay-Raining Bird, Elizabeth, Cleave, Patricia, Trudeau, Natacha, Thordardottir, Elin, Sutton, Ann, & Thorpe, Amy. (2005). The language abilities of bilingual children with Down Syndrome. *American Journal of Speech-Language Pathology*, 14, 187–199.

Kehoe, Michelle, Bourke-Taylor, Helen, & Broderick, David. (2017). Developing student social skills using restorative practices: A new framework called H.E.A.R.T. *Social Psychology of Education*, 21(1), 189–207.

Keles, Serap, Friborg, Oddgeir, Idsoe, Thormod, Sirin, Selcuk, & Oppedal, Brit. (2018). Resilience and acculturation among unaccompanied refugee minors. *International Journal of Behavioral Development*, 42(1), 52–63. https://journals.sagepub.com/doi/pdf/10.1177/0165025416658136

Khan Academy. (2020). https://www.khanacademy.org/

KidTimeStoryTime. (2019–2020). https://kidtimestorytime.com

Kim, Hyun Joo, & Okazaki, Sumie. (2014). Navigating the cultural transition alone: Psychosocial adjustment of Korean early study abroad students. *Cultural Diversity and Ethnic Minority Psychology*, 20(2), 244–253.

Kim, Yanghee Anna, An, Sphyun, Kim, Hyun Chu Leah, & Kim, Jihye. (2018). Meaning of parental involvement among Korean immigrant parents: A mixed-methods approach. *The Journal of Educational Research*, 111(2), 127–138.

King, Kendall, & Bigelow, Martha. (2018). The language policy of placement tests for Newcomer English Learners. *Educational Policy*, 32(7), 936–968.

K'naan. (2012). *When I get older: The story behind "Wavin' Flag."* Toronto, ON: Tundra Books.

Kohnert, Kathryn, Yim, Dongsun, Nett, Kell, Kan, Pui Fong, & Duran, Lillian. (2005). Language intervention with linguistically diverse preschool children: A focus on developing home language(s). *Speech and Hearing Services in Schools*, 36, 251–264.

Kon, Abril, Lou, Elaine, MacDonald, Mary Anne, Riak, Athieng, & Smarsh, Lynn. (2012, August). *Working with South Sudanese immigrant students—Teacher resources*. Edmonton, Alberta: Canadian Multicultural Education Foundation & The Alberta Teachers' Association. https://www.cmef.ca/wp-content/themes/cmef/pdf/CMEF-ATATeacherResourceSudaneseStudents.pdf

Kottler, Ellen, Kottler, Jeffrey A., & Street, Christopher. (2008). *English language* learners in your classroom: Strategies that work (3rd ed.). Thousand Oaks, CA: Corwin.

Krashen, Stephen D. (2009). *Principles and practice in second language acquisition*. Internet Edition, http://www.sdkrashen.com/content/books/principles_and_practice.pdf

Kreuzer, Louise H. (2016). *An educator's guide to aid transitions*. Lanham, MD: Rowman & Littlefield.

Kwok, Jean. (2010). *Girl in translation*. New York: Riverhead Books.

Kyuchukov, Hristo, & New, William. (2016). Peace education with refugees: Case studies. *Intercultural Education, 27*(6), 635–640.

Lahiri, Jhumpa. (2003). *The namesake*. Boston: Houghton Mifflin Harcourt.

Larson, Elizabeth Jean, & Lau, Clarissa. (2016, August 4). *Steps to English proficiency: A review of the framework and its writing continua*. Teachers of English as a Second Language Association of Ontario. http://contact.teslontario.org/steps-to-english-proficiency/

Linares, Rebecca E. (2018). Meaningful writing opportunities: Write-alouds and dialogue journaling with newcomer and English learner high schoolers. *Journal of Adolescent and Adult Literacy, 62*(5), 521–530.

Linton Howard, Lotus. (2017). *Bright ribbons: Weaving culturally responsive teaching into the elementary classroom*. Thousand Oaks, CA: Corwin.

Lotherington, Heather, Paige, Cheryl, & Holland-Spencer, Michelle. (2013). *Using a professional learning community to support multimodal literacies. What works? Research into practice*. Toronto, ON: Literacy and Numeracy Secretariat. http://www.edu.gov.on.ca/eng/literacynumeracy/inspire/research/WW_Professional_Learning.pdf

Lowry, Lauren. (2012a, January 18). Can children with language impairments learn two languages? *The Hanen Centre*, Toronto, Ontario. http://www.hanen.org/Helpful-Info/Articles/Can-children-with-language-impairments-learn-two-l.aspx

Lowry, Lauren. (2012b). *Parents as "speech therapists": What a new study shows*. The Hanen Centre, Toronto, Ontario. http://www.hanen.org/Helpful-Info/Articles/Parents-as--Speech-Therapists--What-a-New-Study-S.aspx

Lum, Zi-Ann. (2017, May 2). *My mom and I don't speak the same language, literally*. Chatelaine. https://www.chatelaine.com/living/my-mom-and-i-dont-speak-the-same-language/

Lynn, Bryan. (2018, October 30). *Number of English learners in U.S. schools keeps rising*. Learning English: Education. https://learningenglish.voanews.com/a/number-of-english-learners-in-us-schools-keeps-rising/4635659.html

Mahoney, Jill. (2007, December 6). Leaping over educational adversity. *The Globe and Mail*. https://www.theglobeandmail.com/news/national/leaping-over-educational-adversity/article699294/

Making Art Making Change. (2020). https://makingartmakingchange.com

Mancinelli, Danielle. (2020, July 7). Using social media to build a personal learning network. *edutopia*. https://www.edutopia.org/article/using-social-media-build-personal-learning-network

Manitoba Education, Citizenship and Youth (2006). *Helping your child succeed at school: A guide for parents and families of Aboriginal students*. Winnipeg, Manitoba. https://www.edu.gov.mb.ca/k12/docs/parents/ab_guide/ab_guide.pdf

Manitoba Education and Training. (2015). *Building hope: Refugee learner narratives*. https://www.edu.gov.mb.ca/k12/docs/support/building_hope/index.html

Markus, Paula. (n.d.). English language learners: Policy and school support in Ontario, Canada. *¡Colorín colorado!* https://www.colorincolorado.org/article/english-language-learners-policy-and-school-support-ontario-canada

Marshall, James. (1998). *Goldilocks and the three bears*. New York: Penguin Books.

Maya's Book Nook. (2020). https://mayasbooknook.com/

McGlynn-Stewart, Monica, Murphy, Shelley, Pinto, Ivorie, Mogyorodi, Emma, & Nguyen, Thien. (2019). Technology supported early learning in a multilingual community preschool. *Education 3–13*(47), 6, 692–704.

Medina, Meg. (2017). *Mango, abuela and me*. Somerville, MA: Candlewick Press.

Medley, Michael. (2012). A role for English language teachers in trauma healing. *TESOL Journal 3*(1), 110–121.

Megan. (2009–2020). *Students create Little Free Library Network stocked with multilingual books.* https://littlefreelibrary.org/students-create-little-free-library-network-stocked-with-multilingual-books/

Mendenhall, Mary, Bartlett, Lesley, & Ghaffar-Kucher, Ameena. (2017). "If you need help, they are always there for us.": Education for refugees in an international high school in NYC. *Urban Review 49*, 1–25.

Menken, Kate, & Sánchez, Marie Teresa (Maite). (2019, September). Translanguaging in English-only schools: From pedagogy to stance in the disruption of monolingual policies and practices. *TESOL Quarterly*, 53(3), 741–767. https://docs.google.com/document/d/1jS3NoyXb-OAfjqT-jiOSKpJ82jQ65SwPzDSrWn9nQQzc/edit

The Metropolitan Center for Research on Equity and the Transformation of Schools. NYU/Steinhardt. (2020). *Resources: Glossaries for ELL/MLL accommodations*, https://research.steinhardt.nyu.edu/metrocenter/resources/glossaries

Metropolitan Toronto School Board. (1996). *Interpreting and translating: A resource guide to assist in the delivery of interpreting and translating services to schools.* North York, ON: Author.

Microsoft. (2020). Flipgrid. https://info.flipgrid.com/

Mohdin, Aamna. (December 18, 2017). *Even if you've forgotten the language you spoke as a child, it still stays with you.* https://qz.com/1155289/even-if-youve-forgotten-the-language-you-spoke-as-a-child-it-still-stays-with-you/

Moll, Luis C., Amanti, Cathy, Neff, Deborah, & Gonzalez, Norma. (1992). Funds of knowledge for teaching: Using a qualitative approach to connect homes and classrooms. *Theory Into Practice, 2*, 132–141.

Montroni-Currais, Maria. (2020). *ESL at home.* https://eslathome.edublogs.org

Moreland Libraries. (2020). https://www.youtube.com/channel/UCUAoPvpkSPvg7vRz5f4oYbw/playlists

Mousa, Salma. (2018, April 16). *Overcoming the trust deficit: Intergroup contact and associational life in post-ISIS Iraq.* https://static1.squarespace.com/static/59a360bacd0f681b1cb27caa/t/5ada01d81ae6cf6be3d6c873/1524236760447/mousa-contact-idps.pdf

Multicultural, Multilingual Interest Group of the Ontario Association of Speech-Language Pathologists and Audiologists. (2010). *Reading develops language skills: A parent handout in eleven languages.* Toronto, ON: https://cdn.ymaws.com/www.osla.on.ca/resource/resmgr/interest_groups/osla-_reading_develops_langu.pdf

Multilingual Families. (2013–2015). https://www.multilingual-families.eu/home

National Association for Multicultural Education. (2020). https://www.nameorg.org

National Association of School Psychologists. (2019). https://www.nasponline.org/resources-and-publications/resources-and-podcasts/school-climate-safety-and-crisis/health-crisis-resources/helping-children-cope-with-changes-resulting-from-covid-19

National Association of Secondary School Principals. (2020). *Undocumented students* https://www.nassp.org/policy-advocacy-center/nassp-position-statements/undocumented-students/

National Education Association. (2020). *Read across America.* https://www.readacrossamerica.org

Nelson, Heidi D., Nygren, Peggy, Walker, Miranda, & Panoscha, Rita. (2006). Screening for speech and language delay in preschool children: Systematic evidence review for the US Preventive Services Task Force. *Pediatrics, 117*(6), 2336–2337. doi: https://doi.org/10.1542/peds.2006-0940

Nelson, Jill R., Hall, Brenda Z., Anderson, Jamie L., Birtles, Caitlen, & Hemming, Lynae. (2018). Self-compassion as self-care: A simple and effective tool for counselor educators and counseling students. *Journal of Creativity in Mental Health*, 13(1), 121–133.

Newsela. (2020). https://newsela.com

Niemann, Christoph. (2008). *The pet dragon: A story about adventure, friendship, and Chinese characters.* China: GreenWillows Books.

Ntelioglou, Burcu Yaman, Fannin, Jennifer, Montanera, Mike, & Cummins, Jim. (2014). A multilingual and multimodal approach to literacy teaching and learning in urban education: A collaborative inquiry project in an inner city elementary school. *Frontiers in Psychology, 5*(33), 1–10.

Ogilvie, Greg, & Fuller, David. (2016). Restorative justice pedagogy in the ESL classroom: Creating a caring environment to support refugee students. *TESL Canada Journal, 33*(10), 86–96.

Olson, Carol Booth, Kim, James S., Scarcella, Robin, Kramer, Jason, Pearson, Matthew, van Dyke, David A., Collins, Penny, & Land, Robert E. (2012). Enhancing the interpretive reading and analytical writing of mainstreamed English learners in secondary school: Results from a randomized field trial using a cognitive strategies approach. *American Educational Research Journal, 49*(2), 323–355.

Olson, Carol Booth, Matuchniak, Tina, Chung, Huy Q., Stumpf, Rachel, & Farkas, George. (2017). Reducing achievement gaps in academic writing for Latinos and English learners in Grades 7–12. *Journal of Educational Psychology, 109*(1), 1–21.

Ontario Council of Agencies Serving Immigrants (OCASI) (2005). *New moves: An orientation video for newcomer students* [Video]. Settlement. org. https://settlement.org/ontario/education/elementary-and-secondary-school/help-your-child-succeed-in-school/new-moves-an-orientation-video-for-newcomer-students/

Ontario Ministry of Education. (2007). *Supporting English language learners in kindergarten: A practical guide for Ontario educators.* http://www.edu.gov.on.ca/eng/document/kindergarten/index.html

Ontario Ministry of Education. (2008). *Supporting English language learners: A practical guide for Ontario educators Grades 1 to 8.* http://www.edu.gov.on.ca/eng/document/esleldprograms/guide.html

Ontario Ministry of Education. (2010). *Parents in partnership: A parent engagement policy for Ontario schools.* http://www.edu.gov.on.ca/eng/parents/involvement/PE_Policy2010.pdf

Ontario Ministry of Education. (2015, November). *STEP: Steps to English proficiency: A guide for users.* http://www.edugains.ca/resourcesELL/Assessment/STEP/STEPUserGuide_November2015.pdf

Ontario Ministry of Education. (2016a, July). *Supporting students with refugee backgrounds: A framework for responsive practice.* Capacity Building Series, Special Edition #45. http://www.edu.gov.on.ca/eng/literacynumeracy/inspire/research/cbs_refugees.html

Ontario Ministry of Education. (2016b). *The kindergarten program.* https://www.ontario.ca/document/kindergarten-program-2016

Ontario Ministry of Education. (2019, July 22). *Parents: Important information in many languages.* http://www.edu.gov.on.ca/eng/parents/multiLanguages.html

Open Culture. (2006–2020). www.openculture.com/freeaudiobooks

Osmond-Johnson, Pamela, Campbell, Carol, & Pollock, Katina. (2020, May 6). *Moving forward in the COVID-19 Era: Reflections for Canadian education.* EdCan Network, Canadian Education Association. https://www.edcan.ca/articles/moving-forward-in-the-covid-19-era/

Oxford, Rebecca L. (2017). *Teaching and researching language learning strategies: Self-Regulation in context.* Boca Raton, FL: Routledge, Taylor & Francis.

Oxford, Rebecca L., Rubin, Joan, Chamot, Anna Uhl, Schramm, Karen, Lavine, Roberta, Gunning, Pamela, & Nel, Carisma. (2014). The learning strategy prism: Perspectives of learning strategy experts. *System, 43,* 30–49.

Paradis, Johanne, Genesee, Fred, & Crago, Martha. (2011). *Dual language development and disorders: A handbook on bilingualism and second language learning* (2nd ed.). Baltimore: Brookes Publishing.

ParentCamp. (2018). https://www.parentcamp.org

Penguin Random House. (2020). *Dorling Kindersley (DK) bilingual visual dictionary series.* https://www.penguinrandomhouse.com/series/ACX/dk-bilingual-visual-dictionaries

People for Education. (2020). *Multi-lingual tip sheets for parents.* https://peopleforeducation.ca/topics/parent-involvement/

Petersen, Jill M., Marinova-Todd, Stefka H., & Mirenda, Pat. (2011). An exploratory study of lexical skills in bilingual children with autism spectrum disorder. *Journal of Autism and Developmental Disorders.* doi: 10.1007/s10803-011-1366-y

Pixabay. (2020). https://pixabay.com/

Popadiuk, Natalee. (2010). Asian international student transition to high school in Canada. *The Qualitative Report, 10,* 1523–1548.

Poza, Luis, Brooks, Maneka Deanna, & Valdés, Guadalupe. (2014). Entre familia: Immigrant parents' strategies for involvement in children's schooling. *School Community Journal 21*(1), 119–140.

Public Domain Pictures. (2007–2020). https://www.publicdomainpictures.net/en/

Puntledge Park Sensory Path. (2019, October 15). https://www.youtube.com/watch?v=EEWH08NZOJA&feature=youtu.be

Radford, Jynnah, & Connor, Phillip. (2019, June 27). *These are the countries that accept the most refugees in the world.* Published with permission from Pew Research Center, World Economic Forum. https://www.weforum.org/agenda/2019/06/canada-now-leads-the-world-in-refugee-resettlement-surpassing-the-u-s/

Raising Awareness of Language Learning Impairments. (2013, November 23). *Bilingualism and SLI* (DLD). https://www.youtube.com/watch?v=g7Sj_uRV7S4

Reading Rockets. (2008). *Reading tips for parents (in Multiple Languages).* https://www.readingrockets.org/article/reading-tips-parents-multiple-languages#english

Roeser, Robert W., Schonert-Reichl, Kimberly A., Jha, Amishi, Cullen, Margaret, Wallace, Linda, Wilensky, Rona, Oberle, Eva, Thomson, Kimberly, Taylor, Cynthia, & Harrison, Jessica. (2013). Mindfulness training and reductions in teacher stress and burnout: Results from two randomized, waitlist-control field trials. *Journal of Educational Psychology, 105*(3), 787–804.

Roessingh, Hetty. (2011). Family treasures: A dual language book project for negotiating language, literacy, culture and identity. *Canadian Modern Language Review, 67,* 123–148.

Rosenthal, Roger. (2016, December 7). *ELLs with special education needs are entitled to both ELL and special education services.* ¡Colorín colorado! https://www.youtube.com/watch?v=bhALmodGuRA&feature=youtu.be

Rousseau, Cécile, Drapeau, Aline, Lacroix, Louise, Bagilishya, Déogratias, & Heusch, Nicole. (2005). Evaluation of a classroom program of creative expression workshops for refugee and immigrant children. *Journal of Child Psychology and Psychiatry, 46*(2), 180–185.

Roxas, Kevin, & Gabriel, María L. (2016). Amplifying their voices. *Educational Leadership 73*(5), 78–81.

Ruiz Soto, Ariel G., Hooker, Sarah, & Batalova, Jeanne. (2015). *States and districts with the highest number and share of English language learners.* Washington, DC: Migration Policy Institute. https://www.tesol.org/docs/default-source/ppt/migration-policy-institute-ell-fact-sheet-2.pdf?sfvrsn=0&sfvrsn=0

Rutu Foundation for Intercultural Multilingual Education. (2019). *The language friendly school.* https://languagefriendlyschool.org/

Saeed, Sitwat, & Zyngier, David. (2012). How motivation influences student engagement: A qualitative case study. *Journal of Education and Learning, 1*(2), 1927–5269. https://files.eric.ed.gov/fulltext/EJ1081372.pdf

Sánchez-López, Cristina. (2017, October 31). *Under- and over-identification of ELLs in special education.* ¡Colorín colorado! https://www.youtube.com/watch?v=AFxDsAtnxx4

Sánchez-López, Cristina, & Young, Theresa. (2018). *Oxford key concepts for the language classroom: Focus on special education needs.* Oxford, United Kingdom: Oxford University Press.

Santa Clara County Office of Education. (2016). My name identity: A declaration of self. *The My Name, My Identity Campaign.* https://www.mynamemyidentity.org/

School Mental Health Ontario. (2020, April 21). *Educator conversations with students and families during COVID-19 school closures.* https://twitter.com/TDSB_Psych/status/1252640472952176640?s=20

Schooley, Skye. (2019, August 12). Lost in translation: 10 international marketing fails. *Business News Daily.* https://www.business

newsdaily.com/5241-international-marketing-fails.html

Seesaw. (2020). Remote learning with Seesaw. https://web.seesaw.me/

Semotiuk, Andy J. (2018, November 16). International students pour into Canada while the U.S. and others lag behind. *Forbes*. https://www.forbes.com/sites/andyjsemotiuk/2018/11/16/international-students-pour-into-canada-ahead-of-projections/#5730c6b753ec

Semple, Jeff. (December 15, 2016). Inuit delegation look to Wales for language preservation lessons. *Global News*. https://globalnews.ca/news/3130639/inuit-delegation-look-to-wales-for-language-preservation-lessons/

Settlement.org. (2016). *Dressing for winter*. https://settlement.org/ontario/education/elementary-and-secondary-school/general-information/dressing-for-winter/

Sinclair, Jeanne, & Lau, Clarissa. (2018). Initial assessment for K–12 English language support in six countries: Revisiting the validity-reliability paradox. *Language and Education*, 32(3), 257–285.

Sioumpas, Angela. (2016, February). *Inspired by Canadian television: Ideas for using identity texts and digital technology in the classroom*. TESOL Video News. http://newsmanager.commpartners.com/tesolvdmis/issues/2016-02-19/2.html

Skelton, Chad. (2014, July 8). ESL students in the majority at more than 60 schools in Metro Vancouver. *The Vancouver Sun*. http://www.vancouversun.com/touch/news/metro/students+majority+more+than+schools+metro+vancouver/10005768/story.html

Social Justice Books: A Teaching for Change Project. (2020). https://socialjusticebooks.org

Soto, Ivannia. (2012). *ELL shadowing as a catalyst for change*. Thousand Oaks, CA: Corwin.

Sousa, David A. (2011). *How the ELL brain learns*. Thousand Oaks, CA: Corwin.

Speech-Language Pathology Services. (2006, September 14). *Collaborative consultation action planning worksheet*. Toronto, ON: Toronto District School Board.

Staehr Fenner, Diane. (2014). *Advocating for English learners: A guide for educators*. Thousand Oaks, CA: Corwin.

Staehr Fenner, Diane, & Snyder, Sydney. (2017). *Unlocking English learners' potential: Strategies for making content accessible*. Thousand Oaks, CA: Corwin.

Stewart, Jan. (2011). *Supporting refugee children: Strategies for educators*. Toronto: University of Toronto Press.

Stewart, Jan, & Martin, Lorna. (2018). *Bridging two worlds: Supporting newcomer and refugee youth. A guide to curriculum implementation and integration*. Toronto: CERIC. https://ceric.ca/resource/bridging-two-worlds-supporting-newcomer-refugee-youth/

Stille, Saskia, & Prasad, Gail. (2015). "Imaginings": Reflections on plurilingual students' creative multimodal works. *TESOL Quarterly*, 49(3), 608–621.

Storyline Online. (2020). www.storylineonline.net/library/

SupportEd. (2020). https://getsupported.net/

Swan, Michael, & Smith, Bernard. (2001). (Eds). *Learner English: A teacher's guide to interference and other problems*. Cambridge, United Kingdom: Cambridge University Press.

Sweeney, Angela, Filson, Beth, Kennedy, Angela, Collinson, Lucie, & Gillard, Steve. (2018, September). A paradigm shift: relationships in trauma-informed mental health services. *BJPsych Advances* 24(5), 319–333. doi: 10.1192/bja.2018.29

TalkingPoints. (2015). https://www.talkingpts.org

Teaching Tolerance. (1991–2020). https://www.tolerance.org

Tello, Angelica M., Castellon, Nancy E., Aguilar, Alejandra, & Sawyer, Cheryl B. (2017). Unaccompanied refugee minors from Central America: Understanding their journey and implications for counselors. *The Professional Counselor*, 7(4), 360–374.

TESOL International Association. (2018). *Community and family toolkit: Engaging the families of English Learners in classrooms, schools, and communities*. https://www.tesol.org/docs/default-source/advocacy/tesol-community-and-family-toolkit.pdf?sfvrsn=0

TESOL International Association. (2020a). *Back to school resources.* https://www.tesol.org/

TESOL International Association. (2020b). *The 6 principles for exemplary teaching of English learners.* http://www.TESOL.org/the-6-principles/k-12

Thames Valley District School Board. (2016). *2016 annual report.* http://annual.tvdsb.ca/gentle-family-reception-centre.html

The Children's Museum of Houston. (2020, July 30). *StoryTime.* https://www.youtube.com/playlist?list=PLPZCH1CZOF9LmzhhOGbLWId5_DUyuxvzi

The Hanen Centre. (2016). http://www.hanen.org/Home.aspx

The Indianapolis Public Library. (2020). *100+ free video read alouds.* https://indypl.org/blog/for-parents/free-video-read-alouds

The Language Friendly School. (2019). *Roadmap for the language friendly school.* https://languagefriendlyschool.org/wp-content/uploads/2019/10/Language-Friendly-School-Roadmap-English.pdf

The Little Free Library. (2009–2020). https://littlefreelibrary.org/

The New York Public Library. (2020). *Multilingual storytimes.* https://www.nypl.org/education/kids/storytime/multilingual-storytimes

The World Bank Group. (2020). *How countries are using edtech (including online learning, radio, television, texting) to support access to remote learning during the COVID-19 pandemic.* https://www.worldbank.org/en/topic/edutech/brief/how-countries-are-using-edtech-to-support-remote-learning-during-the-covid-19-pandemic

Thier, Michael. (2013). Cultural awareness logs: A method for increasing international-mindedness among high school and middle school students. *English Journal, 102*(6), 46–53.

Timson, Judith. (2016, December 14). Immigrant teens and the meaning of home. *The Toronto Star.* https://thestar.com/life/2016/12/14/immigrant-teens-and-the-meaning-of-home-timson.html

Tom, Jessica. (2020). Be a reading role model: If you want your child to be a good reader, be one yourself! *Scholastic Parents.* https://www.scholastic.com/parents/books-and-reading/reading-resources/be-reading-role-model.html

Tools for Schools, Inc. (2011–2019). *Book creator.* https://bookcreator.com/

Toronto District School Board. (2006). *Your home language: Foundations for success* [DVD]. Toronto, ON: Toronto District School Board.

Toronto District School Board. (2007, May 16). *Students without legal immigration status.* (Policy P.061 SCH). http://ppf.tdsb.on.ca/uploads/files/live/98/1555.pdf

Toronto District School Board. (2010). Home Oral Language Activity (HOLA) Program. Toronto, ON: Toronto District School Board.

Toronto District School Board. (2013, May). *Facts: 2011–12 student & parent census.* Issue 1. https://www.tdsb.on.ca/Portals/research/docs/2011-12CensusFactSheet1-Demographics-17June2013.pdf

Toronto District School Board. (2016a). *Use your home language: Building skills with young children for school success* (flyers in 18 languages). Toronto, ON: Toronto District School Board. SLP Google Site for Parents: http://bit.ly/slpconnection

Toronto District School Board. (2016b). *Use your home language: Building skills with young children for school success* (video clips in 18 languages). Toronto, ON: Toronto District School Board. SLP Google Site for Parents: http://bit.ly/slpconnection

Toronto Public Library. (2020). *Dial-a-story.* https://www.torontopubliclibrary.ca/services/dial-a-story.jsp

Trauma Learning and Policy Initiative. (2020, April 20). *Trauma sensitive remote learning: Keeping connections strong.* https://traumasensitiveschools.org/trauma-sensitive-remote-learning-keeping-connections-strong/

Tweedie, M. Gregory, Belanger, Carla, Rezazadeh, Kimberley, & Vogel, Karen. (2017). Trauma-informed teaching practice and refugee children: A hopeful reflection on welcoming our new neighbours to Canadian schools. *BC TEAL Journal, 2*(1), 36–45.

Unite for Literacy. (2014). https://www.uniteforliteracy.com

United Nations Educational, Scientific and Cultural Organization (UNESCO). (2019). *Distance learning solutions.* https://en.unesco.org/covid19/educationresponse/solutions

United Nations High Commissioner for Refugees, Canada. (2020). *Children on the run*. https://www.unhcr.ca/children-on-the-run-experience/

UNHCR. (2019). *Forced to flee: Refugee children drawing on their experiences*. New York, NY: Franklin Watts.

United States Census Bureau. (2020, August 7). *U.S. and world population clock*. https://www.census.gov/popclock

U.S. Department of Education. (1998, August). Appendix D: Project GOTCHA (Project Galaxies of Thinking and Creative Heights of Achievements). In *Talent and diversity: The emerging world of limited English proficient students in gifted education*. https://www2.ed.gov/pubs/TalentandDiversity/appendd.html

U.S. Department of Education. (2005). *Helping your child become a reader*. https://www2.ed.gov/parents/academic/help/reader/index.html

U.S. Department of Education (2015, October 15). *Resource guide: Supporting undocumented youth: A guide for success in secondary and postsecondary settings*. https://www2.ed.gov/about/overview/focus/supporting-undocumented-youth.pdf

U.S. Department of Education. (2017a, May 25). *The federal role in education*. https://www2.ed.gov/about/overview/fed/role.html

U.S. Department of Education. (2017b, September). *Newcomer toolkit*. https://www2.ed.gov/about/offices/list/oela/newcomers-toolkit/ncomertoolkit.pdf

U.S. Department of Health and Human Services & U.S. Department of Education. (2016a, May 6). *Policy statement on family engagement from the early years to the early grades*. https://www2.ed.gov/about/inits/ed/earlylearning/files/policy-statement-on-family-engagement.pdf

U.S. Department of Health and Human Services & U.S. Department of Education. (2016b, June 2). *Policy statement on supporting the development of children who are dual language learners in early childhood programs*. https://www2.ed.gov/about/inits/ed/earlylearning/files/dll-policy-statement-2016.pdf

U.S. Department of Justice and U.S. Department of Education (2015, January 7). *Dear colleague letter: English learner students and limited English proficient parents*. https://www2.ed.gov/about/offices/list/ocr/letters/colleague-el-201501.pdf

Van Viegen Stille, Saskia, Jang, Eunice, & Wagner, Maryam. (2015). Building teachers' assessment capacity for supporting English language learners through the implementation of the STEP language assessment in Ontario K-12 schools. *TESL Canada Journal/Revue TESL du Canada*, 32(9). https://files.eric.ed.gov/fulltext/EJ1092815.pdf

Vargas, Jose Antonio. (2018). *Dear America: Notes of an undocumented citizen*, New York, NY: Dey Street Books.

Vera, Elizabeth M., Susman Israel, Marla, Coyle, Laura, Cross, Joanna, Knight-Lynn, Laura, Moallem, Isabel, Bartucci, Gina, & Goldberger, Nancy, (2012). Exploring the educational involvement of parents of English learners. *School Community Journal*, 22(2). https://files.eric.ed.gov/fulltext/EJ1001618.pdf

Veterans of Foreign Wars. (2020). Patriot's pen contest. https://www.vfw.org/community/youth-and-education/youth-scholarships

Villegas, Francisco J. (2018). 'Don't ask, don't tell': Examining the illegalization of undocumented students in Toronto, Canada. *British Journal of Sociology of Education*, 39(8), 1111–1125. doi: 10.1080/01425692.2018.1467265

Voaden, Jeanette. (2016). *Creating books*. http://bit.ly/CreatingBooks

Vocaroo. (2007–2020). https://vocaroo.com/

Walji, Nazima. (2018, December 30). *Growing number of refugees arriving in Canada as unaccompanied minors*. CBC News. https://www.cbc.ca/news/canada/refugee-shelter-maatthew-house-youth-unaccompanied-transition-1.4922946

Ward, Natalia A., & Warren, Amber N. (2019). "In search of peace": Refugee experiences in children's literature. *The Reading Teacher*, 73(4), 405–413.

Ward Singer, Tonya. (2018). *EL excellence every day*. Thousand Oaks, CA: Corwin.

Welcome to our world. (2013, April 24). CBC News. https://youtu.be/BSA_7jQqNec

Westernoff, Fern. (2014). The Home Oral Language Activities (HOLA) Program:

Building parent partnerships for academic success. *Journal of Interactional Research in Communication Disorders*, 5(1), 97–114.

Westernoff, Fern. (2019). Cultural and linguistic informants. In Jack S. Damico & Martin J. Ball (Eds.), *The SAGE encyclopedia of human communication sciences and disorders* (p. 532–536). Thousand Oaks, CA: Sage.

Westernoff, Fern, Young, Theresa, & Shimotakahara, Joanne. (2018). The Kindergarten Early Language Intervention (KELI) Program: Multiculturalism in action. *Journal of Interactional Research in Communication Disorders*, 9(1), 76–97.

WIDA Can do descriptors. (2020a). https://wida.wisc.edu/teach/can-do/descriptors

WIDA Consortium. (2020b). https://wida.wisc.edu/

WIDA English Language Development Standards. (2020c). *A tool to help educators support language development in multilingual learners.* https://wida.wisc.edu/teach/standards/eld

WIDA (2020d). *Help every student feel included and engaged.* https://wida.wisc.edu/teach/learners/welcoming-classroom

Wiens, Mary. (2018, January 15). *York first Canadian university to give "Dreamers" a chance at a degree.* CBC News. https://www.cbc.ca/news/canada/toronto/canadian-dreamers-york-university-1.4488252

Williams, Karen, & Khadra, Mohammed. (2009). *My name is Sangoel.* Grand Rapids, MI: Eerdmans Books for Young Readers.

Wilson, Amy Alexandra, Chavez, Kathryn, & Anders, Patricia L. (2012). "From the Koran and Family Guy": Expressions of identity in English Learners' digital podcasts. *Journal of Adolescent and Adult Literacy*, 55(5), 374–384.

Wilson, Karma, & Chapman, Jane. (2003). *Medve enne még (Bear wants more).* New York, NY: Little Simon.

Wilson Sanger, Amy. (2003). *Yum yum dim sum.* New York: Alfred A. Knopf Books for Young Readers.

Wong, Sabrina T., Homma, Yuko, Johnson, Joy L., & Saewye, Elizabeth. (2010). The unmet health needs of East Asian high school students: Are homestay students at risk? *Canadian Journal of Public Health*, 101(3), 241–245.

Wong Fillmore, Lily. (1991). When learning a second language means losing the first. *Early Childhood Research Quarterly*, 6, 323–346.

Wong Fillmore, Lily. (2000). Loss of family languages: Should educators be concerned? *Theory into Practice*, 39, 203–210.

World Education News + Reviews. (2020). *Education systems profiles.* https://wenr.wes.org/category/education-system-profiles

World Health Organization. (2018, January 16). *Disability and health.* https://www.who.int/news-room/fact-sheets/detail/disability-and-health

World Health Organization, War Trauma Foundation, & World Vision International (2011). *Psychological first aid: Guide for field workers.* https://www.who.int/mental_health/publications/guide_field_workers/en/

World Health Organization & The World Bank. (2011, December 13). *World report on disability.* Printed in Malta. https://www.who.int/disabilities/world_report/2011/en/

Worlds of Words. (2006–2020). https://wowlit.org/

Worldstories. (n.d.). https://www.worldstories.org.uk

Wright-Maley, Cory, & Green, Jennifer D. (2015). Experiencing the needs and challenges of ELLs: Improving knowledge and efficacy of pre-service teachers through the use of a language immersion simulation. *Cogent Education*, 2(1). doi: 10.1080/2331186X.2015.1030176

Write our World: Multicultural e-books by kids for kids. (2016–2020). https://writeourworld.org

Xing, Lisa. (2018, February 22). *The system is full of holes: Experts say young foreign students left vulnerable by unregulated industry.* CBC News. https://www.cbc.ca/news/canada/toronto/underage-visa-students-falling-through-cracks-in-canada-1.4525664

Yohani, Sophie C. (2008). Creating an ecology of hope: Arts-based interventions with refugee children. *Child and Adolescent Social Work Journal*, 25, 309–323.

Zacarian, Debbie. (2011). *Using RTI effectively with English language learners.* ¡Colorín colorado! https://www.colorincolorado.org/article/rti-and-english-language-learners

Zacarian, Debbie, & Staehr Fenner, Diane (2020). From deficit-based to assets-based. In Margarita Espino Calderón, Diane Staehr Fenner, Andrea Honigsfeld, Shawn Slakk, Debbie Zacarian, Maria G. Dove, Margo Gottlieb, Tonya Ward Singer, and Ivannia Soto (Eds.), *Breaking down the wall: Essential shifts for English learner's success.* Thousand Oaks, CA: Corwin.

Zelasko, Nancy, & Antunez, Beth. (2000, August). *If your child learns in two languages: A parent's guide for improving educational opportunities for children acquiring English as a second language.* Washington, DC: George Washington University (Also available in other languages). https://ncela.ed.gov/resources-library?keys=Zelasko

Author Index

O'Brien, A. S., 38
Ochoa, E., 36
Ogilvie, G., 241, 245, 246
Okazaki, S., 222
Olson, C. B., 193, 195
Oppedal, B., 219
Osmond-Johnson, P., 71
Oxford, R. L., 192, 193, 196

Paige, C., 60
Panoscha, R., 198
Paradis, J., 133, 157, 180, 187, 198, 208
Paw, H. N., 239
Petersen, J. M., 180
Pinkney, A. D., 38
Pinto, I., 117
Pollock, K., 71
Popadiuk, N., 222
Poza, L., 147
Prasad, G., 186

Radford, J., 143
Rao, K., 195
Rauf, O. Q., 38
Ray, R. D., 143, 144
Rezazadeh, K., 238, 240
Riak, A., 239
Richards-Tutor, C., 203
Ringstaff, C., 194, 195
Robinson Kurpius, S. E., 147
Roeser, R. W., 249
Roessingh, H., 60
Rosenthal, R., 206
Ross Anderson, T., 12
Ross, T., 17
Rousseau, C., 242
Roxas, K., 185
Ruiz Soto, A. G., 9
Rumbold, K., 151
Ruurs, M., 38
Ryan, S. V., 249

Saeed, S., 15
Saewye, E., 222
Sajjan, H., 39
Sakkab, A., 145
Sánchez-López, C., 3, 81, 82, 112, 133,
    199, 202, 204–208
Sánchez, M. T., 81
Sawyer, C. B., 219

Scardina, K., 205
Scheller, A., 10
Schneider, S., 194, 195
Schooley, S., 174
Seltzer, K., 81
Semotiuk, A. J., 221
Semple, J., 126
Serrano, D., 205
Shapiro, N., 112
Shimotakahara, J., 81
Sinclair, J., 44, 45, 46
Singh, A., 116
Sioumpas, A., 186
Sirin, S., 219
Skelton, C., 10
Skrypuch, M. F., 38
Smarsh, L., 239
Smith, B., 203
Snyder, S., 12, 14
Soni, E., 183
Soto, I., 126, 127
Sousa, D. A., 122, 133, 205
Spaulding, C., 128
Staehr Fenner, D., 3, 12, 14, 131, 170, 200,
    203, 205, 207, 210
Stewart, J., 237, 238, 240, 242, 245,
    246, 248, 250
Stille, S., 12, 179, 186
Street, C., 3, 112
Suresh, S., 181
Swan, M., 203
Sweeney, A., 181

Tan, S., 38
Tello, A. M., 219, 220
Thier, M., 99
Thoo, L., 239
Timson, J., 183
Tom, J., 162
Toohey, K., 116
Trudeau, J., 144
Tweedie, M. G., 238, 240

Valdés, G., 147
Van Viegen Stille, S., 13
Vargas, J. A., 39, 216
Vera, E. M., 43
Villegas, F. J., 217
Voaden, J., 163–164, 165
Vogel, K., 238, 240

Vogt, M., 203
Vuelvas, S., 181
Vuong, T., 223

Wagner, M., 13
Wah, L. M., 239
Walji, N., 219
Walker, K., 10
Walker, M., 198
Wamariya, C., 39
Warden, D., 184
Ward Singer, T., 81, 112
Weissbourd, R., 12
Westernoff, F., 2, 81, 153, 173, 174, 206
Wiens, M., 218
Williams, K., 128
Williams, N., 164
Wilson, A. A., 186
Wilson, K., 164

Wilson Sanger, A., 148
Wong Fillmore, L., 81, 132, 133, 158
Wong, S. T., 222
Woodson, J., 38
Woomert, A., 184
Wright-Maley, C., 12

Xing, L., 222

Yelich, B., 239
Yeung, W., 39
Yim, D., 208
Yohani, S. C., 242
Young, T., 3, 81, 82, 112, 133, 199, 202, 204, 206–208

Zacarian, D., 3, 204
Zelasko, N., 159
Zyngier, D., 15

Subject Index

A SAGE Publishing Company

Helping educators make the greatest impact

CORWIN HAS ONE MISSION: to enhance education through intentional professional learning.

We build long-term relationships with our authors, educators, clients, and associations who partner with us to develop and continuously improve the best evidence-based practices that establish and support lifelong learning.